Molly,

Towards Awakening

Alg.

April 11, 2019

THE **AGE** OF **AWAKENING**

THE **AGE** OF **AWAKENING**

THE STORY OF
THE INDIAN ECONOMY
SINCE INDEPENDENCE

AMIT
KAPOOR
WITH
CHIRAG YADAV

FOREWORD BY
BIBEK DEBROY,
Chairman, Economic Advisory Council to the Prime Minister

EPILOGUE BY
AMITABH KANT, CEO, NITI AAYOG

PORTFOLIO
PENGUIN

An imprint of Penguin Random House

PORTFOLIO

USA | Canada | UK | Ireland | Australia
New Zealand | India | South Africa | China

Portfolio is part of the Penguin Random House group of companies
whose addresses can be found at global.penguinrandomhouse.com

Published by Penguin Random House India Pvt. Ltd
7th Floor, Infinity Tower C, DLF Cyber City,
Gurgaon 122 002, Haryana, India

First published in Portfolio by Penguin Random House India 2018

10 9 8 7 6 5 4 3 2 1

The views and opinions expressed in this book are the author's own and the
facts are as reported by him which have been verified to the extent possible,
and the publishers are not in any way liable for the same.

ISBN 9780670090891

Typeset in Minion Pro by Manipal Digital Systems, Manipal
Printed at Replika Press Pvt. Ltd, India

www.penguin.co.in

MIX
Paper from
responsible sources
FSC® C016779

To

M.K. Anand
Anurag Batra
Lohit Jagwani

CONTENTS

FOREWORD

I often ask people whether they have read a book by Alexander Campbell, *The Heart of India*. It was published abroad in 1958. They usually haven't because the book is 'banned' in India. The word 'ban' is often used loosely. This book has never been published or printed in India. The ban (Customs Notification No. 49, dated 11 March 1959) is on imports into the country. It is an extremely patronizing book, though that should hardly be a reason for a ban. There is a section on a meeting with Vaidya Sharma of the Ministry of Planning: 'He (Vaidya Sharma) put away the housing-development papers and talked again about the Five Year Plan. "We have now entered the period of the second Plan. The first Plan built up our food resources; the second Plan will lay the foundations for rapid creation of heavy industry. Delhi, as the capital of India, will play a big part, and we are getting ready to shoulder the burden. We are going to build a big central stationery depot, with a special railway-siding of its own. There will be no fewer than 12 halls, each covering 2,000 square feet. They will be storage halls, and," said Sharma triumphantly, "we calculate that the depot will be capable of an annual turnover of 1,400 tonnes of official forms, forms required for carrying out the commitments of the second Five Year Plan!"'

This quote is from 1958. Another from 1940, from a book published by Minoo Masani, called *Our India*, says: 'And so India presents a paradox[:] poverty in the land of plenty. It is a puzzle, but every puzzle has, as you know, a key or clue with which to solve it . . . And simple it really is, though all the statesmen and the politicians and the economists and the captains of industry and the other Wise Men of the East shake their heads woefully and argue interminably

over each little twist and turn of the tangle and just get nowhere!
. . . How are we to make sure that the people who own big workshops
do not use their key positions to send themselves higher up the
mountain? The answer is quite simple. These big factories and plants
should have no owners. Then who will run them? We shall, all of
us, through our own Government . . . Is there any reason then why
the supply of electricity and the manufacture of iron and steel and
machines and chemicals should be left to a few businessmen and not
be undertaken by the State?'

Economists and economic policies fashioned by statesmen and
politicians, in consultation with economists, don't lead anywhere.
They do lead somewhere, but not necessarily where one wanted to
go. There is the famous conversation from *Alice in Wonderland*:
Alice: 'Would you tell me, please, which way I ought to go from
here?' The Cheshire Cat, 'That depends a good deal on where you
want to get to.' Alice, 'I don't much care where.' The Cheshire Cat,
'Then it doesn't much matter which way you go.' Alice, '. . . So long
as I get somewhere.' The Cheshire Cat, 'Oh, you're sure to do that, if
only you walk long enough.'

In the Constitution, the word 'socialism' was deliberately kept
out. B.R. Ambedkar, participating in the Constituent Assembly
debates on 15 November 1948, opposed an amendment that sought
to introduce the word 'socialist' in the Preamble. 'What should be the
policy of the State, how the Society should be organized in its social
and economic side are matters which must be decided by the people
themselves according to [the] time and circumstances. It cannot
be laid down in the Constitution itself, because that is destroying
democracy altogether. If you state in the Constitution that the social
organization of the State shall take a particular form, you are, in my
judgment, taking away the liberty of the people to decide what should
be the social organization in which they wish to live. It is perfectly
possible today, for the majority people to hold that the socialist
organization of society is better than the capitalist organization of
society. But it would be perfectly possible for thinking people to
devise some other form of social organization which might be better

than the socialist organization of today or of tomorrow. I do not see therefore why the Constitution should tie down the people to live in a particular form and not leave it to the people themselves to decide it for themselves. This is one reason why the amendment should be opposed.'

The Constitution apart, at a certain point in time, there was a belief in socialism, not necessarily to be interpreted in the sense of centrally planned economies. After a visit to the former Soviet Union, a reporter from New York famously remarked, 'I have seen the future and it works.' Having witnessed the past trajectory of India's performance since 1947, most economists would now remark, 'We have seen the past and it did not work.' It did lead somewhere, but it certainly wasn't 'Citius, Altius, Fortius'. India was consistently outperformed by a succession of countries, with the costs of state intervention in the 1960s and 1970s no longer commensurate with the benefits. Those were lost development decades for India.

Amit Kapoor is an economist, but this book doesn't lead to nowhere. It captures the trajectory of the past, the promise of the present and, to a more limited extent, the promise of the future. The book isn't a typical economist's book, since it is also about the interplay between politics and economics. Not about what economists call political economy, but politics and economics. It is titled *The Age of Awakening*. This may be a neat turn of phrase. It may be an oblique reference to the famous shloka from the *Katha Upanishad* that Swami Vivekananda was fond of quoting. On the other hand, it may be a more direct reference to the 'Tryst with Destiny' speech, suggesting that it was India that slept while the rest of the world (such as East Asia) had awakened.

The book has four parts beginning around the time of India's independence. Part 1 focuses on the role of Jawaharlal Nehru in shaping the Indian economy. Part 2 covers Lal Bahadur Shastri and Indira Gandhi. Part 3 starts with Rajiv Gandhi and ends with the tumultuous political period of the late-1990s. Part 4 ventures into the new millennium and explores the role of Atal Bihari Vajpayee, Manmohan Singh and Narendra Modi in taking India's growth story forward. With such a terrain to cover, across more than seven decades, generalizations are inevitable. No reader will agree with every statement made. But every reader will agree that it is a very good read.

Bibek Debroy

INTRODUCTION

The Indian commitment to the semantics of socialism is at least as deep as ours to the semantics of free enterprise . . . It is regularly averred by the government and, indeed, by nearly all articulate Indians. Even the most intransigent Indian capitalist may observe on occasion that he is really a socialist at heart.

John Kenneth Galbraith, economist, in 1958

India is an elaborate mix of contradictions and complexities. It is rare to find other countries in the world that embrace such an extraordinary diversity of religions, a multitude of ethnic groups, a disparate assortment of languages and a range of economic development levels in society. For these reasons, there was considerable scepticism surrounding the idea of India as a nation.

The British were especially doubtful that any unity of the Indian state could outlast their reign. A 'Balkanization' of the region was widely expected as soon as they left. When the renowned writer Rudyard Kipling was asked in 1891 about the possibility of self-government in India, he exclaimed, 'Oh no! They are 4,000 years old out there, much too old to learn that business. Law and order is what they want and we are there to give it to them.'[1]

Among others, Sir John Strachey, a British civil servant who gave a series of lectures in Cambridge in 1988 that were later compiled in a book titled *India*, also held a similar view. In the lectures he argued that 'India' was merely 'a name which we give to a great region including a multitude of different countries'.[2] He pointed out that the differences among European nations were much smaller than those that existed across the Indian landscape. All the nation states that had formed in Europe arose from a shared identity of language or territory. India displayed no comparable sense of national unity.

Most popularly, Winston Churchill, the formidable prime minister of United Kingdom during the Second World War, once infamously remarked that 'India is merely a geographical expression . . . no more a single country than the Equator'.[3] But, against all cynical assessments of the possible establishment of an Indian state, when the country gained independence in 1947, speculations arose on how long it would stay united. With the death of every leader, eruption of new secessionist movements, or even failure of monsoons, the survival of India as a single entity was vehemently questioned. But the Indian experiment remained resilient through it all.

It also remained puzzling how a poor nation like India could sustain its democratic institutions. The idea of political equality seemed comically out of place in a society stratified by the hierarchical order of the caste system. Unlike other democratic experiments in the West, India and Indians hardly had any awareness of the mechanisms of a democratic state. Macaulay in his characteristic exaggerated, but for once justifiable, outcry described India as 'the strangest of all political anomalies'.[4]

India has truly been an anomaly in its existence. Most of the nations that gained independence in the twentieth century eventually succumbed to autocratic or military rule. So, the democratic routines that India takes for granted after over seven decades of independence were once hard to fathom. Time certainly has a way of trivializing successes. It is, therefore, crucial to revisit history and contextualize the times.

The latter is important because it is simplistic to pass judgements with the perfect hindsight of history. This is fairly common in the field of economics, when the leaders in power at the time of independence are criticized for adopting a model of development that failed to place the economy on a high-growth trajectory. But as John Rawls, arguably the greatest political philosopher of the twentieth century, rightly pointed out—the giants of the past need to be understood in the context of their times and not ours. Just as it is difficult to realize that the very existence of India was in doubt, it is also difficult to imagine a time when economic ideas of socialism and state control were the preponderant notions of the day.

Considering the conversations and interest surrounding the Indian economy in contemporary times, it was deemed necessary to similarly put our place in the world in context. With a per capita income of less than USD 2,000, India is probably the poorest nation that is posited as the next economic superpower. Gazing so far ahead into the future, one needs to understand why the nation stands where it is today.

The birth of the Indian nation was fittingly marked by the stirring words of India's first prime minister, Jawaharlal Nehru, in his famous 'Tryst with Destiny' speech:

> Long years ago, we made a tryst with destiny, and now the time comes when we shall redeem our pledge, not wholly or in full measure, but very substantially. At the stroke of the midnight hour, when the world sleeps, India will awake to life and freedom. A moment comes, which comes but rarely in history, when we step out from the old to the new, when an age ends, and when the soul of a nation, long suppressed, finds utterance. It is fitting that at this solemn moment we take the pledge of dedication to the service of India and her people and to the still larger cause of humanity . . . The service of India means the service of the millions who suffer. It means the ending of poverty, ignorance, disease and inequality of opportunity. The ambition of the greatest man of our generation [Mahatma Gandhi] has been to wipe every tear from every eye. That may be beyond us, but as long as there are tears and suffering, so long our work will not be over.

Nehru's words were more of a call to action for a nation that had long been suppressed under foreign rule and exploitation. It was a declaration to the world that India's independence had marked its age of awakening from the prolonged slumber that was imposed upon it. But these eloquent words were not merely a credulous world view of an overeducated leader. India was a melting pot of human striving, a place which would prove all doomsayers wrong in their judgements. In all its failings and successes, the country would hold lessons for all mankind.

CHAPTER 1

RADCLIFFE AND HIS LINE

It had been only two years since the end of the Second World War when India won her independence. Today, the world at the time can be hard to imagine. In a span of less than half a century, two of the biggest wars in history and one of the largest financial crises had caused widespread devastation and ruin. India was much worse off. After almost two centuries of colonial rule, it had become an indistinguishable shadow of the former trading power that it had once been on the world stage.[1]

Moreover, the world economies were divided into two ideological camps, one led by a communist Soviet Russia and the other by a capitalist United States. The former model was undoubtedly more appealing, not just because it strived for a just and equitable society but because it was working. It had also managed to remain relatively unaffected by the Great Depression of 1929 that had brought financial ruin to most of the closely interlinked Western world.[2] These geopolitical realities were bound to be highly crucial in the choices made by the newly independent nations at the time.

For India, however, the liberty of making such choices would come much later. Her first challenge was not to fall apart. It all began in February 1947, when British prime minister Clement Attlee declared that his country would withdraw from India by June 1948. He sent Lord Mountbatten to complete the transfer of power with crisp instructions: 'Keep India united if you can. If not, save something from the wreck. In any case, get Britain out.'[3]

Mountbatten had little idea of the complications involved in the process, where multiple groups divided along regional and communal lines carried a unique vision of independence. His predecessor, Lord

Wavell, had no words of reassurance to offer him on his arrival to India. When the two met, Wavell commented, 'I am sorry indeed that you've been sent out here in my place . . . You've been given an impossible task. I've tried everything I know to solve this problem and I can see no light.'[4]

Mountbatten, however, proved quite enterprising. He went about trying to chalk out a compromise that was acceptable to the towering personalities of the Indian freedom struggle, on the one hand, and the British cabinet, on the other. The Indian side was harder to appease. Two major parties needed to be brought on board: the Congress party led by Mohandas Karamchand Gandhi and Jawaharlal Nehru and the Muslim League led by Mohammed Ali Jinnah. In a broad sense, the former wanted a united, independent India, while the latter had been adamant about a separate nation for the Muslims. There was also the question of the 565 Princely States, which were primarily vassal states under the British. Now, many of them were eyeing independence.

Mountbatten worked at remarkable speed and came up with a plan by May, which was approved by the British government. The 'Mountbatten Plan', as it would be popularly known, was to divide British India into two fully sovereign dominions of India and Pakistan, and the Princely States would be given an option to join either of the two nations. The dominion status implied that the British Crown would remain the symbolic head of the state, represented by the Governor General. The formation of the two nations would involve a division of the provinces of Bengal and Punjab on sectarian lines. Both parties were forced to compromise a bit to come to terms with the plan—Congress accepted Partition,[5] while Jinnah accepted a Pakistan separated from the vast expanse of India without a connecting corridor, which he had always demanded.

After the plan had been accepted by all parties concerned in a meeting with Mountbatten on 3 June, the Viceroy unexpectedly revealed that the transfer of power would take place ten months in advance of the June 1948 deadline, on 15 August 1947. Things were moving so fast that Mountbatten saw it fit to move the date of British withdrawal forward. He chose that date for no particular reason but to mark the two-year anniversary of Japan's surrender and Britain's victory in the Second World War. The first day of independent India, therefore, was marked with a colonial overhang. Even astrologers felt that the day was quite inauspicious. Working around the technicality in an amusing display of Indian *jugaad*,[6] it was suggested that the transfer of power in the final minutes of 14 August be punctuated by the blowing of the holy conch at the stroke of the midnight hour. Jawaharlal Nehru obediently stuck to the allotted timeline when he delivered his landmark 'Tryst with Destiny' speech, marking an age of awakening for a nation that had been forced into insignificance under a foreign rule. Soon after he finished his speech, the sound of a holy conch reverberated across the room, signalling the stroke of the midnight hour. India was free, and Nehru was its first prime minster.

India became the second-largest country in the world in terms of population, while the two chunks of Pakistan on its eastern and western edges combined to make up the sixth-largest country. However, no borders existed between the two nations yet. At least not to anyone's knowledge, except for a man named Sir Cyril Radcliffe and his secretary. Radcliffe was a British jurist who had been sent to India on 8 July to undertake the onerous task of drawing the lines of Partition between the two nations. He was entrusted with one of the most sensitive acts of sociopolitical surgery and was only given five weeks to complete it. He also knew very little about India and its people, having never visited the country before. The British saw that as a suitable qualification for the job as his ignorance would make him objective and impartial on the matter.

Radcliffe was to consult with a committee consisting of four members of the Indian National Congress and four members of the Muslim League. But the members hardly ever saw eye to eye on anything, and, since time was a constraint, Radcliffe had to take most crucial decisions on his own. Nevertheless, he completed his work by 12 August and handed it over to Mountbatten who decided to wait until after Independence to make it public.

On 16 August, Nehru wound up celebrations by afternoon and made his way to the Government House for a meeting where the lines of Partition, or the Radcliffe Award, were disclosed to Indian leaders. Expectedly, there were expressions of dissatisfaction all around the room, but it was agreed that Mountbatten would issue the Award the following day. Radcliffe had written to his stepson three days earlier: 'Nobody in India would love me for my award about Punjab and Bengal and there will be roughly 80 million people with a grievance who will begin looking for me; I do not want them to find me.'[7]

As he expected, the serpentine line that Radcliffe drew on a piece of paper brought about the largest mass migration in history, which was marred by utter chaos and bloodshed. Communal tensions ran high on either side of the border and gruesome reports of mobs systematically burning down villages and homes of other communities emerged from both sides of the border. No accurate estimates of the migration exist, but estimates claim that out of the 10 million people that migrated, somewhere between 200,000 to a million perished in the violence that ensued.[8]

Along with a nation, an economy was also carved into two. In the days between Mountbatten's announcement and India's independence, a Partition Council finalized the finer details. It was decided that Pakistan would receive 17.5 per cent of all the monetary and liquid assets and liabilities of British India while India would get the rest. All the movable and non-liquid assets, were to be divided between India and Pakistan in the ratio of 80:20. Railway assets and government vehicles were divided in the proportion of the railway and roadway network inherited by each country.[9]

As for irrigation waters, the Indus river system was of particular importance, especially for Pakistan. The water system, which includes the Indus river itself and its various tributaries, flows through Kashmir into Pakistan and finally drains into the Arabian Sea. It had been used for irrigation since time immemorial, and under the British rule large canal systems had been built making them indispensable for the fertile northern plains of the Punjab region. In the Partition, the headworks of the water system went to India while the canal systems along with a major portion of Punjab's fertile, irrigated lands went to Pakistan.

Meanwhile, foodgrains were in short supply after Second World War, and the Partition exacerbated the problem for India. India was deprived of 75 per cent of its most important foreign exchange–earning crop, jute; 40 per cent of its raw cotton; and a primary source of its wheat. However, India had the upper hand on resources that were necessary to run heavy industry. Mining sites of high-quality coal, iron ore, manganese and other precious minerals were primarily located in India.[10]

Likewise, every public asset was meticulously divided, sometimes at ludicrous levels of detail. An amusing dilemma was faced by the Punjab Government Library that had only one copy of each book. Dictionaries were ripped apart, with the portion carrying words from A–K going to India and the rest to Pakistan. Other books were to be divided based on which nation had a greater interest in the subject. Things got heated when it became difficult to ascertain which country had a greater interest in *Alice of Wonderland* and *Wuthering Heights*, and ended in a physical confrontation between the librarians.[11]

Tensions ran high all around and the issue of Kashmir added fuel to the fire. The Princely State of Jammu and Kashmir presented a unique situation. It was a Muslim-dominated region with a Hindu ruler, Maharaja Hari Singh. In the whimsical hope of independence, Hari Singh had not joined any side yet. Also, his troops were helping create a buffer zone of uninhabited land between Kashmir and Pakistan by forcing Muslims living near the border to flee to the other side. The refugees, mostly Muslim, carried horrific tales of atrocities, from arson, physical violence to genocide.[12] The Pathan tribes on the other side of the border sympathized with the displaced population and prepared to retaliate. Thousands of Pathan tribesmen carried out a truck-mounted incursion on 22 October 1947. They headed for the capital, Srinagar, ransacking towns and villages on the way. The Maharaja's army failed to halt their rampage. He asked for military assistance from India. In turn, Mountbatten asked India to agree only if Kashmir acceded to India. The Maharaja complied.

However, Hari Singh had deserted the capital and had practically lost control of the state by the time he signed the Instrument of Accession. The British High Commissioner in Pakistan urgently telegraphed London instructing that the accession should not be recognized by India until a plebiscite took place.[13] But it was too late. India had airlifted troops to Kashmir and Pakistan, not recognizing the accession, sent its own army in response. Attacks and counter-attacks from both sides would continue for almost a year until a UN resolution on 13 August 1948 would enforce a ceasefire. Until then, India had gained control of two-thirds of Kashmir while Pakistan held the rest.

While the Kashmir conflict was on, the domestic situation in India was no better. Communal tensions between the Hindus, Sikhs and Muslims showed no signs of relenting. The only glimmer of hope for peace was Mahatma Gandhi. At the time of independence, he was busy maintaining peace on the streets of Calcutta, which had been a hotbed of communal violence for almost a year now. Due to his efforts, Bengal was relatively more peaceful than Punjab at the time of Partition, but by the end of August armed gangsters ruled the streets of Calcutta once again. Gandhi resorted to applying moral pressure on the perpetrators by going on a fast on 2 September. The impact was profound. In a little less than a day, a sense of calm spread over the city and leaders from all parties and faiths came to appeal to the Mahatma to end his fast. Finally, when all of the city had pledged to refrain from resorting to violence, he broke his fast on 4 September. Calcutta would keep its word for months. Mountbatten commented: 'In the Punjab, we have 55,000 soldiers and large-scale rioting on our hands. In Bengal, our forces consist of one man, and there is no rioting.'[14]

Gandhi then left for Delhi on 7 September, hoping to proceed to the Punjab and quell the violence there. However, by the time he arrived in Delhi, the situation had started deteriorating. Hindu and Sikh refugees arriving from Punjab were vying for the blood of the

Muslims and forcibly occupying their homes.[15] Large-scale riots were becoming commonplace. Nehru described the situation as being 'analogous to war'.[16] Gandhi visited refugee camps and hospitals to console the victims and publicly appealed for peace so that he could proceed to both East and West Punjab. He said that he wanted to go to the Punjab to end the atrocities committed by the Muslims there but could not do so before securing justice for the Muslims in Delhi.[17]

Meanwhile, another issue also became a cause of distress for Gandhi. The Congress party had developed two power centres. On the one side, there was a left-wing Jawaharlal Nehru and on the other a right-wing Vallabhbhai Patel. In the first Cabinet, Patel had taken up the position of deputy prime minister, but it was no secret that he did not quite get along with the prime minister. He only accepted the position without protest because Gandhi had made that choice. However, he had a different way of handling things from Nehru and found it difficult to unquestioningly accept the latter's decisions. In the matter of Muslims, for instance, he was of the view that the party should not consciously shed its Hindu image to reach out to the Muslims. Nehru's biographer, Sarvepalli Gopal, noted that, 'The old stalwarts of the Congress . . . such as Patel, Rajendra Prasad, with the backing of the leader of the Hindu Mahasabha, Shyama Prasad Mookerjee, believed not so much in a theocratic state as in a state which symbolized the interests of the Hindu majority.'[18] In fact, Patel assumed that some Muslim officials, even though they chose to stay in India, would be disloyal and should be dismissed. He, therefore, felt that Nehru's non-judgemental treatment of Muslims was a threat to national security.[19]

The deep ideological differences between the two also came out in the open during the election of the party president. Patel backed a Hindu nationalist Purshottam Das Tandon, a man who openly advocated an aggressive policy stance towards Pakistan while Nehru pitched Acharya Kripalani, merely to take on Tandon. When Patel's candidate won, Nehru's supporters walked out of the party in protest, leaving Patel isolated and placing him at the centre of the party. The animosity reached a point where, on 6 January, Nehru told Gandhi that either Patel had to go, or he would. Gandhi was of the view that India needed both men to lead the country. Despite all their differences in style and temperament, the two gave the country a perfect balance of leadership.

A week later, Gandhi went on a fast that surprised even his confidantes. Unlike previous instances, he had made no clear indication of the intention of his fast. Presumably, it was an effort to stop the Hindus from attacking the Muslims in Delhi. But the British High Commissioner noted that some 'sources suggest that the fast is due to the bad state of relations between Nehru and Patel which they say have been worse in the last week than ever before.'[20]

One of the demands of Gandhi's fast was also that India fulfil a monetary obligation to Pakistan that it had made before Independence. As part of the partition process, India was to transfer a sum of Rs 75 crore to the Pakistani government as compensation. The first instalment of Rs 20 crore had already been paid, but after the Kashmir issue arose Patel froze the remaining Rs 55 crore on the grounds that they would be used to sponsor the conflict and, thus, used against India itself. This would have been a death blow to Pakistan. But Mahatma Gandhi felt that India should not back down on commitments made earlier and should honour the agreement. When the frail old man went on a fast Patel had no choice but to relent.

The fast also proved effective in curbing the senseless violence that had taken over the streets of Delhi. Representatives from across Delhi sent assurances to the Mahatma that no more harm would come to the Muslims. And he gave up the fast on 18 January. Gandhi's efforts won the hearts of Muslims on both sides of the border, but not everyone agreed with him.

His pro-Muslim stance eventually led to his assassination. On 30 January, as the Mahatma made his way to his evening prayer meeting, Nathuram Godse, a Bombay Brahmin, pulled out a Beretta pistol and fired three shots at point-blank range into his chest. He would later state in court that he did so because the government was becoming unfairly favourable towards Muslims due entirely to the presence of Gandhi.[21] In his delusional fight for Hindu rights, Godse committed the biggest disservice to his community. If Gandhi had carried on with his mission for peace into Pakistan, as he had planned, a lot of Hindu lives would have been spared.

Nehru knew exactly how to address a bereaved nation. 'The light has gone out from our lives and there is darkness everywhere,' he lamented over the radio. Then he soon corrected himself:

> The light has gone out, I said, and yet I was wrong. For the light that shone in this country was no ordinary light. The light that has illumined this country for these many, many years will illumine this country for many more years, and a thousand years later that light will still be seen in this country, and the world will see it, and it will [give] solace to innumerable hearts. For that light represented something more than the immediate present; it represented the living, eternal truths reminding us of the right path, drawing us from error, taking this ancient country to freedom.[22]

The name that came to be associated with peace around the world succumbed ironically to a shameless act of violence. That year, the Nobel Committee declined to award the Peace Prize on the grounds that 'there was no suitable living candidate that year'. The Committee would later comment in 2006 that 'the greatest omission in our 106-year history is undoubtedly that Mahatma Gandhi never received the Nobel Peace Prize . . . Gandhi could do without the Nobel Peace Prize; whether [the] Nobel Committee can do without Gandhi is the question'.[23]

CHAPTER 2

A MIDDLE GROUND

India at the time of Independence was predominantly rural and agricultural in character. Nearly 85 per cent of the Indian population lived in villages and supported their livelihoods mainly with agriculture and related activities. Even with such a large proportion of the population engaged in agriculture, the country was not self-sufficient in food. Despite importing 2 to 3 million tonnes of foodgrains annually, the daily grain consumption fell below 250 grams per person. The sector was marked by traditional, low-productivity techniques, with modern inputs like fertilizers hardly in use and irrigation facilities available to merely one-sixth of the area.

The industry was an inconsequential part of the economy. About a tenth of the workforce was employed in it, with a bulk of them in the traditional cottage and small-scale processing activities. Even modern factories, which employed merely 3 million of the 140 million in total, catered predominantly to jute, cotton and other agriculture-based industries. Factories producing steel, cement, paper and basic chemicals did exist but accounted for very little of the national output.

On the social side, illiteracy was abysmally high, at about 84 per cent, and about 60 per cent of children in the age group of six to eleven years did not even attend school. An average Indian at the time lived to about thirty-two years of age. Mortality rate was as high as 27 per 1,000 people, as the prevalence of mass communicable diseases was widespread and good public healthcare services were virtually non-existent. These problems of the economy, of rampant poverty, ignorance and disease, were accentuated by an unequal distribution of resources between groups.[1]

Thus, a newly independent India was a typically underdeveloped economy, and the responsibility of chalking out its developmental path rested on the shoulders of the leaders who had fought for its independence. However, they had not waited for Independence to do so. Discussions had been taking place more than a decade ago, both within and outside Congress, on the broader socio-economic questions.

Two things were clear from the outset. The idea of capitalism was a taboo as it was seen as an extension of imperialism. As economist John Kenneth Galbraith put it, '[A] good deal of capitalist enterprise in India was an extension of the arm of the imperial power—indeed, in part its confessed *raison d'etre*. As a result, free enterprise in Asia bears the added stigmata of colonialism, and this is a formidable burden.'[2] Second, there was widespread agreement that the role of the state was paramount. This view was not limited to the political class alone. As we shall note, even the business community at the time argued strongly in favour of the necessity of state intervention and control for economic development.

The debate on which economic policy best suits India became apparent around the 1937 general elections that were held for the provincial assemblies. These were the first elections in which large masses of the population were allowed to participate, accounting for a restricted franchise of about 12 per cent of the Indian population.[3] Congress, the Muslim League and Unionist Party were the main contenders. Young men and women working for these political parties were particularly enthusiastic about the elections and were devising new and innovative ways to showcase their leaders. One of them, Minoo R. Masani, prepared a campaign film called *Pandit Jawaharlal's Message*. On 19 May 1936, Nehru sat down in front of the cameras to share the core of his political philosophy in his usual intelligible tone:

> At present, there are two groups of people in the world. On one side, there are people who want to advance the world further and free the people from the chains of imperialism and capitalism.

On the other side, there are a handful of people who are deriving
benefit from . . . the present state of things. There is a conflict going
on between these two groups. The question is, on which side our
country, our people, are going to stand. Out of these two groups,
I have no doubt that our country will side with that group which
stands for independence and socialism.[4]

Nehru's fascination with socialism had begun during his time in
Cambridge. His ideological beliefs were reinforced when he visited
Soviet Russia in 1927 at the age of thirty-eight. Nehru along with
his family was visiting the country for the tenth anniversary of
the Bolshevik Revolution. What he saw impressed him deeply.
Dr Sarvepalli Gopal points out in Nehru's biography that 'He sailed
from India as a dedicated disciple of Gandhi but returned as a self-
conscious revolutionary radical . . . It is significant that the change
was not affected by the revolutionary situation in India but by what
he saw and heard and read in Europe'.[5]

In fact, he returned to India so full of revolutionary fervour that
Gandhi had to snub him for his naiveté. However, this did not stop him
from convincing Congress as early as 1929 in its All-India Congress
Committee resolution that 'in order to remove the poverty and misery
of the Indian people and to ameliorate the condition of the masses, it
is essential to make revolutionary changes in the present economic
and social structure of society and to remove gross inequalities'.

After Congress won the elections in 1937, Subhash Chandra
Bose was elected as the party president the following year in the
Haripura Congress Session. In October 1938, he called a conference
of the party's ministers of industries. It was agreed upon that
industrialization was the key to the economic revival of the country.
The National Planning Committee was set up on its recommendation
with Nehru as its chairman.

This was India's first attempt at planning, and quite evidently
there was general consensus on the same. Contrary to what would be
expected, Nehru was quite apprehensive about what the committee
could achieve. He wrote : 'It was a strange assortment of different

types and it was not clear how such an odd mixture would work. I accepted the chairmanship of the committee not without hesitation and misgiving; the work was after my own heart and I could not keep out of it.'[6] Nevertheless, between December 1938 and September 1940, the committee met seventy-two times, and Nehru only missed it once.

The committee's professed aim was to create an adequate standard of living within ten years. A total of Rs 50,000 was allotted for its expenses. It created twenty-nine subcommittees that worked in seven main areas of economic interest: agriculture, industry, demography, transport and communication, finance and commerce, public welfare, and education.

Gandhi did not comment on these activities of the party until the Quit India resolution was passed in 1942, demanding full independence from the British. The realization that independence was imminent seemed to have woken him up. In his speech after the passing of the resolution he said: 'In Jawaharlal's scheme of free India, no privileges or privileged classes have a place. Jawaharlal considers all property to be state-owned. He wants [a] planned economy. He wants to reconstruct India according to plan. He likes to fly; I don't. I have kept a place for the princes and the zamindars in the India that I envisage.'[7] He went on to appeal to the princes to renounce ownership of their properties and become 'servants of the people'.

Gandhi's idea of how an independent India should run its economy was quite different from that of Nehru. Gandhi's approach was more centred on the individual while Nehru's more on the state. While Gandhi dreamed of a utopian world where an individual was responsible enough to need little from the state, Nehru imagined a world where the state would create a fair and prosperous world for all.

On 5 October 1945, Gandhi decided to take up the issue directly with his heir. He wrote to Nehru in a letter:

The first thing I want to write about is the difference of outlook between us . . . I am convinced that if India is to attain true freedom, and through India the world also, then sooner or later the facts must be recognized that people will have to live in villages . . . Crores of people will never be able to live at peace with each other in towns and palaces. They will have no recourse but to resort to both violence and untruth. I hold that without truth and nonviolence there can be nothing but destruction of humanity. We can realize truth and nonviolence only in the simplicity of village life.[8]

Gandhi's idea of economic development might seem out of place in today's world, but that is why it is so crucial to understand history in the context of the times. Gandhi firmly believed that villages were the future and the entire world was 'going the wrong way'. Nehru was slightly taken aback by Gandhi's stand and promptly replied from Anand Bhawan four days later:

[T]he question before us is not one of truth versus untruth or non-violence versus violence . . . The whole question is how to achieve this society and what its content should be . . . A village, normally speaking, is backward intellectually and culturally and no progress can be made from a backward environment . . . I do not think it is possible for India to be really independent unless she is a technically advanced country. I am not thinking for the moment in terms of just armies but rather of scientific growth. In the present context of the world, we cannot even advance culturally without a strong background of scientific research in every department.[9]

The two letters need to be read in their entirety for a better understanding of the economic thinking of the two most revered personalities of Indian history. They are reproduced in the Appendix. Gandhi and Nehru discussed the issue further in person, and within a month the former wrote back citing threads of similarity between their viewpoints and a longing to carry on the discussion further.[10] However, that was not to be due to quick political changes and, then, the outbreak of communal violence around the country.

Nevertheless, it is safe to say that in this exchange of ideas, Nehru's approach seems to be more pragmatic. Gandhi's idea was to lay emphasis on spiritual satisfaction. He emphasized on minimizing wants and keeping away from luxuries. He claimed that 'True economics stands for social justice; it promotes the good of all including the weakest and is indispensable for decent life'. It must be kept in mind that he did not advocate the destruction of factories and machinery but sought for a regulation of its excesses.

In the fast-paced modern times, it might seem like a refreshing change to imagine going back to the idyllic Gandhian village. However, it might have been as revolutionary and impractical to adopt the Gandhian economic model as it would have been to turn into a communist nation. Nehru chose the middle ground.

* * *

Around the time Nehru and Gandhi were discussing the optimal economic plan for India, there were other official and non-official schemes being devised. The 'Bombay Plan' was one of the most interesting—both because of its member composition and its ensuing recommendations. The authors of the Plan were some of the leading figures of the industrial and financial worlds of undivided India. It included five businessmen (Sir Purshottamdas Thakurdas, J.R.D. Tata, Ghanshyamdas Birla, Kasturbhai Lalbhai and Sir Lala Shri Ram), two economists (Dr John Mathai and A.D. Shroff) and a former civil servant (Sir Ardeshir Dalal). Together, these eight men carried enormous clout in Indian commercial circles.

They met on 11 December 1942, at Bombay House, the Tatas' headquarters, to lay out a plan for the development of an independent Indian economy. By this time the business community had become completely disillusioned with the colonial state after coming to the realization that their interests would always remain subordinate to Britain's economic interests. A national government seemed like the best bet to 'safeguard India's economic and financial interests'.[11]

The group published a 90-page document in two parts. In the words of its authors, the Bombay Plan was 'a statement . . . of the objectives to be kept in mind in economic planning in India, the general lines on which development should proceed and the demands which planning is likely to make on the country's resources'. It aimed to double the per capita income of the country within fifteen years and achieve a minimum standard of living that it defined in terms of basic necessities of life. The Plan proposed an investment of Rs 10,000 crore over the course of fifteen years to bring about a 130 per cent increase in agricultural output, a 500 per cent rise in industrial output, and an increase in services by 200 per cent.

The most interesting aspect of the Plan was that the state was expected to play a critical role. It argued that 'the existing economic organization, based on private enterprise and ownership, has failed to bring about a satisfactory distribution of the national income'. The state has to intervene to help 'diminish inequalities of income'.[12]

It also called for the state to invest in infrastructure and protect domestic businesses from the influence of foreign capital. In fact, the authors were of the opinion that 'central planning, central coordination and central direction' were crucial for the successful economic development of the country, especially in the initial stages. Interestingly, India's first Five-Year Plan that came into effect much later incorporated many of the features of the Bombay Plan, but none of the authors were ever invited or consulted during its formulation. Nevertheless, this shows that there was a widespread belief at the time that a poor nation that had recently gained independence needed massive state intervention to support and protect itself.

The official line of thinking was also beginning to shift towards higher levels of state involvement even before Independence. In 1944, the British Indian government set up a Department of Planning and Development with Sir Ardeshir Dalal, who was one of the eight Bombay Planners,[13] as its head. The department produced the Industrial Policy Statement in 1945 that suggested licensing of twenty-nine industries of national importance, nationalization of public utilities and public ownership of 'basic industries'.[14]

Independent India would go on to adopt a very similar strategy, but at the time it did not bode well with the British, as Dalal and his colleagues wanted to ensure that maximum benefits from India's industrial development accrue to Indians and proposed that foreign capital should be allowed to hold only a minority interest in domestic companies. The British government rejected New Delhi's proposals, and the department was eventually disbanded in 1946. However, it was replaced by an Advisory Planning Board which recommended that an apolitical Planning Commission be created to coordinate economic management of the country. Not much could be done related to economic matters after this as more demanding matters of Independence and Partition gained primacy.

However, as India gained independence and post-Partition riots were raging, the government did not forget planning. In November 1947, the Constitution and Economic Programme Committee was set up, which submitted its report on 25 January 1948. Among other things, it recommended setting up of the Planning Commission. Vallabhbhai Patel was not in favour of it at the time as he felt that business interests would be tread upon after the creation of such a body. The Indian business class at the time did want state intervention but only to a limited extent. It must be highlighted that the state and the business class at the time shared close links as they had played an integral part in the freedom struggle. The fact that Mahatma Gandhi spent the last 144 days of his life in the house of G.D. Birla is testament to the influence that the business class wielded at the time.

Patel was of the view that strongly established and entrenched interests should be respected—especially those of the bureaucracy and private businesses. Naturally, Nehru, who wanted to establish a modern, socialist nation state, disagreed with him. Patel, on the other hand, felt that it was dangerous to rapidly take a traditional economy down a reformist path. Gandhi, being a powerful force of reconciliation between the two, was trying to convince them to get along until his final days. In fact, the day Gandhi was assassinated, he had gotten late to the tragic prayer meeting because he was in a meeting with Patel to hear him out on his issues with Nehru.

It turns out that Gandhi did ultimately succeed on that front. On 3 February 1948, Nehru wrote to Patel, 'Now, with Bapu's death, everything is changed, and we have to face a different and more difficult world. The old controversies have ceased to have much significance and it seems to me that the urgent need of the hour is for all of us to function as closely and cooperatively as possible. Indeed, there is no other way.'[15] Patel reciprocated two days later with an affectionate response of mutual respect. Neither of them went against Gandhi's wishes and worked together until Patel's abrupt death two years later.

As for the report submitted by the Constitution and Economic Programme Committee, Patel was not the only voice of dissent. The socialists within Congress were also unhappy with the report for reasons that were exactly the opposite of those of Patel. They felt that the report was watered down in favour of private businesses and wanted greater state control over private assets. After consistent ideological disagreements, they left the party to form the Socialist Party in March 1948.

As a result of these developments, Congress published its first Industrial Policy Resolution on 6 April 1948 that adopted a less stringent approach than what even the colonial government had recommended in 1945 under Dalal. It emphasized that India was to have a mixed economy which would reserve an important place for private capital. A monopoly of the state was established only for the manufacture of defence equipment, atomic energy and railways, and rights of the government were reserved for setting up of any new enterprise in industries related to coal, steel, minerals, shipbuilding, aircraft and communications. The rest of the industrial fields was left open to private enterprise. Business houses were also promised that no nationalization would take place for at least ten years.[16]

Thus, India set out on an economic path that tried to include the best of both worlds. It was a society that was trying to establish state control while respecting private property rights, along with having a strong commitment to equality and democracy. This, in fact, broadly defined Nehru's economic vision. While he believed in the steady expansion of the public sector, he also believed in a mixed economy that provided substantial scope for development of private enterprises. His economic approach was, therefore, pragmatic rather than dogmatic. This is best evidenced in his own words from an address to a meeting on 26 December 1950:

> We should try to understand our problems in as realistic a manner as possible, avoiding for the moment words which have long histories behind them and which confuse the mind. When we throw these 'isms' about as arguments, we get lost ... Here in India, there is so much we want – food, clothing, housing, education, health – in fact, all the important things of life. How are we to get them? Surely, not by shouting slogans or passing resolutions about socialism or capitalism or any other 'ism.' We will have to produce goods and distribute them properly.[17]

This was the economic strategy that independent India went on to follow for the first few decades. It did not involve any premature commitment to any ideology but, rather, an emphasis on the maximization of production with distributive justice and equality of opportunity. It was necessary for the nation to adopt the middle ground because any misstep towards extremes at that point would have threatened the very existence of India as a nation.

* * *

The ideological middle ground also seeped into the country's foreign policy. In the formidable cold war dynamics, Nehru advanced the concept of non-alignment. As early as September 1946, he proposed to 'keep away from the power politics of groups aligned against one another, which have led in the past to world wars and which may again lead to disaster on a wider scale'.[18]

There were, in fact, more pragmatic concerns for India's neutral foreign policy: a close border with Soviet Russia, aid requirements from both the West and the Eastern bloc, and, most importantly, with its political, economic and military weakness, it could not afford to make powerful foes. India's left leanings and its policy of non-alignment often put it at odds with the US, especially when it came to matters of foreign aid. American diplomats and leaders found it hard to fight for India's case whenever the need arose and even more so with Nehru's virtual disdain for the country.[19]

The first requirement for American aid came soon after Independence when the government began enforcing a series of economic projects that made external help desirable. In early 1949, the 'Grow More Food' (GMF) campaign was implemented with an aim to raise foodgrain production in the short run and achieve self-sufficiency by 1951. In April, Indian officials made a formal request to the US for aid. Later in the year, Nehru also made his first ever visit to the United States. Even though the Truman administration was quite sceptical of extending aid to India, Ambassador Loy Henderson had suggested the US provide India with an economic aid of USD 500 million as an interest-free loan to help increase food production, and also endorsed India's request for 1 million tonne of wheat.

However, when Nehru arrived in Washington on 11 October after weeks of speculation and rising expectations, it proved to be a major disappointment for everyone concerned. Nehru found little common ground with the Americans and viewed them to be quite materialistic. In fact, the matter of aid was never raised in the interactions with Truman. C.D. Deshmukh, India's finance minister who accompanied Nehru, wrote in his memoirs that probably Nehru saw it beneath India's dignity to appear to be too eager a supplicant. On his return, he explained to his chief ministers that the Americans 'expected more than gratitude and goodwill and that more I could not supply them'.[20]

Nehru's mindset also becomes clearer from an account by T.N. Kaul, a young civil servant, who had also accompanied Nehru on his US visit. When Kaul asked Nehru why he was not taking the US offer for supplying India with a million tonne of food when the nation was in dire need of it, Nehru exclaimed, 'Do you know that I am sitting on an explosive situation? Any country in Asia which cannot feed its people cannot be stable, can't last long. So, we have got to be self-sufficient in foodgrains in the next two or three years, and we must depend on ourselves and not depend on others, particularly when there are strings attached.'[21] Nehru's economic policies carried a reflection of his mind throughout his term in office.

CHAPTER 3

PLANNING AHEAD

The mid-point of the twentieth century was a massive turning point for India. One of the biggest achievements right at the beginning of the second half of the century was the formal acceptance of the Constitution on 26 January 1950. India had transformed itself from a 'dominion', where the British monarch was the head of the state, to a full-fledged republic.

After much debate and discussion for three years, between December 1946 and December 1949, the Drafting Committee wrote the longest constitution in the world with 395 Articles and eight Schedules. Granville Austin, the leading authority on the Indian Constitution, claimed that it was 'a gigantic step for a people previously committed largely to irrational means of achieving other-worldly goals'.[1]

As the constitution-building process was winding up, Nehru once again revived the question of establishing a Planning Commission. Patel was still not in favour of it, but this time Nehru prevailed due to the private sector's inability to effectively better the poor economic situation at the time. The Directive Principles of the Constitution also strengthened the case for setting up of the institution. The government was required to ensure that 'the ownership and control of the material resources of the community are so distributed as best to subserve the common good' and that 'the operation of the economic system does not result in the concentration of wealth and means of production to the common predicament'.

A month after the formal adoption of the Constitution, the finance minister, John Mathai, announced in his budget speech on 28 February that the government had decided to set up the Planning

Commission. Less than a month after that, on 15 March 1950, the government passed a resolution for its formal establishment with Nehru as the chairman. The declared objective of the body was to bring about a rapid rise in the standard of living through efficient exploitation of the nation's resources and increased production.

The Planning Commission was set up as an advisory body, but the extent of powers given to it raised a few questions. John Mathai resigned as the finance minister on the grounds that it was an extra-constitutional authority with too much power. The press statement issued by him upon his resignation read:

> I consider the Planning Commission not merely ill-timed but in its working and general set-up ill-conceived. The Planning Commission was tending to become a parallel cabinet . . . it would weaken the authority of the Finance Ministry and gradually reduce the Cabinet to practically a registering authority.

Mathai cannot be faulted for feeling so at the time. Even though the Five-Year Plans produced by the body were only guidelines and not the force of law, the Commission did acquire some weight because the prime minister was its chairman and a few key ministers were its members. Also, it gained considerable heft in shaping investment decisions as it became a convention that financial sanctions for projects were contingent on its approval.

Most importantly, the Commission would be responsible for devising a national plan and, hence, play a decisive role in settling any competing claims between states and ministries. However, these issues were usually subject to larger political considerations. Also, in many critical areas of policy—for instance, procurement and distribution of food, foreign exchange allocation and the regulation of the private sector—the Commission's influence was merely marginal.

The Commission got to work on the Five-Year Plans immediately, asking the Central and state governments to submit a budget of their resources and development projects so that the First Plan could be formalized by 1951. However, before the landmark year which had given India the Constitution and the Planning Commission could come to an end, tragedy struck.

Vallabhbhai Patel, the only politician who could stand up to Nehru, passed away on 15 December 1950. The twin axis on which Congress revolved, and along with it the nation's fortunes, was broken with his demise. A notable weekly summed up the mood of the nation:

> What makes [Patel's] death such a tragic and such an ominous event is the lack of sufficient indication that what has been rocking us has not yet taken a clear shape. We are still groping in the dark and gaping for the light. Hence the loss of a guide becomes an even greater calamity than it need be. The forces of disruption have not yet been overcome to the extent that we can still hold together without someone powerful enough to hold us together.[2]

It is evident that even three years after Independence there still existed some scepticism and doubt about the continued existence of India as a nation, an idea that Churchill called 'merely a geographical expression' and 'no more a single country than the Equator'. After Patel's death, Nehru was left all alone to hold the nation together. Just a few weeks before the latter's death, Nehru visited Patel at his home on account of his illness. Patel said: 'I want to talk to you alone when I get a little strength . . . I have a feeling that you are losing confidence in me.'

'I have been losing confidence in myself,' answered Nehru.[3]

Thus, without Gandhi and Patel, the following decade and a half were defined by one man: Jawaharlal Nehru. All the successes and failures of the country during this time have to be largely attributed to him. On the economic front, one of his most significant legacies were the Five-Year Plans that the Planning Commission was working on.

Nehru witnessed the implementation of the first three Plans during his lifetime. The draft outline of the first Five-Year Plan (1951–56) was presented in July 1951 and a final version later in December 1952. The First Plan was only meant to be a reconstruction effort to remedy the immediate economic situation of the country that had just gotten itself out of war and Partition. The Plan had some obvious weaknesses as it was formulated in a hurry and with insufficient data. Nehru's speech in the Lok Sabha on the release of the final version of the Plan accepted that the Plan was 'not perfect', but there were broader motives behind enforcing the idea of planning:

> This is the first attempt in India to integrate the agricultural, industrial, social, economic and other aspects of the country into a single framework of thinking. It is a very important step, and even if the thinking is partly faulty, it does not detract from the magnitude of what has been attempted or accomplished. It has made the whole country planning-conscious. It has made people think of this country as a whole. I think it is most essential that India, which is united politically and in many other ways, should, to the same extent, be united mentally and emotionally also.[4]

Despite the accepted inadequacies, the Plan did result in some positive economic changes. Over the Plan period, foodgrain production increased by 20 per cent, exceeding the target expectations. Moreover, the national income of the country rose by 18 per cent, per capita income by 11 per cent and per capita consumption by 9 per cent. These were unprecedented rates for an economy that was practically stagnant for the first half of the century.[5]

A particular highlight of the Plan was an evident emphasis on the role of the state in economic development. Even though the Planning Commission did accept that the public and private sectors could complement each other, it considered a system of quantitative controls over capital issues, industrial licensing, imports and exports, and prices and movement of foodgrains to be of vital importance.

The Plan document asserted that:

> Whether one thinks of the problems of capital formation or the introduction of new techniques or the extension of social services, or the overall realignment of productive forces and class relationships

within society, one comes inevitably to the conclusion that a rapid
expansion of the economic and social responsibilities of the State
will alone be capable of satisfying the legitimate expectations of
the people. This need not involve complete nationalization of
the means of production or elimination of private agencies in
agriculture or business or industry. It does mean, however, a
progressive widening of the private sector to the needs of a planned
economy.

At the same time, the planners also conceded that 'the expansion
of industrial production during the period of the Plan would be
largely the responsibility of the private sector'. They also were quite
welcoming of foreign capital 'when finance was the main handicap
in the progress of industry'.[6] The mixed economy was working at its
fullest.

* * *

The First Five-Year Plan had Nehru written all over it. During his
time, India's plans were Nehru's plans. Also, he carried substantial
popular support for his ideas with regard to the economy. The extent
of public backing behind Nehru was reaffirmed in the very first
general elections that independent India held.

Elections seem quite commonplace in modern India, but back
in 1951, it was a big step for a newly independent nation to directly
delve into universal adult suffrage at a time when most Western
countries reserved voting rights for a selected class. The Indian
electorate consisted of about 176 million Indians aged above twenty-
one, of which 85 per cent could not even read or write. Each of them
had to be identified, named and registered, and that was only the
beginning. A colossal effort lay ahead of the Election Commission
to conduct nationwide elections for almost 3,800 seats—about
500 parliamentary seats and the rest for the provincial assemblies.

The elections were slated for the first few months of 1952 and
Nehru campaigned extensively in the months leading up to it. In fact,

in a space of nine weeks, beginning on 1 October 1951, Nehru covered the country from end to end, travelling approximately 25,000 miles in all: 18,000 by air, 5,200 by car, 1,600 by train, and even 90 by boat.[7]

His efforts really paid off. About 60 per cent of the electorate exercised their franchise. Among these voters, 45 per cent cast their ballot for Congress in the parliamentary elections and a little more than 42 per cent in the contest for state assembly seats. As a result, the party won 364 out of 489 seats in Parliament and 2,247 out of 3,280 seats in the state assemblies.

The results, therefore, established Nehru's authority over questions of economic and social policy in an even stronger way. As a result, when the final version of the First Plan was published in December 1952, it was stronger in its tone and approach, especially towards industrial development. The most striking of these was the mandate that the private sector would have to operate within the provisions of the Industries (Development and Regulation) Act, 1951. As per the Act, no new industrial unit or subsequent expansions to existing plants could be made without a licence issued by the Central government. Thus, began the infamous 'licence and permit raj', a term popularized by C. Rajagopalachari[8] who was motivated by its fallacies to exit Congress and launch his Swatantra Party at the end of the decade.

The pursuit of creating a socialist society where the state guided production created a Frankenstein's monster in the form of the licence raj. The long-term repercussions of this very legislation were deleterious to India's growth prospects. No private business could set up a new firm or aim for expansion without the approval of government authorities. This opened up avenues for corruption and exploitation by government officials, which only accentuated with time, and infused lethargy in the Indian business environment.

Another notable change in the final version of the First Plan was in regard to the agricultural sector. The planners felt that the basic cause of India's agricultural backwardness was not inadequate technology per se, but the exploitative socio-economic factors that had throttled the dynamism of rural India. Higher levels of output, therefore, depended less on the application of modern scientific methods, which few cultivators could afford, but on the transformation of the existing institutional framework to provide small farmers with proper incentives to enhance production through efficient application of traditional farming techniques.

It would seem puzzling that a person like Nehru, who admired the advances in the field of science and technology, did not favour the modernization of agriculture. But, there was a unique aspect of the Indian agrarian economy that needed to be dealt with first. Throughout the British rule, the landlord class (called the zamindars) was the instrument of exploitation for the colonists. In most villages across India, the British delegated the duty of collecting taxes to these feudal zamindars who, in turn, used any means necessary to fulfil their financial obligations. This class expectedly generated a sense of disgust among everyone, from the leaders who led the freedom struggle down to the poorest farmer. Since these zamindars owned vast tracts of rural land even after Independence, resources were denied to the agricultural sector as any such transfer would only empower the rural rich. Therefore, increasing imports were more acceptable to sustain the food economy rather than modernizing agriculture.

The planners also realized that agricultural productivity was affected by the inequitable distribution of land holdings in India. Approximately 61 per cent of households held no land or held marginal holdings, and so were effectively uneconomic. The rest of the households accounted for 92 per cent of the country's agricultural holdings. These lands were usually so large that landowners had little incentive to make investments that would improve farm productivity.

So, the final version of the Plan proposed land reform that would involve a significant redistribution of land. In a reversal from the Draft Outline, the final document stated that it was now 'in favour of the principle that there should be an upper limit to the amount of land that an individual may hold'. As a result, the state governments passed laws with the aim of abolishing landlordism, distributing land through the imposition of ceilings and protection of tenants.

However, at that point of time, Right to Property was guaranteed as a Fundamental Right, and the ceiling legislations met with lawsuits across the country from affected landlords.

Therefore, the contradiction between legislature and judiciary proved to be a serious impediment to land redistribution and reform. A series of constitutional amendments were passed to address the situation.[9] Nevertheless, such persistent legal issues prevented any effective land reforms. Also, by 1954, the Planning Commission shifted its focus to formulating a design for rapid industrialization of the country under the Second Plan.

* * *

Despite some failures, the First Plan was largely seen as a success as it had been implemented at a time of institutional instability and economic uncertainty. The agricultural sector, which accounted for over half of the national product, also benefitted from good monsoon seasons in 1953–54 and 1954–55 and from the modest but significant irrigation investments. The resultant surge in agricultural output dampened inflationary pressures within the economy and stimulated demand for manufactured goods. This easing of economic conditions after 1954 allowed for a more ambitious approach with the Second Five-Year Plan (1956–61).

The leading architect of the Second Plan was Professor Prasanta Chandra Mahalanobis, a Cambridge-trained physicist, and statistician, who was Nehru's most trusted adviser on planning. Mahalanobis had become acquainted with Nehru on his trips to Shantiniketan in the 1930s. In 1931, he set up the Indian Statistical Institute (ISI) that went on to become a world-class centre of training and research within a decade. He was appointed as an honorary statistical adviser to the Union Cabinet in 1949. In the years that followed, he established the National Sample Survey (NSS) and the Central Statistical Organization (CSO). Since then, these institutions have played a key role in recording the most reliable statistics for the Indian economy.

He became involved in the process of planning when the government approached the ISI in 1954 to study the problem of unemployment. The note that Mahalanobis sent back on the subject left an indelible impression on Nehru, so much so that he asked the ISI to prepare a draft of the Second Five-Year Plan.

The formulation process of the Plan marked the pinnacle of Nehru's personal influence in the government and the planning process. In 1952, the National Development Council (NDC) had been set up to involve chief ministers in the process of economic planning. However, as Congress was in power in the majority of states, there was a virtual absence of a countervailing voice within the Council. In regular letters to the chief ministers, Nehru described the socialist approach in planning as an 'adventure worthy of this country'. None of these ministers would dare interfere in a project that was so close to Nehru's heart. Planning, therefore, had become a Nehru-run show.

In a meeting of the Council on 9 November 1954, Nehru decided to reaffirm the idea that he had in mind for India and the upcoming Plan:

> The picture I have in mind is definitely and absolutely a socialistic picture of society. I am not using the word in a dogmatic sense at all. I mean largely that the means of production should be socially owned and controlled for the benefit of society as a whole. There is plenty of room for private enterprise provided the main aim is kept clear.[10]

Nehru's speech also went on to establish that mere expansion of the consumer goods industry based on imported machinery could not address India's poverty problems. Rather, the country needed to follow an import substitution strategy that would strengthen the domestic capacity of capital formation. He added that 'the basic things'—metals, power and heavy machinery—had to be produced in India. The first hints of the Second Five-Year Plan were beginning to appear.

A month after that, the Lok Sabha committed itself to 'a socialistic pattern of society'. The Congress Steering Committee that met on 8 January 1955 decided to present an official resolution on economic policy before the 60th Session of the party at Avadi, near Madras, that was to be held between 17 and 23 January. Avadi would go on to enter the history books.

Quite expectedly, Nehru was the one to move the resolution at Avadi. More than 300,000 people had gathered to hear him speak. He took pride in the historical role that the party had played in the country's freedom struggle, claiming that the history of the country was the history of the Congress. Now, the party was navigating the nation through a new phase of development and growth. He added that everything 'we now do should be governed by the ideal of a socialistic society'. However, he went on to say:

> We are not going to get socialism by resolutions, even by a decree, or by saying that there is socialism. We can only get it by hard work, by increasing our production and distributing it equally. . .
> I put this resolution because I think it represents the hopes and aspirations of the Indian people and much more than that. It is a pledge which you and I take—not a pledge, but a challenge to the future that we are determined to conquer.

The Avadi Session marked the ideological shift of Congress and the nation towards a socialistic pattern of society of Nehru's dreams, along with a hint of the Gandhian principle of cooperation. His vision had the complete backing of the masses. On the second day of the Session, a fifty-year-old woman walked up to him and placed a golden crown on his head, calling him the real Lord Krishna of modern India. M.J. Akbar writes in his biography of Nehru: 'Till 1919 the Congress was Hume's party. Till January 1955 it was Gandhi's party. After 1955 it became a Gandhi-Nehru party.'[11]

Mahalanobis put Nehru's idea into practice based on a model that the polymath had first described in an essay on growth.[12] Assuming a closed two-sector economy that produced only capital and consumer goods, it could be shown that a higher level of initial investment in capital goods (or goods that are utilized for production of other goods and services, instead of being directly bought by consumers) resulted in higher levels of output and growth, different from a scenario where the initial allocation was skewed towards consumer goods. The key to economic growth, therefore, lay in investment in the production of capital goods by means of a public sector–dominated 'industry-first' policy. The Second Five-Year Plan was based on this line of thinking.

The focus on capital goods was deemed necessary for two reasons. First, it would rapidly industrialize the country and safeguard its economic, and hence political, independence. Second, it was expected to address the problem of unemployment. Mahalanobis was of the view that 'Unemployment is chronic because of [the unavailability of] capital goods'. The most efficient way to create jobs is to build dams and factories.

The contrast between the First and the Second Plan could be evidently seen in the distribution of outlay towards agriculture and industry.[13] Between the two Plans, the total outlay towards agriculture and irrigation fell from 26.3 to 14 per cent, while that of industry escalated from 7.6 to 18.5 per cent.[14] The Second Plan also reinforced the importance of the public sector as an instrument of industrialization. While private investment in organized industries had been more than twice that of the public outlay in the First Plan, the Second Plan reversed the order and allocated more to the public sector—mainly to the 'heavy goods' sector.[15]

The Plan aimed to rapidly industrialize India, which expectedly demanded a Herculean effort of resource mobilization, the single largest instance of it during the Nehru era. The most notable aspect of the method of financing was the role that the public sector was expected to play in the matter. The early planners expected the public sector to foray into industrial and commercial activities so that its profits could provide the required resources for public use. Therefore, the expected role of the public sector was not welfare-oriented, but to raise resources for public purposes.

The second point to note is that the planners made no attempts to be populist in nature, even though the elections were around the corner. Increased taxation was seen as the obvious recourse by the policymakers to raise resources for the Plan. Mahalanobis provides the clearest stand on these two aspects:

> In the highly developed countries of the West, taxes on commodities are usually looked upon as 'regressive,' as being a burden on the poor. Public enterprises are also expected to be run on a no-loss-no-profit basis. Fortunately, our outlook is changing, and it is being realized that in an underdeveloped country like India, excise and custom duties, purchase tax on commodities or a levy on services would be convenient and adaptable methods to raise resources. It is also agreed in principle that public enterprises should earn and contribute increasing returns for purposes of national development.[16]

The viewpoint adopted by the economic planners of the time—that which is devoid of populism and which perceives the public sector as a viable source of revenue—stands in stark contrast to much of the contemporary thinking of modern politicians.

The Plan expectedly faced severe criticism from the business community. The sole point of agreement was the increased outlay and higher allocation to basic and heavy industry. Everything else in the Plan was fervently challenged. The association of business organizations Federation of Indian Chambers of Commerce and Industry (FICCI) even called for a revision in the official approach towards the all-pervasive role of the public sector in the economy.[17]

It must also be noted that a solitary economist, B.R. Shenoy,[18] on the panel of economists who submitted the draft of the Second Five-Year Plan, wrote a comprehensive note of dissent. He made two very crucial points. First, he feared that considering the massive size of the Plan and the excessive dependence on borrowing will be particularly inflationary. Adopting a pace of growth that is not matched by availability of real resources would only result in inflation. Second, he pointed out the growing role of the government would undermine democratic processes. He was of the view that excessive usage of legislative and administrative measures to control the economy infringes upon the personal liberty of the individual. In hindsight, his assessment proved to be fairly accurate. The ambitious Plan, which called for higher imports, especially that of capital goods, would go on to create a problem of balance of payments in 1957. Indian exports stagnated that year and the country found it increasingly difficult to finance its import bill.

Despite the criticisms, the government did not change its stance, but instead the private sector was assured 'the opportunity to develop and expand' with a new Industrial Policy Resolution in 1956. The resolution then classified industries into three categories: all new units in seventeen industries of 'basic and strategic importance'[19] were reserved for the public sector. Another twelve 'essential' industries[20] were left predominantly to the public sector, while the private sector was only expected to supplement the efforts of the state. The rest were open to both public and private sectors subject to the targets of the national plan and the licensing provisions and import controls.

The industrial policy, therefore, focused on 'capital goods as the leading sector and the state as the leading actor'.[21] This would be India's economic strategy for industrial development for at least the next three decades.

* * *

The Indian planning process and its extensive focus on capital goods ascribed particular focus to two economic activities: the production of power and the production of steel. Nehru regarded them as the 'essential bases' of planning. A newly independent economy with an urgent need to expand necessitated the development of these sectors.

Construction of large dams was seen as means to build the country's power-generating capacity. It would also provide indispensable water for irrigation and prevent flooding, making India self-sufficient in food production. Even before independence was gained, Indian scientists and engineers visited America and Russia to understand how dams were built. They were absolutely impressed by what they saw.[22]

The first Plan proposed three major hydroelectric projects—the Bhakra–Nangal dam in Punjab, the Hirakud dam in Orissa and the Nagarjuna Sagar dam in Andhra Pradesh. Bhakra dam was one of the biggest projects of the time as, at 680 feet, it was expected to be the second-highest in the world after the Grand Coulee Dam on the Colorado River. The project would generate nearly a million kilowatts of energy and irrigate about 7.4 million acres of land. It was a colossal effort. When Nehru inaugurated the dam on 8 July 1954, he famously declared:

> For me, the temples, the gurudwaras, the churches, the mosques of today are these places where human beings labour for the benefit of other human beings, of humanity as a whole. They are the temples of today. I feel more, if I may use the word, religious-minded when I see these great works than when I see any temple or any place of pure worship. These are the places of worship because here we worship something; we build up India; we build up the millions of India, and so this is a sacred task.

Political scientist Henry Hart wrote a detailed account of the event in *New India's Rivers*. He noted that as Nehru switched on the powerhouse of the Bhakra dam, planes of the Indian Air Force dipped their wings overhead, and as he opened the gates of the dam and the water began to flow, villagers set off hundreds of fireworks downstream. Hart called these projects 'the greatest of the monuments of free India'.[23]

The production of steel was the second monumental aspect of Indian planning. While the Second Plan was in the works, the Indian government signed three separate agreements with three countries for the construction of steel plants. The Germans would build a plant in Rourkela in Orissa, the British in Durgapur in West Bengal and, most significantly, the Russians in Bhilai in Madhya Pradesh. The last one particularly caught American attention. Things got more worrisome for them when Soviet Prime Minister Nikolai Bulganin and Communist Party Secretary Nikita Khrushchev decided to visit India in November 1955. On his visit, Nikita called Bhilai the 'Magnitogorsk of India',[24] and Russian media hailed it as a symbol of Indo-Russian cooperation.

Apart from the economic logic behind the domestic production of capital goods, these large-scale projects to build formidable dams and steel plants were meant to imbibe a spirit of self-reliance and self-sufficiency among Indians and provide a living refutation of the belief that they were backward in any sense of the word. The sense of pride that came with these projects is difficult to imagine in hindsight. But, after years of being subjugated by a foreign power and being treated as an inferior race, the sight of such monumental projects built by the same countrymen must have been an inspiring experience.

CHAPTER 4

FIRST SIGNS OF CRISIS

The efforts to rapidly industrialize India in the Second Five-Year Plan did not come without a price. The proportion of total amount allocated to agriculture and irrigation in the Plan had to be reduced from 26.3 to 14 per cent in the Second Plan. Even in absolute terms, the outlay for agriculture witnessed only a marginal increase while that for irrigation fell![1]

This was despite the fact that the planners had estimated that India's foodgrain requirement would double over a ten-year period. However, given the extent of outlays on agricultural production programmes, the Planning Commission itself estimated that total production could only expand by 15 per cent during the Five-Year Plan period. Such a discrepancy arose due to different ideas of the pace of agrarian reform between the planners and the state leadership.

The Planning Commission was of the view that agricultural production could be substantially improved, given the investment outlays, merely through an efficient use of resources. In fact, V.T. Krishnamachari, the deputy chairman of the Planning Commission, even circulated a note in a meeting of the National Development Council claiming that, given the allocation in the Second Plan, agricultural production could be increased by 40 per cent. A.P. Jain, the Union Food and Agriculture Minister at the time, expressed strong disagreement with Krishnamachari's figures, claiming that, given the Plan allocation, the maximum possible increase could only be a little over 15 per cent.

The Commission's stance was strengthened by reports from China that showed that, as a result of agrarian reorganization and mobilization of idle manpower, the country would be able to boost agricultural output by 35 to 40 per cent over five years. Nehru picked up on the contrast between the planned outcomes of India and China: 'Our original estimate was for a 15 per cent increase in agricultural production during the Second Plan. This manifestly is too little. The Chinese estimate is between 35 and 40 per cent in five years, and they start with a higher yield per acre. There is absolutely no reason why, if we are serious enough and work hard, we cannot equal the Chinese rate of progress in this matter.'

To study China's methods, both the Planning Commission and the food ministry sent delegations to the country in July 1956. Both delegations did come to similar conclusions that the mere establishment of cooperatives across China had led to vast improvements in agricultural output through utilization of surplus labour power. By December 1956, the National Development Council gave way and voted to adopt higher targets of foodgrain production without any increase in investment outlays, though not as high as the planners would have wanted. Later, the NDC also voted to establish 2,000 cooperative farms during the Plan period.

However, reality proved to be a difficult taskmaster for the Planning Commission. The summer of 1957 proved to be a particularly difficult year for the Indian agricultural sector. The monsoons failed to make an impact, affecting production and escalating prices. The government had already imported 2 million tonnes of foodgrains in 1956-57, which was one-third of the total amount allowed for the five-year period. In the following year, it had to import another 4 million.

These food imports also included the first PL480 agreement[2] with the US to import rice, wheat and cotton over a three-year period. The agreement with India was not reached easily as critics in the US vociferously attacked the government's efforts to assist non-aligned nations. President Eisenhower, however, argued that a neutral stance by a nation does not necessarily imply 'a position between right and wrong'. Instead, in most cases, it simply signifies an aversion to military alliances.

However, despite the import of foodgrains by the Indian government, the food minister, A.P. Jain, admitted in the Lok Sabha that, 'we could not make up the total deficit [and] prices did go up to a level which was quite unprecedented'.[3] Hoarding activities by traders worsened the situation. The Planning Commission was convinced that the country should undertake 'progressive and planned socialization of the wholesale trade in foodgrains'.[4]

A.P. Jain was simply not convinced with the idea of price controls and state trading as he felt that it would be akin to what Stalin and Mao had done by force in Russia and China.[5] Nehru, however, told the chief ministers, in August 1957, that he saw no other solution to the problem of food shortages other than government purchase of foodgrains at controlled prices.

As foreign exchange was getting depleted, the option of continued commercial imports was also slipping away. So, the food ministry ultimately agreed to begin its own procurement and distribution operations along with the implementation of price controls. This marked the beginning of the public distribution system (PDS), through which foodgrains were distributed cheaply through a network of 'fair-price shops'. Also, no effort was made to replace the private trader with a state trading organization. However, the food crisis continued as prices rose and shortages remained chronic. By September 1958, the government had signed another PL480 agreement with the US, further deteriorating India's foreign exchange position.

The economic cost of these efforts had a drastic impact on the Second Plan. The inflationary pressures also pushed up the costs of planned industrial projects. As higher financial outlays were not feasible, the Planning Commission had to lower the physical targets. However, the 'core projects'[6] were protected through a reallocation of funds. As Shenoy had predicted, the Plan was too ambitious, keeping India's resource constraints in perspective.

To make matters worse, serious budgetary shortfalls were realized two years into the Plan, which depressed the Plan outlay far lower than originally expected. The sterling balances, which had proved to be an effective cushion against any balance of payment problems, had already been spent by 1956. Taxation proved to be the only dependable source of revenue. In fact, mobilization of resources from taxation exceeded the planned targets. But that was not pleasing to the masses for obvious reasons. A culmination of these factors led to the emergence of the first signs of political discontent across India.

In the general elections of 1957, even though the Congress won both at the Centre and the states, there was a marked difference to the victory from the ones in the previous elections. A shift in voter sentiment towards the left was quite prominent. The Communist Party of India (CPI) emerged as the largest opposition party in the Lok Sabha. In fact, the party also left a mark in the state assemblies. In Kerala, Congress had to witness the formation of the first communist ministry in India. In Madras, C. Rajagopalachari broke away from Congress after being disillusioned with the party's socialist leanings and formed a new party, which emerged as the second-largest party in the state. Nehru warned that 'if the forces released by democracy and adult franchise were not mastered, they would march on, leaving the Congress aside'.[7]

The major issues raised by most political parties at the time revolved around the economic discontent of the masses, including increased taxation, rising unemployment levels and rampant poverty.[8] Clearly, Indian voters were beginning to develop a sense of disappointment with the economic mismanagement by the national leadership. A noteworthy takeaway from the voting pattern is that Indians were not sceptical of the idea of socialism but were growing dissatisfied with the failures of its implementation.

Later in the year, the Nehru government was also rocked by the first corruption scam of free India, which eventually led to the resignation of the finance minister, T.T. Krishnamachari. It emerged that in June 1957, the public sector company Life Insurance Cooperation (LIC) had made the largest investment yet of Rs 1.24 crore in six companies owned by Haridas Mundhra, a Calcutta-based businessman. The Investment Committee had not even been consulted on the investment, against regular protocol. The order seemed to have emerged from the highest offices of the government and the investment was made despite the fact that Mundhra's companies were bleeding money and he was siphoning off huge chunks of money.[9]

Nehru's son-in-law, Feroze Gandhi, demanded an explanation for LIC's puzzling decisions. In early 1958, Nehru set up a one-man enquiry commission under former chief justice M.C. Chagla, who submitted a report within a month. The hearings were held in public where crowds used to gather in such huge numbers that loudspeakers had to be set up outside the courtroom. When Chagla finally filed his report, and it emerged that Mundhra's companies were obnoxiously rotten, Krishnamachari had to resign while the businessman was arrested and sentenced to twenty-two years in prison.[10] Nothing seemed to be going right for Nehru.

* * *

The Second Plan was proving to be disastrous. The issues ailing the agriculture sector, combined with a stark limitation of financial resources, was becoming severely problematic. The National Development Council met again in November 1958 to discuss the economic situation. Nehru revived the issue of establishing agricultural cooperatives on the lines of China's and also recommended socialization of foodgrain trading. The NDC endorsed both the moves and gave its formal approval for the reorganization of the village community into cooperatives and immediate implementation of state trading in foodgrains.

In the following annual session of the Congress held at Nagpur in January 1959, the party unanimously approved the formation of cooperative farms. The resolution stated that:

> The future agrarian pattern should be that of cooperative joint farming, in which the land will be pooled for joint cultivation, the farmers continuing to retain their property rights, and getting a share from the net produce in proportion to their land. Further,

those who actually work the land, whether they own the land or
not, will get a share in proportion to the work put in by them on
the joint farm.

The resolution also endorsed state trading of foodgrains and setting
of minimum floor prices at which farmers could sell crops directly to
the government. Although all of these policies of agrarian reform were
already a part of the Five-Year Plans, the resolution set a concrete
timeline for its implementation. The transition to cooperative village
management was supposed to be undertaken by 1962—the second
year of the Third Plan.

Such an urgent and revolutionary tone of the party was not
accepted without dissent. In the months following the Nagpur
resolution, the media widely attacked the Plan to collectivize Indian
agriculture by 'Sino-socialist minded planners'.[11] Veteran leaders
like C. Rajagopalachari, who had already left the party, and N.G.
Ranga, who was organizing dissidents inside the Congress party to
break away, spoke and wrote strongly against the idea of agrarian
cooperatives.[12]

There were also fears about the means the government would
adopt in establishing cooperatives. Even though Chinese-style
coercion was not expected, Nehru was aware of the fact that some
unwilling peasants would have to be overruled. He clarified in
Parliament that, 'There is no question of coercion. There is no
question of a new law . . . But I do believe in cooperation, and I do
firmly and absolutely believe in the righteousness of joint cultivation.
Let there be no doubt. I do not wish to hide my own beliefs in this
matter. I shall go from field to field and peasant to peasant begging
them to agree to it, knowing that if they do not agree, I cannot put it
into operation.'[13]

The ground reality proved to be far more complex than Nehru's
belief. In order to meet the targets of the Nagpur resolution, around
6,000 new cooperatives had to be set up each month over a period of
three years, and about 70,000 workers had to be trained annually. But
when Indira Gandhi, Nehru's daughter and Congress Party President,

at the time, called for volunteers for training to organize cooperatives, merely 600 members of Congress came forward.

Due to the utter lack of enthusiasm among party workers, targets had to be revisited. The Working Committee realized that universal membership into cooperatives could not be achieved before the end of the Second Plan and joint farming could not be implemented until after the Third Plan. However, the idea of cooperative farming met its inevitable end when the training camps, which were supposed to begin from 1 June, had to be discontinued due to lack of support at all levels of the party.

On the other hand, the plan to implement state trading hardly found a better start. A.P. Jain, who had never been supportive of the idea, cited various administrative and logistical difficulties in the process, with the biggest being a lack of storage space for buffer stocks. He also made no effort to address these challenges in his remaining tenure as food minister until his resignation in August 1959. Moreover, food shortages and price rises continued throughout 1958-59 despite limited efforts by the government to implement state trading, which did not make a strong case for the policy.

As for the remainder of the Plan period, the new food minister, S.K. Patil, gave up on any attempts to take things forward on the socialization of foodgrain distribution. Instead, the government relied on imports under PL480 and the like. In fact, in May 1960, India got into a new agreement with the US for import of rice and wheat over a four-year period.

Such consistently high dependence on imports during the entire Plan period deteriorated India's external sector. During the five-year period, imports cost the country Rs 537 crore, which was far in excess of the target of Rs 434 crore. On the other hand, India's share in the total world exports, which stood at 1.5 per cent in 1953, when trading conditions stabilized after the Korean War, declined to 1.4 per cent in 1956, to 1.3 per cent in 1958 and, eventually, to 1.2 per cent in 1960.[14]

In all, during the Second Plan period, the national income increased by about 20 per cent against a target of 25 per cent. The increase was more muted in per capita terms as the population grew by over 2 per cent, as compared to the original estimate of 1.2 per cent. Against a target of 18 per cent, the rise in per capita income turned out to be merely 9 per cent during the Plan period. Also, due to the unexpected rise in population, unemployment also rose to the tune of 9 million by the end of the Plan period.

However, considering the fact that India was a virtually stagnant economy in the first half of the century, the economic performance in the first decade after Independence was quite significant. During the first two Plan periods, national income rose by about 42 per cent, and per capita income rose by over 16 per cent. This improvement in income levels was experienced across sectors. Agricultural production increased by 41 per cent in this span of ten years, industrial production by about 94 per cent and power sector by 148 per cent. The standard of living also improved in terms of life expectancy, which rose from 32 to 47.5 years.

Also, through the decade, Nehru, who was a fervent believer in the merits of science and technology, famously worked towards establishing technical institutions for higher learning, including laying the foundation of the famed Indian Institute of Technology (IIT).[15] The number of engineering colleges and polytechnics over the decade shot up from 134 to 380.[16] On a related note, Nehru also encouraged two Cambridge-educated scientists to establish institutions that would prove to have historic legacies in the country. The first was the setting up of the Atomic Energy Commission by Homi J. Bhabha, which proved to be key in building India's nuclear capability. The other institution was the Committee for Space Research (COSPAR) by Vikram Sarabhai, which would evolve into the Indian Space Research Organisation (ISRO) and put India on the map of space science research and planetary exploration.

* * *

The latter half of the 1950s was proving to be disappointing, and not just for economic reasons. A new border dispute with China was rearing its head—one which Nehru had not anticipated. Over the years, Nehru had shown that he held a soft spot for China. He ensured that India was one of the first countries to recognize the People's Republic of China and even refused an American offer for a permanent seat in the United Nations Security Council as he felt that China's status in UN should be given priority. Nehru saw these moves as a moral debt that China would repay in due time with favourable policy adjustments towards Indian concerns.

In 1954, the two countries even agreed to 'Five Principles of Peaceful Coexistence', famously known as the Panchsheel Treaty, which called for non-interference in each other's internal affairs. The next year in the Bandung Conference, when Asian and African countries met together to put on a display of strength and cooperation against colonial forces, India and China put on a united front.

However, a possible issue of discord between the two countries was the border that separated India's north-eastern region from China's Tibetan region. In 1914, a British colonial administrator, Henry McMahon, got into a border agreement with Tibetan representatives without Chinese participation. When Chinese Prime Minister Zhou En-lai visited India in 1956, he urged Nehru to formally recognize the 'colonial' McMahon Line as the border between the two nations, but the latter did not take up the offer for reasons unknown.

Things began to turn sour when, in 1958, India discovered that China had completed the construction of a road linking Xinjiang with Tibet, which passed through Kashmir (an area locally known as Aksai Chin), across the other border that the two countries shared. The territorial intrusion was formalized when a map appeared in *China Pictorial* that showed Aksai Chin as a part of China. Nehru was expectedly furious and traded a series of letters with Zhou over the next few years, expressing surprise over the Chinese act.

Around this time there were also protests in eastern Tibet against the forced occupation by Chinese troops. The revolt was successfully put down by Chinese troops, but the Tibetan god-king, the Dalai Lama, felt threatened. Perhaps out of annoyance with the Chinese intrusion into India, Nehru decided to give political asylum to the

Dalai Lama in 1959. Zhou felt that India had crossed a red line by interfering in China's internal matters. By the end of that year, border troops on either side had also begun to exchange fire.

Zhou visited India in 1960 on India's invitation to discuss the border question and spent a week, meeting Nehru every day. He finally offered Nehru the option to accept India's claim on the eastern front (the north-eastern region) if India accepts China's claim on the western front (the Kashmir region). However, Nehru viewed China's gains in Kashmir as illegal and did not accept the offer. Talks broke down with no solution in sight. Thus, at the turn of the decade and into the final lap of the Nehru years, India was sailing in troubled waters on both economic and geopolitical fronts.

CHAPTER 5

WAR AND DISSENT

As the Second Plan was nearing its end, discussions had begun around the specifics of the Third Five-Year Plan. It was recognized that agriculture needed to be brought back into focus to correct the missteps of the Second Plan. In a meeting of the National Development Council held in April 1959, Nehru stated that the main aim of the Third Plan should be to 'bring about institutional change'.[1] This implied setting up of village cooperatives and state trading of foodgrains. The state leaders again chose not to oppose Nehru's stand on the matter and put on an appearance of a united party.

However, forces outside Congress found legitimate grounds to attack the Congress leadership. The newly formed Swatantra Party portrayed the actions of Congress as an attack on free enterprise while the Jana Sangh denounced its policies as ones that would impoverish agriculturalists and push India towards communism. The United States weighed in as well, suggesting that the Plan should prioritize agriculture over heavy industries, but not in the manner that the government wanted. The Ford Foundation issued a 'Report on India's Food Crisis and Steps to Meet It' and criticized the government's approach to agrarian reform through institutional change. Instead, it called for a technocratic approach that would be based on price incentives to farmers and higher investment in modern inputs.

Despite all external criticism, the final version of the Plan went ahead with its policy of institutional change. The timeline for implementation of these policies was, however, kept less ambitious than what the Planning Commission would have wanted, as state leadership cited numerous administrative and organizational difficulties. In fact, the Planning Commission acquiesced to watering down some aspects of the Plan almost to the point of immobilization. The concessions that were decided to be given to the propertied class to win their cooperation were so large that it almost became impossible to carry out any meaningful implementation of land reforms.

The expectations from the Plan were further compromised when the 1961 Census showed that the population was growing at a higher rate than the estimates that were used during the planning process (2.3 per cent instead of 2 per cent annually). Therefore, the per capita (or, per person) gains expected out of the budgeted expenditure of the Plan had to be toned down. The Census findings also pointed to the pressing problem of unemployment.[2] Despite these issues, no further allocations could be made for additional financing as the cost of the physical programmes was already about Rs 500 crore higher than the financial provisions of the Plan. In all, the total outlay towards agriculture and irrigation was around 17.8 per cent of the Plan finances while industry was awarded 20 per cent. Both of these sectoral distributions were higher than that of the Second Plan.[3]

Implementation of the Plan proved even more difficult. The efforts to mobilize local idle manpower for community development projects met with little success. Local officials realized that it was impossible to mobilize labour for unpaid work, even for minor projects like construction of approach roads or drinking water wells, as the greatest beneficiaries were usually the richer sections. Roads linking villages to nearby markets only benefitted cultivators while social amenities like common wells were of no use to lower castes due to widespread social discrimination.

As the Third Plan was being implemented, preparations were also being undertaken for the third general elections. Unlike the first two general elections where Congress pitched itself as the party that had won the nation her independence, the 1962 election campaign focused more on its achievements. There was also the development of strong opposition parties that catered to the demands of specific sections of society, unlike Congress, which had been politically accommodative of all communities. There was the Swatantra Party that stood for the interests of the business community, and the Jana Sangh that fancied itself on representing the Hindus. There were also regional parties like the Dravida Munnetra Kazhagam (DMK) that stood for the Tamil community against the northern domination in politics.

All of these parties attacked the Congress aim of establishing a socialistic pattern of society and its performance until now. In response, Nehru reinforced the party's goal in the election manifesto from a Gandhian-sounding 'cooperative commonwealth' to a more Marxist-sounding 'establishment of a socialist state'. He also ran another strong election campaign, travelling about 14,000 miles by road, rail and air, appearing before an estimated 20 million people. He even gave personal endorsements to candidates committed to the socialist cause for the first time in his political career.

Even though Congress retained its majority in Parliament, winning 361 out of 494 seats, support for the party had clearly dipped. About 45 per cent of the electorate voted for the Congress, compared to 48 per cent in the previous election, resulting in a loss of 18 seats. In states, the tally had fallen from 45 per cent to a little over 43 per cent. A closer inspection revealed a worsening situation. The party had managed to win only 1 out of every 3 additional votes cast in 1962 over 1957. Therefore, young voters were beginning to get disillusioned with the policies of the Congress.[4]

The Jana Sangh managed to increase its membership in the Lok Sabha from 4 to 14, while the new party Swatantra put up an impressive show with 18 seats. The rise of the two parties in the Indian political arena was seen as a reaction of the propertied class to protect their position against Nehru's policies of socialism and planning.[5]

* * *

Nehru's political stature further weakened with the unfortunate events that took place in the summer of 1962. Since India gave asylum to the Dalai Lama, China was quite sceptical of its neighbour's territorial aims towards Tibet. The feeling grew stronger as India increased military presence on its borders in disputed areas to prevent further advances by Chinese troops like the one in Aksai Chin. Due to these developments, China's belief of India's expansionist aims were strengthened and border clashes increased. In the third week of July, Indian troops and Chinese troops clashed in the Galwan valley of Ladakh, and then in early September, conflict ensued over the disputed Dhola ridge[6] that was about sixty miles west of Tawang, the region where the Indian, Tibetan and Bhutanese border meets. A stand-off began at the ridge with troops from both nations on either side of a narrow river waiting for their leaders to signal the next move.

Angry letters were exchanged between the two nations, yielding no results. Finally, on the night of 19 October, Chinese forces launched a simultaneous attack on the western and eastern fronts, taking India by surprise. They moved deeper and deeper into Indian territory, taking control of over eight posts in Ladakh and almost twenty in the north-east, ultimately reaching Tawang.[7]

The Chinese halted their advance on 24 October, and Nehru received a letter from Zhou who wanted to reopen border negotiations as 'our two peoples' common interest in their struggle against imperialism outweighs by far all the differences between our two countries'. In his response, Nehru poured out his sense of betrayal and shock:

> Nothing in my long political career has hurt me more and grieved me more than the fact that the hopes and aspirations for peaceful and friendly neighbourly relations which we entertained and to promote . . . worked so hard . . . should have been shattered by the hostile and unfriendly twist given in India-China relations during the past few years.[8]

He went on to add that India would only resolve the differences 'on the basis of decency, dignity and self-respect, and not under threat of military might'. The Chinese offer of a ceasefire, therefore, came to a nought and military offensive resumed on 15 November. Meanwhile, America, Britain, France and Canada came to India's military aid. By 20 November, Chinese forces were poised to reach the plains of Assam, and panic spread. Surprisingly, on 22 November, China abruptly announced a unilateral ceasefire and began withdrawing troops by 1 December. In the north-east, they withdrew behind the McMahon Line, and in Kashmir reinstated troops at positions that they had held before the war.

The sudden retreat could have been due to a mix of reasons. The West was coming to India's support, and arms and ammunition were already being flown in. Winters were also setting in and passes in the eastern Himalayas usually get blocked by heavy snowfall. So, continued intrusion would have lengthened supply lines and resulted in severe losses for the Chinese.

The Chinese attack exposed Nehru's foreign policy of Panchsheel and non-alignment to widespread criticism. There were strong calls both within and outside Congress to dismiss V.K. Krishna Menon,[9] Nehru's longtime friend and defence minister. Nehru had to comply. The war and India's weak war preparedness also brought forth arguments for a reduction in the Plan expenditure on industries in favour of defence.

The Third Plan was already off to a rough start. The agriculture sector had stagnated, with foodgrain production even declining in 1962-63. Production in the industrial sector, meanwhile, was growing at a healthy pace but much below the average annual target of 14 per cent.[10] The average annual growth rate of the economy in the first two years of the Plan was about 2.5 per cent, which was roughly the same as the country's population growth. Moreover, as war expenses rose, the country's balance of payments worsened.

Therefore, the case was strong to reduce the public outlay on developmental expenditure and boost defence spending. When the National Development Council met in November 1962, they were prepared to give the private sector a larger role in undertaking developmental projects. However, Nehru had other plans. He argued that the development of heavy and intermediate industries was strongly connected to the country's defence efforts and so the allocations to these projects should be increased instead.

The chief ministers, still unsure of opposing Nehru, acquiesced to his proposals and formally accepted that the Plan was imperative to national security. They even agreed to make a modest increase in outlays to power, industry and minerals by cutting down expenditure on social services, irrigation projects and village and small-scale industries.

When Morarji Desai, the finance minister, presented the budget in 1963, he reaffirmed the government's commitment to increase both defence and developmental outlays. Since the scale of taxation had already been expended, he proposed two measures—first, a super profits tax of up to 60 per cent to be imposed on companies when their income after paying taxes still exceeded 6 per cent of their capital and reserves and, second, a compulsory deposits scheme for individual taxpayers, urban property owners and landowners, withdrawable after five years with a simple interest of 4 per cent per annum.[11]

The business community was expectedly unhappy with yet higher taxes. The Federation of Indian Chamber of Commerce and Industry accused the government of failure on all economic fronts and called out the Planning Commission for being more interested in meeting higher investment targets than in actually boosting production levels. The Swatantra Party and the Jana Sangh joined the attack and asked the government to keep out of business and industry and abolish the system of permits, licences and quotas.[12]

The verdict against government policies was further strengthened in the parliamentary by-elections of 1963 that were held to fill elected offices that had become vacant due to unforeseen circumstances in three constituencies which were considered safe for the Congress party. Two of them, Amroha and Farukhabad, were in Nehru's home state of Uttar Pradesh, and the last one was in Rajkot, Gujarat. Congress lost in all three constituencies, despite fielding some of its strongest candidates. Nehru's prestige was shaken. Things got to a point that the Parliament witnessed its first no-confidence motion, introduced in the Lok Sabha by socialist Acharya Kripalani in August 1963 against Nehru.

In fact, Nehru's authority had begun to decline to a point where his own ministers were openly going against his will. The most illustrative of these incidents was Nehru's altercation with S.K. Patil, the minister of food and agriculture. Patil had until now refused to move things forward on the Planning Commission's recommendation of state trading. The stand-off between the food ministry and the Planning Commission climaxed in the summer of 1963 when Patil was supposed to attend the World Food Congress in Washington. India was facing acute food shortages, and the Planning Commission suggested addressing the issue partly through imports and partly through internal procurement that would involve state trading. Patil, on the other hand, wanted to rely on renewed PL480 agreements with the United States.

Nehru, aiming to achieve self-sufficiency, supported the Planning Commission and advised Patil only to talk for an extension of current agreements. However, while in America, Patil chose to ignore Nehru's instructions and got involved in detailed discussions for new agreements. Nehru was furious and asked Patil to resign on his return.[13]

Patil's resignation came when the Kamraj Plan was implemented in August, a plan that originated in discussion with chief ministers on the need to revitalize the party after the humiliating defeat in the by-elections. The plan was named after K. Kamraj, the chief minister of Madras at the time, who resigned from his post on 2 October 1963 and advised other senior party members to do the same and delve into full-time organizational work. The idea was to dispel the lure of power from the minds of Congressmen and instil a dedication to the objectives and policies of the party. Nehru offered his resignation which was summarily rejected. The resignation of six Cabinet ministers and six chief ministers was, however, accepted. Lal Bahadur Shastri, Morarji Desai and S.K. Patil were among the Cabinet ministers who resigned.

Not everyone was of the view that the Kamraj Plan was only meant to strengthen the Congress party at its roots. S.K. Patil minced no words in an interview soon after his resignation: 'The prime minister does not like violence, but he is a 100 per cent communist in my mind. He wants a leftist pattern. He practically gave everything to the leftists. All six [Cabinet ministers] removed were considered from the communists' side to be on the right. All these things that are being done are not honest. They are camouflage. They are not really to strengthen the organization at all.'[14]

It remains a matter of speculation whether the Kamraj Plan was Nehru's attempt at reasserting his position in the party, but the plan did have one eventuality beyond doubt. Morarji Desai was the second in command in the Cabinet after Nehru, and, since the latter's kidney ailment that had flared up in 1962, speculations had been rife regarding who his successor would be. Desai, on account of his seniority, stature and experience, was treated as the obvious choice. However, Desai preferred a free enterprise approach and found Nehru's goal of a classless society to be unattainable. Kamraj claimed that Nehru saw in Morarji a Vallabhbhai Patel with 'too much on the side of vested interests and big business'.[15] Therefore, due to vast ideological differences, Nehru hardly felt comfortable with Desai succeeding him as the prime minister. The Kamraj Plan significantly dented his chances after being relegated to the political sidelines.

* * *

Another effort by Nehru to reinstate his power in the party came in the annual session of the Congress held at Bhubaneswar in January 1964 where he passed a resolution to establish the 'basic ideas underlying the Congress approach' to a 'revolution in the economic and social relationships in Indian society.'[16] The resolution laid special emphasis on the point that every Indian should have equal opportunity to share the fruits of success, and that disparities should be eliminated.

Apart from building a strong industrial base backed by a growing public sector, the resolution also recommended a ceiling on individual income and private property. Other significant recommendations included the completion of land reforms within two years and securing the basic needs of every individual, with respect to food, shelter, clothing, health and education, by the end of the Fifth Plan period. These were the first time-bound commitments undertaken by the government.

The resolution was passed by a unanimous vote by the party. In the final days of the Bhubaneswar Session, Nehru suffered a mild stroke. All the efforts that Nehru had put in to accelerate the progress towards socialism lost momentum as he was forced to exit the political scene.

For the first time since Independence, the country was rife with speculation on the question, 'After Nehru, Who?' Nehru's immediate aim, in turn, was to find a candidate who would cause the least damage to his legacy. So, Morarji Desai was out of the equation.[17] Fortunately for him, many state leaders also preferred a less controversial candidate.

Back in October 1963, four such men met at the Tirupathi Temple to offer worship at the shrine, but also to secretly discuss the future of the country after Nehru. These were K. Kamraj, the former chief minister of Madras; Sanjiva Reddy, an Andhra leader; Atulya Ghosh, the president of the Bengal Congress Committee; and Nijalingappa, the chief minister of Mysore. Later, along with the Maharashtrian leader S.K. Patil, they would be popularly known as the Syndicate. They could not immediately agree on who would succeed Nehru, but they agreed on who should not—Morarji Desai. He was the most prominent leader after Nehru and this very aspect of his was a threat to the Syndicate. They wanted someone more malleable, whom they could control.

Meanwhile, there was also a sense that Nehru was trying to groom his daughter, Indira Gandhi, for succession after she was made the Congress President in 1959. However, quite interestingly, Nehru was appalled by the idea of dynastic succession. He once publicly declared, 'The concept of dynastic [succession] is altogether foreign to a parliamentary democracy like ours, besides being repulsive to my own mind.'[18] In fact, a few days before his death, he also gave a statement in a foreign television interview, saying 'it was very unlikely' that Indira would succeed him and he was 'certainly not grooming her for anything'.[19] In the same interview, Nehru also went on to say that if he 'nominated somebody that is the surest way of his not becoming prime minister. People would be jealous of him, dislike him'.[20]

So, Nehru refrained from publicly backing a successor. But after Nehru suffered the stroke in January, Lal Bahadur Shastri, who had been in a self-imposed exile under the Kamraj Plan, was asked to rejoin the Cabinet as a minister without portfolio and help Nehru undertake his onerous responsibilities. Shastri's selection was not a matter of chance. He was the most preferred successor by both Nehru and party members alike. Shastri had been a central figure throughout the freedom struggle since he had decided to join the Non-Cooperation Movement in 1921 and had been in Nehru's Cabinet since the first general elections of 1952. He was, therefore, a man with considerable experience to run the country and, most importantly, he shared Nehru's ideological vision and was sympathetic to his goals.

Nehru passed away on the morning of 27 May 1964, at his official residence in New Delhi. The same day, Gulzarilal Nanda was sworn in as Interim Prime Minister. Kamraj immediately began the search for a new prime minister, meeting over a dozen chief ministers and over 200 Members of Parliament (MPs) in four days. Desai pushed for his candidature but was persuaded to withdraw while the Congress Working Committee approved the appointment of Lal Bahadur Shastri. Kamraj later explained the selection to veteran journalist Kuldip Nayar: 'It became clear to all of us that no single leader could fill the gap left by Nehru and that a collective leadership of persons who had worked under his guidance had to bear the responsibility of leading the nation. It was possible to do so with flexible Shastri, but not with conservative and rigid Morarji.'[21] The Syndicate had found the perfect candidate in Shastri.

* * *

Much has been discussed and debated about Nehru's economic legacy. However, not a lot of it remains favourable. In a world of free marketeers, his posthumous reputation seems to have taken a hit. It is interesting to note the contrasts in public perception of Gandhi and Nehru before and after their deaths. Gandhi during his lifetime was respected for the influence that he held among the masses, but little consideration was given to his ideas by the intellectuals of the time. This changed after his death as Gandhian principles seem to have been rediscovered. On the other hand, Nehru found immense adulation and respect for his views during his lifetime among the masses and the intellectuals alike, which seem to have been lost since the time of his death.

However, any discussion on Nehru's legacy needs to begin with a recognition of the fact that the job on the hands of Jawaharlal Nehru at the time of Independence was unimaginably difficult. In a newly independent nation that was not expected to hold together for long, riots had to be contained, refugees settled and food shortages tackled, along with writing a Constitution and building an electoral system in a highly diverse society. Finally, an economic policy had to be formulated to revive a virtually stagnant economy.

Amidst all of these complexities, India managed to grow at the rate of 4.1 per cent between 1950 and 1964. In comparison, China had grown at the rate of 2.9 per cent during the same period. Therefore, Nehru did not leave the nation at any disadvantageous position at the time of his death. In hindsight, his persistence in following the socialist model of development might seem worthy of blame for all that followed in terms of slow economic growth. But there was popular support for the adoption of a socialist approach across society and even among the business community, as evidenced in the Bombay Plan.

His focus on capital accumulation by strengthening India's heavy and basic industries was also in line with the popular development economics thinking of the time. The Estonian economist Ragnar Nurkse in his *Problems of Capital Formation in Underdeveloped Countries*, published in 1953, placed capital accumulation at the very centre of economic development. Renowned Indian economists like A.K. Dasgupta, who groomed Amartya Sen, also carried a similar opinion. Also, since India met most of its needs for machines and even machine tools through imports, it implied that despite political independence, the country would have remained dependent on the advanced nations for its economic growth. So, the logical step was to make the economy self-reliant in the production of capital goods.

Another issue that is generally attributed to the Nehru era is the origin and growth of the inefficient public sector. However, the idea that the state should take the lead in industrialization was also quite popular in intellectual circles of the time. The early successes of the Soviet model had made it even more acceptable. As for the performance of the public sector during the Nehru era, public investment during the fifteen-year period surged at a level that has still not been surpassed.[22] The sector's evolution into inefficient employment-granting welfarist agencies was the work of a subsequent generation of political leaders.

The one area where Nehru did falter was the neglect of primary education. In the focus on planning to build heavy industries and massive dams, education was always short-changed. It cannot be denied that had the policy focus from the start been on educating the masses to develop human capital, the current scenario would have been vastly different. However, even more than half a century after Nehru's death, not much has changed on that front. In fact, many other developing countries shifted their economic development strategy after 1965. India failed to do so. Nehru can hardly be blamed for it. He was merely hostage to the thinking of his times.

Lord Mountbatten had an interesting take on why Nehru could not retain his popularity. He pointed out that Nehru had lived too long. Considering the fact that a lot of the blemishes in Nehru's political career, from failing economic to foreign policies, came towards the end, had he died early, he would have been remembered as the greatest statesman of the twentieth century.[23]

CHAPTER 6

A SMALL INTERLUDE

In his final days, Nehru made last-ditch efforts to resolve the one issue that continues to be an irritant for the country long after his death: the problem of Kashmir. After the war with China and given his own deteriorating health, Nehru decided to put an end to the border conflict with Pakistan. He began by reaching out to the one man who carried significant political heft in the Princely State of Jammu and Kashmir, Sheikh Abdullah. Nehru had first met Abdullah in the early 1930s, when the latter was trying to build an alternative political voice in Kashmir to oppose Maharaja Hari Singh. Both of them had instantaneously hit it off on account of having similar leanings towards socialism and secularism.

Since 1953, Abdullah had been in prison for showing an inclination towards an independent Kashmir. Nehru began by pushing for his release in 1964, which took place on 8 April amidst much fanfare in the state. Nehru then invited Abdullah to stay with him in New Delhi and work towards a possible resolution. There was expected backlash against these developments as Abdullah was perceived as a traitor by many. Jana Sangh led a large procession in the capital the day before Abdullah was scheduled to arrive. Even within his party the sole senior supporter of Nehru was Lal Bahadur Shastri. However, only a leader like Nehru could afford to ignore the critics and stay committed to the plan.

Abdullah stayed with Nehru for five days and the two got into intensive discussions on the issue whenever the latter found time. After meeting Nehru, Abdullah set off for Madras to seek advice from C. Rajagopalachari, who had been surprisingly supportive of Nehru on the issue. They spoke for three and a half hours and worked out a solution that would be a win-win for both the nations. The details were not revealed to the press, but Abdullah found support for the plan in Nehru.[1] An informal committee of advisers was formed on Nehru's directive to explore the viability of the proposed plan and all other possible alternatives.

Meanwhile, while Abdullah was in Madras, the president of Pakistan, Ayub Khan, extended an invite to him. Abdullah visited the country in May and convinced Ayub Khan to meet Nehru and discuss the Kashmir issue. The meet was supposed to happen in Delhi in the middle of June, but Nehru died before it could take place. Even though Ayub's stance on the matter at the time remains unknown, Nehru took away with him all possibilities of any conflict resolution.

The man who succeeded him, Lal Bahadur Shastri, had an entirely different persona. He was a simple man cast into a major role. He had experienced poverty first-hand, even losing his daughter to typhoid after being unable to buy medicines for her. A lot of his economic policy during his term would be influenced by his understanding of the struggles of the common man.

An endearing account of Shastri's humility and simplicity can be found in journalist Kuldip Nayar's autobiography, *Beyond the Lines*. Nayar was Shastri's press secretary when the latter served as the home minister in the Nehru government. The two were travelling by car on a hot day when they arrived at a railway crossing. One single security guard sat in the front seat. Shastri spotted a man selling sugarcane juice and got out of the car to buy two glasses and paid for it himself. Nothing about Shastri's demeanour gave a hint to the juice vendor or anyone around them that the little man was, in fact, the second-most important man in Indian politics.

Shastri's first interaction with Ayub Khan is also quite telling. The newly appointed Indian prime minster stopped at Karachi on his way home from Cairo in October 1964. The Pakistani counterpart, who was clearly unimpressed, turned to his aide and wondered aloud, 'So this is the man who succeeded Nehru!'[2] Surely, he was not a man who could take forward Nehru's efforts in resolving the Kashmir issue with Pakistan or, for that matter, bring about any major policy reversals. However, Shastri's brief tenure of twenty months would surprise many.

* * *

Shastri was no socialist. He did declare in Parliament within minutes of being elected that 'socialism is our objective',[3] but he was not ideologically wedded to the idea like Nehru. His belief in socialism stemmed from a personal empathy with the problems of the poor rather than an overarching outlook on the world that guided his policy choices. He also lacked any formal training in economics or prior experience with planning, which probably worked to his advantage as it made him more receptive to external opinion and criticism.

In fact, Shastri was more Gandhian than he was Nehruvian in his economic thinking. He believed in striving towards self-sufficiency at the village level and committing to hard labour. He put it simply in the first Cabinet meeting: 'I am a small man and believe in small projects with small expenditure so that we get quick results.'[4] This was quite unlike Nehru who believed in mechanized industries and large dams. Shastri felt that they delayed benefits and used little labour. It was not that he wanted to completely depart from Nehru's policies, but he did not want to follow the beaten track either. He once drew on an example of Stalin's successor, Khrushchev, and commented, 'No real leader ever walked the beaten tracks. Conditions change, and it is for the leader to respond to them.'[5]

The stance he took was understandable. Over the last few years, it had become clear that a change was in order. The economy which Shastri had inherited was not in a hopeful state. Even though the Third Plan (1961–66) was technically only halfway through when Shastri came in, it was headed for failure. The annual increment in national income since the beginning of the Third Plan had barely kept pace with the rate of population growth. To make matters worse, price levels had risen by almost 50 per cent during the period. The suffering was worse for lower-income groups due to the paucity of foodgrains. Some of the big river-valley projects were also showing poor results and a lot of them were incomplete due to poor planning.

Public sector undertakings were also operating well below their capacity. For these enterprises, Nehru used to be of the view that 'the real test is how far this adds to our productive capacity'. But his solution to their idle capacities was an expansion of the public sector. 'It is far better to use our resources for new state enterprises, leaving the old ones to carry on as they are, subject to some kind control by the State. Thus, production grows, and the public sector grows till it becomes the dominant sector.'[6] Thus, expansion of the public sector was the cornerstone of his economic policy. On the contrary, for Shastri, the solution lay in maximizing production of the public sector and not expanding it.

So, in the spirit of infusing change, one of Shastri's first acts was to reduce the all-encompassing power of the Planning Commission. He divested members of the Planning Commission from their long-standing privilege of indefinite tenure and placed them on fixed contracts instead. Also, unlike Nehru, he preferred to consult ministers individually rather than meet the Planning Commission in its entirety. In fact, most of the differences were resolved in this manner before they reached the Cabinet discussion stage. He effectively reduced the stature of the Commission from an extension of the Prime Minister's Office to a subordinate group of advisers. Simultaneously, he established a National Planning Council with the deputy chairman of the Planning Commission as its head but excluding the rest of its members. The Council brought together fifteen–twenty experts from various fields of policy concern, including economics and science, who would 'help the Planning Commission' in carrying out its tasks.[7] It gained formal importance when chief ministers raised concerns about various aspects of the Fourth Plan and Shastri advised that the Council establish five committees on different policy issues and advise the Planning Commission in the respective areas. The locus of power on economic policy immediately shifted from the planners to the respective ministries and chief ministers of the states.

Shastri also saw that agriculture was the key to India's economic problems and decided to reorient the focus of the Third Plan in favour of the sector. This move was in sharp contrast to Nehru's incessant focus on heavy industry. Shastri also displayed a similar approach when the Fourth Plan was being taken into consideration. The investment priority of the Plan was shifted from industry to agriculture. Foodgrain production had barely kept pace with the growth of population and successive droughts in 1964 and 1965 only worsened the situation. He regarded the first draft of the Plan, which had been approved by Nehru less than three weeks before his death, 'as essentially a first approximation' and called for a concrete action plan to revive agriculture.[8] In the end, however, the increase in Plan outlays, towards agriculture and irrigation were merely increased by 2 per cent, from 22 per cent in the draft plan to 24 per cent in the final document. Shastri also transferred the successful minister of steel C. Subramaniam to the Ministry of Food and Agriculture. This was a decision that would revolutionize Indian agriculture. The decisions that the new agriculture minister would take during his tenure would play a key role in ushering in the Green Revolution.

Soon after Subramaniam took office, food prices started rising again and the Planning Commission along with the prime minister and his Cabinet agreed that it was due to hoarding rather than actual supply shortfalls. They proposed imposing price controls and state trading of foodgrains as a short-term solution. But, Subramaniam took a different stand. He felt that the real solution lay in increasing production. To do so, he advised a market-based approach that provided price incentives to private players and encouraged the use of yield-enhancing inputs, especially chemical fertilizers. All short-term needs could be met with higher imports under PL480. Shastri set up an expert committee under L.K. Jha, a distinguished civil servant and an eminent economist, to find an acceptable solution to the immediate crisis. The committee's recommendations lined up with the stance of the food minister. It urged the policymakers to consider establishing a government trading organization at a future date and not disturb established trade patterns. Instead, it asked the government to carry out purchases within the framework of the market mechanism.

Subramaniam put the plan in action in July 1964. He established a foodgrain trading organization, the Food Corporation of India, with branches spread throughout the country. However, contrary to the long-standing official position, the new institution would not depend on price controls and compulsory procurement but compete with private traders in the open market. For the short-term, S.K. Patil took a trip to the United States to negotiate a five-year deal, for the provision of about 20 million tonnes of grain under PL480.

The food situation, however, failed to improve in a drought year. These issues with the economy were beginning to result in incessant political attacks. In September, the Shastri government faced a no-confidence motion over its failures on food policy. Congress ministries in the states were also subjected to similar no-confidence motions. This also created fissures within the Congress party, which were on complete display during the annual session of Congress at Durgapur in early January 1965. It witnessed 'the most ruthless criticism of the government ever to be witnessed at a Congress session'.[9] The resolution adopted by the session also reflected the internal contradictions developing within the organization. It called for rapid advancement towards 'the goal of socialism' and also a 'period of consolidation' over the next two years. This reflected a developing dilemma among the national leadership, which was inclined towards economic and social reform but also faced practical constraints on their implementation due to the dominance of the landed and business classes at every level of the organization.

Two days after the Durgapur Session, Kamraj, who had taken over as the Congress President in 1964, made a surprising address questioning the economic policy of the government and the financial feasibility of the entire Fourth Plan. He felt that a plan of that magnitude would only add to inflationary pressures. He also seemed to suggest an alternative approach when he pointed out that 'there is plenty of room for the private sector to grow'.[10] In response to Kamraj's remarks, Shastri immediately called for a meeting of the Planning Commission to reconsider the size of the Plan. The Commission, however, saw no possibility of cutting the allocations for the Plan. It was slowly becoming clear that the Commission's authority was being eroded and the business community was managing to increasingly influence economic policy at the highest levels of the government.

Around this time, the World Bank began a six-month study of India's economic policy under the Third Plan. They sent out a mission in September 1964 under the leadership of Bernard Bell. The World Bank had long argued that India's public sector programmes were too ambitious, and the private sector should be given a larger role. They had also endorsed the view that agriculture should be prioritized in investment allocations.

The experts after coming to India argued that given the limited knowledge of India's land distribution, achieving improvements in agricultural productivity was only possible by providing price and cost incentives to farmers for higher investment in modern inputs. The mission also stressed on the higher role of the private sector in the industrial sector and recommended India do away with the system of industrial licensing and import substitution. In order to provide strong price incentives to the export sector, the mission also advised devaluation of the rupee, or a deliberate reduction in the value of the rupee as compared to the dollar.[11] If the value of the rupee were corrected, Indian exports would become cheaper on the world market and the country's foreign reserves would receive a much-needed boost. All of these recommendations were in stark contrast to the Nehruvian view of economic planning. But, they were the conditions that India was expected to fulfil for receiving substantial inflows of aid.

Even though there was general resentment at the foreign pressure on matters of economic policy, most of the officials at the highest levels of the government and within the Congress party were in favour of the suggestions for economic reform. The idea of devaluation, however, was met with considerable resistance. In fact, T.T. Krishnamachari, who was the finance minister under Nehru and had a sentimental attachment to his legacy, took to the radio on 18 July 1965, and adopted a firm stand against the devaluation of the rupee. He felt that it could create foreign exchange difficulties for India and would do more harm than good to domestic industries.[12]

The devaluation issue was put to rest thereafter for the time being. The World Bank's arguments, however, left an indelible impression on Subramaniam. With respect to agriculture, they had suggested that the food problem could be solved using modern technology backed by price incentives to farmers. Subramaniam built a concrete action plan to reorganize the agricultural sector. Most significantly, he did away with all plans of community development that had been the ultimate goal under Nehru. He argued, 'Where cooperation is not in a position to deliver the goods, shall we wait indefinitely for the cooperatives to become effective instruments?'[13]

He recommended the adoption of modern techniques in agriculture with the help of American assistance and strengthening agricultural research within India. For the latter part, he began by infusing new life into the Indian Council for Agricultural Research. The pay and working conditions of scientists were improved and they were protected from bureaucratic interference. States were also encouraged to open agricultural universities, which would focus their research on the crops of their respective regions. He also set up the Seed Corporation of India that would produce quality seeds in bulk for boosting agricultural productivity.

* * *

Subramaniam formally presented his plan to reinvent agriculture to the Lok Sabha in April 1965 in a 71-page document. His idea was to shift the country's agricultural strategy from a community-based labour-intensive approach to one that imbibed an entrepreneurial spirit with heavy private investments in modern inputs. The strategy would go on to be incorporated into the Fourth Plan.

But other concerns had begun to take primacy in the summer of 1965. Trouble had started brewing on the Indian borders. A conflict had broken out in the first week of April between Indian and Pakistani troops over the Rann of Kutch, a barren salt marsh in Gujarat that was claimed by both the countries at the time. Pakistan was successful in gaining some ground using American tanks. Angry telegrams were exchanged between the two countries, but before the situation could escalate any further, British Prime Minister Harold Wilson intervened and successfully convinced the two nations to end hostilities and set up a tribunal to resolve the dispute.

However, the successes of the Pakistani army in Kutch led Ayub Khan to believe that the Indian defences were weak and a quick military campaign in Kashmir could bring the issue to a decisive end. The Indian loss to China in the 1962 war was also fresh in their minds and reaffirmed their view of military superiority. Pakistan also incorrectly believed that the local Kashmiri population was unhappy with the Indian rule and that a minor spark could ignite a resistance movement. In the first week of August, 'Operation Gibraltar' was put into action where Pakistani troops crossed the border dressed as locals and went on to blow up bridges and bomb government installations. The intent was to create a sense of unrest and revolt against the Indian government. Radio Pakistan even announced that a popular uprising had broken out on the other side of the border. The operation turned out to be a failure after the local population handed over some of the intruders to the police.

In a sensible display of political maturity, Shastri took the entire Cabinet into confidence on 12 August and sought consensus on the broad outlines of his stance: India would refrain from approaching the UN; Pakistan would be warned against infringing on Indian sovereignty; and plans would be prepared for possible contingencies. He also gave the army chief, General J.N. Chaudhuri, permission to cross the ceasefire line and attack the infiltrators' bases if the need arose, knowing fully well that it would lead to a full-blown war.[14] The hostilities continued and, by the end of the month, both sides had gained some territories with the Indian army capturing the strategic Haji Pir pass and some tactically crucial heights in Kargil from where it could look out for infiltrators.

Pakistan, then, launched its reserve plan which was codenamed 'Operation Grand Slam' on 1 September. Using an armoured-cum-infantry attack, the Pakistani army caught the Indians by surprise and captured over thirty square miles in less than twenty-four hours. They aimed to capture the Akhnoor sector, which would seal off Kashmir from India. To Pakistan's surprise, India's defence minister, Y.B. Chavan, backed by Shastri, gave the army and the air force permission to go ahead and launch attacks beyond the ceasefire line. This was unlike Nehru who had hesitated to call in the air force in a comparable situation in 1962.

As the situation in Akhnoor became tense, the Indian army opened a second front on the border of Punjab to relieve the pressure up north. As several tank regiments rolled on straight for the city of Lahore, Pakistan troops and tanks were diverted from Kashmir and one of the biggest tank battles since the Second World War ensued between the two nations. The escalation of hostilities alarmed the superpowers and, on 6 September, the United Nations Security Council meeting was called to discuss the matter. Following the meeting, the UN secretary general, U. Thant, flew down to get the two sides to agree to a ceasefire. He succeeded in doing so and, on 22 September, the guns went silent.

India had captured about 1,920 square kilometres of Pakistani territory and lost almost 550 square kilometres of its own at the cost of over 11,000 casualties. But the morale in New Delhi was high. The damning memory of defeat in 1962 had been somewhat replaced with pride. As a result, Shastri's political capital soared. The small man who believed in the Gandhian philosophy of peace had handled war much better than his predecessor.

When the bleak food situation in a drought year was adding to the miseries of the war, Shastri stepped up to the occasion and appealed to the masses. In a public rally held at Ramlila Maidan, he famously coined the slogan 'Jai Jawan, Jai Kisan' (Hail the Soldier, Hail the Farmer) to boost the morale of both soldiers on the borders and farmers on the fields. The latter was especially needed to reduce India's import bill so that more could be spent on defence.

However, as the monsoons failed, and agricultural production declined by 17 per cent that year in comparison to the previous one, and food prices jumped upwards by 14 per cent, mere motivation could not alleviate the distress.[15] Subramaniam explained to the Congress Parliamentary Committee in November that all the government buffer stocks had been exhausted as well. The only option that remained was to depend on imports. Meanwhile, the United States had suspended all aid to both India and Pakistan as it felt that scarce resources had been wasted on an unproductive war. It had resorted to sending food sufficient to fulfil the requirements of a few months. The aid was also contingent on the reforms that India would undertake in its agricultural policy. This only strengthened Subramaniam's case for market-based orientation of the sector. He drafted a programme for revamping Indian agriculture and met officials in the US Department of Agriculture to seek assurance that the new agricultural strategy would suffice in resuming American food shipments.

The plan was to achieve self-sufficiency in foodgrains through a three-pronged approach that included use of high-yielding variety seeds, price incentives to farmers and concentrated use of improved inputs in irrigated areas. As pressure mounted to revive foreign aid, the Cabinet approved the plan in December, despite objections from the finance minister and the Planning Commission to reform agriculture.

A major problem was the production of fertilizers, which was largely controlled by the public sector. The public sector factories were operating with inefficient technology and low rates of utilization, due to which the government had to subsidize the cost of fertilizers. So, simultaneously, along with approving Subramaniam's plan, the Central government passed a new policy to provide concessions to foreign private companies willing to invest in the Indian fertilizer industry. In addition, any foreign company doing so before 31 March 1967 would also be allowed to set its own prices and distribution channels, provided that the Indian government holds majority of the equity in the firm.

The only part of the World Bank recommendation that was needed to resume aid was the aspect of currency devaluation. T.T. Krishnamachari was the only man who stood against the move.[16] Shastri's view on the matter was still not public. But, Braj Kumar Nehru, an Indian diplomat and Nehru's nephew, later revealed that a few members of the Cabinet, including Subramaniam, had convinced Shastri that devaluation was imperative.[17] Shastri also removed Krishnamachari from the picture on different grounds.

Since February, Krishnamachari had been under fire for misusing office in favour of a firm that was managed by his sons. By the end of November, an official inquiry had been called into the matter. Shastri showed no support for his finance minister and planned to set up an independent judicial authority that would examine the issue. Krishnamachari resigned on the last day of the year, reasoning that if the prime minister had to consult someone else, he had clearly lost confidence in him.[18] After the infamous Mundhra scandal, his resignation came for a second time under two different prime ministers.

By this time, Shastri had gone abroad to Russia as the Soviets had offered to work out a peace settlement between India and Pakistan after the war had ended. The meet was to happen in Tashkent between Shastri and Ayub with Soviet Prime Minster Alexei Kosygin as the chief mediator. After a week of talks, the two sides agreed to withdraw their forces to the positions they held before the war began. This meant that India would have to give up the strategic positions it had captured, such as the Haji Pir pass. But not coming to an agreement would have meant alienating Russia, which was the only friendly veto India could always count on in the Security Council. So, Shastri signed the 'Tashkent Agreement' on the afternoon of 10 January 1966 and peace was restored, at least for the time being.

That night itself Shastri suffered a heart attack in his sleep and passed away. His body was flown back in a Soviet plane to a shocked nation. If it was said for Nehru that he died too late, for Shastri death came too early. 'Lal Bahadur Shastri died at a pinnacle of popularity that no one in India believed possible when he succeeded the late

Jawaharlal Nehru as Prime Minister barely nineteen months ago,' reported the *New York Times* the next day.[19]

The popularity that he had gained towards the end of his life had stemmed from his response to the war with Pakistan. But he had also made indispensable contributions to the economy that would put him on the right side of history later. He realized that the emphasis on physical controls instead of prices, the focus on industry instead of agriculture and the crushing web of controls spread across the economy by Central planners was proving inimical to national development. Despite all the criticism, Shastri began dismantling it piece by piece. He was trying to infuse fresh thinking into India's development strategy. In that he could be termed as India's first economic reformer.

It helped that Shastri wore no ideological blinkers. He saw facts as they were and looked for a practical solution to all economic problems in his own quiet way. In response to the problem of chronic food shortages, he shifted the investment focus from basic industries to agriculture; to contain the growth of black markets, he encouraged the setting up of a system of incentives instead of controls; and to address the numbing inefficiencies of the public sector, he gradually allowed for a larger role for the private sector and foreign investment. He also shifted the locus of economic decision-making away from the Planning Commission and towards the states. His actions significantly reduced the influence of the Planning Commission, which had become extremely rigid in its outlook on economic policies. Such policy decisions were unimaginable in Nehru's India.

Apart from these moves towards economic reform, he also began embracing a policy of export promotion instead of import substitution. It is interesting to note that South Korea had almost the same level of average incomes as India in 1964, but it pulled ahead following a similar strategy that Shastri had favoured. Therefore, there remain legitimate grounds to speculate how the Indian economy would have developed had Shastri lived longer. India went on to adopt similar reform measures twenty-five years later, which put the economy on a higher growth trajectory. The little man was just way ahead of his times.

CHAPTER 7

THE DUMB DOLL[1]

As the plane carrying Shastri's body cut through Delhi's winter clouds on the afternoon of 11 January 1966, an astrologer popular among political circles waited among the sea of mourners at Palam airport. A high-ranking Congress leader ventured to ask him, 'What do the stars foretell?' The holy man replied curtly, 'A hat-trick.'[2] The atypical sports reference was suggestive of the fact that after Nehru and Shastri, who were both closely associated with Allahabad, India's third prime minister was also expected to be from the same city—Nehru's daughter, Indira Gandhi.

Despite such prophecies, the question of who would succeed Shastri remained unresolved for quite a while. Merely nineteen months ago, Kamraj, the Congress President, had perfectly orchestrated a behind-the-scenes consensus on Nehru's successor. But this time, an open and heated conflict seemed inevitable. Morarji Desai, who failed to make the cut in 1964, was determined to take up the role this time. But Desai was his own man and quite rigid in his beliefs. The Syndicate, as before, was not in favour of him assuming power. The acting prime minister, Gulzarilal Nanda, also pitched for the candidacy, but he was so lacking in political stature that Desai could have easily defeated him. Another serious candidate was Y.B. Chavan, the then defence minister, who had a strong political base in Maharashtra and also a progressive image, unlike Desai's. But his limited regional appeal would not have sufficed against Desai. Some Congress members in the Cabinet also tried to build a consensus on Kamraj himself. He was convinced, though, that he could not become a national leader with his limited ability to speak either English or Hindi.

The challenge was to find a candidate who could defeat Desai in an open contest and had a national appeal that could come in handy during the general elections slated for the next year. Indira Gandhi fit the bill perfectly. Her first qualification was that she was Nehru's daughter and his closest confidante. This inspired adulation among the masses, and gave her the rare ability to draw large crowds merely through her presence. Over time, she had also developed her own group of supporters within the party, especially among young workers. Most importantly, the greatest asset she had was the perception that she was weak. Kamraj convinced the top brass of the party that after she was elected, she would do as they bid, allowing them to enjoy political power without owning up to any of the responsibilities.

Apart from Kamraj, Indira also had some powerful allies within the Congress. One was D.P. Mishra, the then chief minister of Madhya Pradesh, who had a strong influence over other chief ministers. In fact, just a few hours after Shastri's death, Indira called Mishra at 5.30 in the morning, on 11 January, to immediately fly to Delhi since she needed all the support she could get in the oncoming power struggle. Mishra proved quite resourceful and managed to persuade eight out of the fourteen chief ministers to back her. On 15 January, they issued a statement in her support.

Indira also had an ally in the Indian president, Sarvepalli Radhakrishnan. As a non-partisan member of the government, he was supposed to be neutral in the struggle between the two contenders, but he favoured Indira on account of being an old friend of Nehru. Radhakrishnan's son, Sarvepalli Gopal, claimed that his father even went to the extent of advising Indira on the timing of key moves and also kept her informed of which Congress leader supported her after privately speaking to them.[3]

Indira, therefore, emerged as the candidate of choice not because of her merits but because of the shortcomings of other contenders in the fray, especially Desai. She was very well aware of this fact and once admitted that 'they are not so much for me as against him'.[4] She was simply the right person at the right place at the right time.

Desai himself believed that Indira was certain to win as 'these people had gone around and cornered everybody and promised them everything'.[5] But, he was not one to give up so easily. He called for a secret ballot to be held on 19 January. The meeting began at 11 a.m. on that day and dragged on for four and a half hours as 526 Congress MPs voted one by one. As the counting process began, a crowd had gathered around the Parliament building. When the Congress Whip finally emerged on the balcony to announce the results, someone shouted, 'Is it a boy or a girl?' It was a girl. Indira had beaten Desai by 355 votes to 169.[6]

As she emerged from the Parliament, she was greeted with a roar of approval from the crowd, along with shouts of 'Indira Gandhi Zindabad!' Five days later, she was sworn in as the third prime minister of India. At forty-eight, she was ten years younger than both her father and Shastri when they took over that position. She also gained the distinction of being only the second female prime minister in the world after Sri Lanka's Sirimavo Bandaranaike.

On the same day Indira was sworn into power, an Air India plane headed for Vienna crashed into the snow-covered Swiss Alps in perhaps an omen of the trials that lay ahead for the nation. In it was Homi J. Bhabha, the father of Indian nuclear science and a family friend of the new prime minister. The cause of the crash was attributed to miscommunication between the pilots and the Air Traffic Control (ATC). Curiously, Homi Bhabha had announced over All India Radio just a few months ago that if he were given the go-ahead, India would be capable of making a nuclear bomb in less than two years.[7]

*　*　*

The economic situation of the country in January 1966 was worse than it had ever been under Nehru or Shastri. Two wars in less than three years and two leadership changes in almost half the time had taken a heavy toll on the nation. Inflation was rampant and foreign reserves were low. To add to the misery, the monsoons had failed in 1965 and the spectre of famine loomed across large parts of the country. Due to chronic shortage of foreign exchange, commercial imports of foodgrains had become practically impossible and concessional aid from the US under PL480 had also not yet resumed since the war with Pakistan. Food riots had taken place in Kerala and West Bengal and even the army had to be called in in the latter case to restore order.

On the international front, the situation was only slightly less dismal. The heydays of global prestige that India enjoyed during the Nehru era sharply deteriorated after the 1962 war with China. Relations with the US were already strained after the use of American weapons by Pakistan in the war that had taken place barely a few months ago. Even the Soviet Union, which usually had India's back against Pakistan, was beginning to display a more even-handed policy between the two neighbours.

In the backdrop of such adverse circumstances, Indira took to power, having virtually no experience in government or administration. She was unprepared for the tasks that had fallen to her and, unlike her father, she was shy, diffident and lacked conversational flair. She could also not count on her party for support. The Congress was slowly developing fissures as various power centres were growing within it over time. On the one hand, there was the Syndicate, which mainly constituted the senior leaders of the party. On the other hand, there was Morarji Desai, who had proved in his power struggle with Indira that he had the support of at least a third of the party, even though not of the Syndicate. Desai's group of supporters became vehement in their opposition to Indira over time, which made her seem to be at the mercy of the Syndicate.

As she began to feel vulnerable in her own party, she started distancing herself from the Syndicate and chose to rely on a group of friends and advisers whom she had become acquainted with during the Shastri period, when she was heading the Ministry of Information and Broadcasting. This coterie was popularly nicknamed as her 'Kitchen Cabinet' in the media.[8] The existence of the Kitchen Cabinet was perceived as a symbol of Indira's inadequacy rather than an essential requirement for her to get accustomed to the big shoes of her predecessors that she was called upon to fill.

Barely a month after becoming prime minister, she had to address the All India Congress Committee (AICC) at Jaipur in Rajasthan. The food crisis was the most pressing issue before the AICC. Since people of Kerala were the hardest hit as they were highly dependent on rice for consumption, which was now practically unavailable, Indira dramatically declared that she will neither eat nor serve rice until it was adequately available to the state. Such a commitment made for a good symbolic gesture, but it needed strong policy backing to improve food procurement and distribution channels.

Since Independence, India had been divided into over half a dozen food zones, each consisting of a food surplus state and a couple of deficit ones. Trade was allowed to take place freely within a food zone, but movement of grains was strictly prohibited across zones. These restrictions were imposed to prevent avaricious traders from diverting scarce food supplies to affluent areas where the purchasing power of buyers was high.

However, over time, chief ministers of surplus states, who drew much of their political backing from rich farmers, had come to oppose the concept of food zones. They wanted grain to move to places where it would fetch the highest price but were unable to muster up the courage to say so when Nehru was alive. He would have flown into rage at the suggestion of a policy change in favour of the rich at the expense of the poor. Shastri would have been easier to convince but he had died before much could be done on the issue.

So, it fell upon Indira to decide if food zones should be abolished. Public sentiment was in favour of abolition as the people were generally tired of controls. But for the Central government, abolishing food zones would have implied compulsory procurement of grains on a massive scale, which could have been enforced only with strong political will and large-scale administrative resources, both of which the government was lacking at the time.

Despite these issues, the demand for scrapping food zones was put to vote at the AICC in Jaipur. It was evident from the show of hands that the amendment would pass. But T. Manean, who was counting the votes, panicked and declared that the amendment had been rejected. As hundreds of delegates rose in protest, Indira was forced to try her best to calm the situation. She took to the stage, visibly shaken, and promised the delegates that the entire food policy would be reviewed, and appealed to them to withdraw the amendment. She left in a haste after that. Amidst all the confusion, Kamraj announced that the amendment had been withdrawn following the prime minister's assurance.

After she returned to Delhi, mortified with her poor performance at Jaipur, her performance on the Parliament floor deteriorated. She became even more inarticulate and nervous than she had been in Parliament during the Shastri days. She lapsed into silences and failed to think on her feet. Her colleagues tried to help her by passing notes on slips of paper, but she kept faltering. Her performance might not have been so bad had the Opposition extended her some consideration, usually shown to a new prime minister. But she was consistently heckled. The socialist leader Ram Manohar Lohia was her main tormentor. It was Lohia who called her 'goongi gudiya', or the 'dumb doll', and the name stuck to her even after she began finding her voice.[9]

It was this bad start for Indira that led her to develop a contempt for Parliament. Her father had used the Parliament as a sounding board to lead and educate the nation on matters of national importance. He had valued it for the very embodiment of democracy that it represented. On the other hand, Indira treated the Parliament with a similar kind of disdain as it had shown towards her. Over time, she attended Parliament less and less and skipped even important debates. In the years of her supremacy, she would even begin to overrule and circumvent the Parliament.

* * *

The first budget that the Indira government introduced had a lower overall outlay than the budget presented a year earlier. This was the first time since the start of the planning process that the amount of expenditure by the government in a particular year had to be reduced. The financial situation of the country was at a new low. Even the trimmed-down budget could go through only if adequate foreign aid was available. But the World Bank along with the US was only willing to resume aid if India accepted the conditions laid down by the mission they had sent when Shastri was prime minister.

Shastri had almost accepted all the recommendations in principle except the devaluation of the rupee. But he had almost cleared all the decks to make that move, including removing T.T. Krishnamachari, who had been dead against it. So, Indira had to ultimately make the final decision on the matter.

Since her economic knowledge was limited, she relied on the advice of some members of the Kitchen Cabinet, mainly C. Subramaniam, the food minister; Asoka Mehta, then the deputy chairman of the Planning Commission; and L.K. Jha, Indira's personal secretary. They enthusiastically supported devaluation. Even B.K. Nehru, Indira's cousin and India's ambassador to the US, advised her in favour of it. She was assured that adopting the World Bank recommendations would lift the economy onto a higher growth path and getting additional aid now would reduce the need for it in the future. In other words, the economy could be made self-reliant. These prospects seemed like the fulfilment of her father's dream. It was too alluring an outcome to ignore, especially since it was becoming clear that the Fourth Plan couldn't be implemented that year, and for the first time since Nehru initiated the planning process, a 'Plan Holiday' was taken. The Plan Holiday took the form of an Annual Plan until the Fourth Plan could be hammered out.

Finally, what clinched the deal was the word of the then Reserve Bank governor, P.C. Bhattacharya, who made the assessment that India urgently needed a USD 200 million loan to save the country's financial system from collapsing. He was soon sent to the US to secretly commit to the World Bank that India would devalue its currency. The Bank released part of the required loan amount as a first instalment in a total package of about USD 321 million.[10]

In those days, the rupee was pegged to the pound, which was in turn pegged to the dollar. It was decided that the rupee would be effectively devalued from Rs 4.76 against the dollar to Rs 7.50 amounting to a correction of 57 per cent. The quantum of devaluation had been barely decided before a cable arrived for B.K. Nehru that it might not take place since the prime minister was having second thoughts about it. She had finally consulted Kamraj about devaluation and he was strongly opposed to it. B.K. Nehru replied, saying that it was too late to back out now since the World Bank had already sent out the money based on Bhattacharya's commitment.

However, before taking the final plunge, Indira decided to visit the United States—her first foreign visit as prime minister. She made it a point to maintain public perception that this was only a goodwill visit and she was not going with a begging bowl for food and aid. The very opposite was true in actuality. She privately told Inder Malhotra that her main motive behind the mission was 'to get both food and foreign exchange without appearing to ask for them'.[11]

At the time, her visit to the US was regarded as a resounding success. There was an unprecedented media build-up around her trip in both countries and it really helped that President Lyndon Johnson responded well to Indira's subtle charm and candour. He was so enchanted by Indira that after a private meeting at the house of B.K. Nehru, he stayed on for drinks even as guests arrived for the evening banquet, which was to be hosted by the vice president. When the dinner couldn't be delayed any longer, Indira politely asked Johnson to join them and, breaking protocol, he agreed.

Despite her public claims about not seeking aid during her visit, she agreed to key American demands required for the resumption of aid. She promptly agreed to the devaluation of the rupee and also accepted an American proposal to set up an Indo-American Educational Fund using the rupee funds that the US had accumulated due to its massive shipments of PL480 wheat. Earlier, both Nehru and Shastri had rejected the proposal since it would have given the Americans undue influence over higher education and research in

India. But Indira did not have the liberty to disregard American wishes.

India also changed its tone on the Vietnam War. Earlier, India had been openly critical of America's actions in Vietnam, much to their annoyance. But, to Johnson's delight, Indira was publicly supportive of him on the issue during her visit. She issued a statement claiming that 'India understood America's agony over Vietnam'. The only thing that Indira refused to do was to join Johnson on the dance floor when he invited her to do so during the White House dinner hosted in her honour. She explained that 'her countrymen wouldn't approve of their Prime Minister dancing in a ballroom'. Johnson understood and said that he wanted to ensure that 'no harm comes to this girl'. In the end, he promised over three million tonnes of foodgrains and USD 900 million in aid. He also assured that the World Bank would be persuaded to be more responsive to Indian needs.[12]

Indira was pleased with what she had achieved. So she did not expect the response she got when she returned to India. She was criticized both within and outside her party for being a sell-out to the Americans in her economic policies as well as her stance over Vietnam. She defended herself by arguing that no developing country could do without aid and its acceptance did not imply foreign domination. 'Even Lenin,' she pointed out, 'had taken American aid after the Russian revolution.'[13]

However, the stalwarts of the party were disappointed at the realization that they could not control Indira Gandhi as they had believed at first. A powerful attack was launched against her for deviating from her father's policies. As her critics became increasingly virulent, she lashed out at them while addressing a Congress workers' meeting in Poona:

> Do not tell me I do not know Nehru's ideology. We worked together. I was intimately connected with all his thinking. In any case I do not see myself in the role of an imitation of Nehru. If I think it is necessary to depart from his policies in the interest of the country, I shall not hesitate to do so . . . If you do not like my

policies, you have every right to remove me and have your own leader . . . The Congress is big, but India is bigger.[14]

This was the beginning of Indira's political strategy to appeal to the masses over the senior members of Congress themselves. Whenever Indira faced a political problem with the party barons, she would go over their heads to the people. She had grasped a key element of Indian politics: mass support mattered more than organizational support. Indira would go on to perfect this approach later, whenever she found herself isolated. But at the time, hardly anyone called her out on it, since no one expected Indira to last very long on the political scene.

Until now, the nation did not have a hint of the biggest assurance that Indira had given to the Americans: the devaluation of the rupee. All negotiations had been enshrouded in secrecy. Even the Indian Cabinet was taken into confidence at the last moment. On 6 June 1966, she announced the decision to the nation. She got into even more trouble than she had been in before. She had not realized that the people she had relied on for advice were mere administrators and bureaucrats who could not have foreseen the political consequences of devaluing the rupee. The entire Opposition from the extreme left to the extreme right was vocal in their criticism of the move. Kamraj despondently commented, 'A big man's daughter, a little man's mistake.'[15] Indira had to respond. She got on the radio on 12 June to address the nation in a style reminiscent of her father:

Let me be frank with you. The decision to devalue the rupee was not an easy one. It was taken after the most anxious and searching consideration. How much easier would it have been to have evaded a decision, to have drifted along – waiting, hoping! There are times in the history of every nation when it will be tested, and its future depends on its capacity for resolute action and bold decision. This is such a time in India.[16]

But it turned out that the government had not followed up the act of devaluation with any measures to counter its effects on the economy.

The devaluation of the currency implied that Indian exports would become cheaper on the world market but, on the other hand, imports would be costlier. So, the cost of capital goods and inputs that were imported would go up. A rise in price levels was inevitable. Air India, the state-controlled airline unit, was the first to react by raising its fare prices. Although most of the Indian population had not seen the inside of an airplane, the announcement had an adverse psychological impact. Simultaneously, imported goods started disappearing from the market and there was an acute shortage of even essential commodities like kerosene.

It was even more tragic that the increase in exports that was expected due to the devaluation failed to materialize. Since there was a shortfall in agricultural output and a recession in the industry, India hardly had anything to export. It did not help that the monsoons failed again that year. To add to the misfortune, the Americans also failed to keep their word. The war in Vietnam escalated and the US had to divert funds to the country at the expense of foreign aid. So, even the immediate motive behind devaluation, to resume economic assistance from abroad, could not be fulfilled. Indira had taken pride in the fact that she had managed to obtain aid without strings. Now, she was mocked for being stuck with strings without any aid.

She felt betrayed by Johnson for not keeping his word and decided to revise her stance on Vietnam. On a visit to Russia, she condemned the 'imperialist aggression' in Vietnam and called for an immediate halt to the bombing of its cities. Johnson was livid. He immediately saw to it that each shipment to India carried his personal authorization, which was always late in coming. India lived from ship to mouth, and each consignment was a humiliating reminder of its inadequacy.

The country's food requirements became so severe that some food ships on the sea bound for other ports were routed to India instead. When Chester Bowles, the US ambassador in Delhi, pointed out to Johnson that India was not saying anything very different from what the UN Secretary General, U. Thant, and the Pope were saying, he curtly responded by saying that the Pope and U. Thant 'do not want our wheat'.[17] That year, the government could be credited for preventing a famine from taking place across the country through its proactive efforts in ensuring adequate food supplies. Just twenty-five years ago, one million had starved to death in the infamous Bengal Famine during the British Rule. Such a catastrophe was avoided.

Nevertheless, the series of events in the early months of Indira's tenure as prime minister took a toll on her. This period would have a lasting effect on her personality and style of leadership. She was overcome with a deep sense of paranoia and insecurity and came to believe that she could not trust anyone. Also, after incessant attacks and an utter lack of support from her own party leaders, she realized that she had to destroy the Syndicate before it destroyed her. But she needed political capital for that and so decided to wait it out till the time was right. Finally, after the altercation with America, she decided that self-reliance should be the ultimate goal for the nation. Herein grew the seeds that would be necessary to spark the Green Revolution.

* * *

On the twentieth anniversary of Indian independence in 1967, Indira turned fifty. Most prime ministers usually age faster in office, but not Indira. She thrived on the job. As a child, she was prone to sickness and had even suffered from tuberculosis a year ago. But, in 1967, she was healthier than ever before. It was also the year India was to have its fourth general elections and she knew it would make or break her. She was convinced that she would be removed once the elections were over. After the devaluation episode, Gulzarilal Nanda had openly said that she would not be prime minister after the next general elections.

So, she turned the tables on those who wanted her out of office. In her typical approach of appealing to the masses over the head of the party bosses, she told the press: 'Here is a question of whom the party wants and whom the people want. My position among the people is uncontested.'[18]

Indira was also aware of the fact that she was no great orator and lacked her father's deep intellect and breadth of vision. So, she avoided the ideological rhetoric and focused on issues that affect the daily lives of people instead. She made it seem as if there were no other leader who cared for them half as much as she did. To do so she travelled relentlessly, trying to reach every corner of the country, covering almost 25,000 kilometres and speaking at hundreds of public meetings. She managed to draw crowds even larger than those that Nehru could attract.

She even braved some hostility during her strenuous campaign. In Orissa, which was a stronghold of the right-wing Swatantra Party, some hecklers started pelting stones soon after she began her address. She continued with her speech despite pleas from her security staff to wind it up. She finally managed to finish her speech, but when the stoning resumed as another Congress candidate came forward to speak, she took to the microphone to reprimand the perpetrators, asking the crowd if those are the kind of people they would wish to vote into power. Several stones were then hurled at once and one of them hit her on the nose, fracturing the bone. This made headlines the next day and her courage through the ordeal garnered immense admiration, especially when she resumed her campaign with the top half of her face covered in bandages.

The affectionate outpouring of the crowds, however, failed to transform into any electoral gains, at least for the party. The elections were held in February and, even though the Congress retained power, the results were disappointing. The Congress vote share was down to 41 per cent from 45 per cent in 1962 under Nehru. The mere reduction of 4 per cent in vote share had resulted in a disastrous loss of 21 per cent in terms of the number of seats. The party had won only 283 seats in a house of 520.

Incidentally, this was also the last instance of the general and state elections being held simultaneously. The performance of Congress in the states was no better than at the Centre. It lost power in eight major north Indian states, which prompted a remark from the journalist Inder Malhotra that one could travel 'from Calcutta to Amritsar without having to traverse an inch of Congress-run territory'.[19]

Quite paradoxically, the poor show of Congress in the elections only strengthened Indira's position in the party rather than weaken it. The Syndicate suffered spectacular defeats. Kamraj lost his seat in Madras to an unknown student leader of the regional Dravida Munnetra Kazagham (DMK), P. Seenivasan. S.K. Patil in Bombay, Biju Patnaik in Orissa and Atulya Ghosh in Bengal had similar experiences. On the other hand, Indira secured her parliamentary seat from Raebareli by a huge margin. Such a turn of events meant that all of the Syndicate's plans to oust Indira as prime minister lay shattered. She emerged as the most acceptable choice for prime minister yet again.

Unfortunately for Indira, Morarji Desai put up a strong performance in the elections and he was still vying for the prime minister's seat. Another power struggle was on the cards. But Kamraj intervened and tried to chalk out a compromise. After much back and forth, it was agreed that Indira would be unanimously elected as the prime minister while Desai would hold the finance portfolio along with being the deputy prime minister, a post that had last been held by Vallabhbhai Patel. It was an uncomfortable set-up that was bound to blow up with time. Indira even had a last-minute realization that she had made a mistake but Kamraj argued that it was too late and that she was 'the prisoner of her own commitment'.[20]

However, what mattered was that Indira had managed to retain power and, in fact, seemed in a much stronger position than where she was a year ago. The Syndicate's dominance had been shattered and most of their favourites had been dropped or downgraded in the new government. They were replaced by ministers who were nominees of chief ministers who had remained steadfast in their support of Indira. This would become another characteristic of Indira's government. Just as in a feudal court, dissidents would be eased out only to be replaced by people who would unquestioningly do the bidding of the one at the top. This was not exactly the case for now. Indira knew that the senior party members could pose a legitimate threat to her in the future and she had to prepare herself for it.

CHAPTER 8

SHARP LEFT AHEAD

In some ways it could be said that Indira Gandhi's job in the Prime Minister's Office[1] was more challenging than it had been for Nehru. It is true that Nehru had to lay down the very institutional framework for economic and social development of the nation and create a cooperative federal structure. But Nehru had colleagues who had fought the freedom struggle alongside him and who shared a common outlook on the nation and strived to keep most of their differences at manageable levels. Nehru's stature as a leader of the masses, his intellectual supremacy, his liberal approach and his confidence in publicly discussing policy issues, combined with the early demise of Vallabhbhai Patel and the exit of C. Rajagopalachari from the party, ensured that he mostly had political consensus on his policies and that his government functioned smoothly. It also helped that Congress was in power in almost all of the states.

Indira, on the other hand, had to face numerous challenges in the decision-making process. Keeping aside the fact that she was quite unpopular among the senior members of her own party, she had to undertake policymaking among politicians and civil servants who offered her conflicting and confusing advice. She was in dire need of someone who could sift through the plethora of advice that she was receiving and come up with pragmatic, politically feasible policy suggestions. She needed someone who could give her definite views on matters. Her secretary L.K. Jha, who usually gave her conclusive advice, had lost her confidence since the devaluation fiasco.

It was finally in P.N. Haksar that she found such an aide. Haksar had been a friend of Indira's and her late husband, Feroze Gandhi, since their university days in London. He used to practise law in

Allahabad until Nehru convinced him to join the Indian Foreign Service soon after Independence. Since then he had been abroad, serving as a diplomat, until Indira summoned him.

Haksar was a man of unimpeachable integrity and proved to be a prized asset for Indira with his sage advice and dedicated assistance. She would completely trust his intelligence and judgement, and over time he would become the most powerful and influential person in the government. He would also provide Indira with the necessary support that she needed to counter the strenuous relationship that she had with the party bosses, and especially Desai.

The tenuous compromise that had been hashed out between Indira and Desai was beginning to come apart. Desai truly believed that he was more capable than her in policy and administrative matters and openly undercut her every move. His high-handed and patronizing behaviour towards her particularly irked Indira. For instance, at a meeting of the Planning Commission in May 1967, while a discussion was taking place to find resources for the Fourth Plan, which had been delayed due to the war with Pakistan, Indira had barely begun to speak when Desai interrupted. 'Indiraben (Sister Indira),' he said, 'you don't understand the matter. Let me deal with it.' Indira was understandably 'livid with anger but let him have his say'.[2]

She was, however, able to assert herself when the choice of the party for the next President of India turned into a power struggle. Even though the president is only the constitutional head of state in India, he enjoys considerable discretion in times of political uncertainty and instability. So, it was in the best interests of both Indira and Desai to have a friendly face in office.

Indira backed Dr Zakir Husain, who was the vice president at the time and next in line for office after the outgoing president, Dr Radhakrishnan. She felt that the choice of Husain would be welcomed by Indian Muslims. She also did not want Radhakrishnan to be re-elected since she had still not forgiven him for criticizing her father during the China war. But the party bosses felt that Husain might not get enough votes in a presidential election. So, Desai convinced the

Syndicate to push for a second term for Radhakrishnan. This meant that in a closed ballot for the presidential poll, Congress members might not vote for the party nominee.

Meanwhile, the Opposition chose the Chief Justice of the Supreme Court, K. Subba Rao, to be their candidate. He was deliberately chosen because only a few days ago, Subba Rao, in a landmark judgment, had deprived the Parliament of the power to amend the Fundamental Rights enshrined within the Constitution. Indira had been vocally critical of the judgment as she felt that the elected representatives of the people should have the authority to amend all parts of the Constitution.

She could not do much about Subba Rao's candidacy, but she managed to have her way with the Congress nominee. She simply asked her opponents, 'When people want to know why was Zakir Sahib bypassed, what answer will you give?' When right-wing groups expressed reservations about appointing a Muslim to such a high public post, she said, 'To me, Muslims and Hindus are Indians first and foremost.' Everyone was shamed into silence and Husain was elected with a comfortable majority. Indira had emerged triumphant in the first tussle with her adversaries in the party.

* * *

The electoral performance of Congress in the 1967 elections had come as a shock to everyone. It was a rude reminder for the party that a change was in order. Haksar, who had strong ideological leanings to the left, interpreted the results as the electorate rejecting Shastri's push towards liberalization. He further argued that the Syndicate had completely lost public support because of the public suspicion that they were deviating from Nehru's policies.

There were radical factions within the party who seconded Haksar's point of view. The 'Young Turks', as they were popularly known, highlighted that it was not only young people exercising their franchise for the first time who had voted against Congress, but also their traditional support base among the minorities and the poor.

The only way to regain lost ground was to rededicate the party to its old objectives of socialism and to reinstate the socialistic programmes that had been downgraded during the Shastri years. This was the point in history when the Indian economy diverged from the other Asian economies in the East that would adopt more liberal policies and a different trajectory of economic growth.

Indira, who had already been tilting left-wards since the disastrous decision of the devaluation of the rupee, saw it fit to strengthen the commitment of the Congress towards the left. The conservative and the radical forces within the party reached a compromise to adopt a Ten-Point Programme on 12 May 1967. This called for: (1) 'social control' of the banks, (2) nationalization of general insurance, (3) progressive take-over of export and import trade by state agencies, (4) state trading in foodgrains at the wholesale level, (5) organization of consumer cooperatives in urban and rural areas, (6) effective steps to curb monopolies and concentration of economic power, (7) provision of minimum needs to the entire community by the earliest feasible date, (8) ceilings on individual holdings of urban property, (9) prompt implementation of land reforms, and (10) abolition of the princes' privileges as well as privy purses.

The first and the last point were the most contentious. There had been talks of nationalization of banks since as far back as 1950. But even Nehru had not encouraged the idea. In 1967, however, the government was more receptive to it. The Young Turks expectedly favoured outright nationalization of banks but the more conservative elements in the party reined in their ambitions. Desai, as the finance minister, was completely opposed to it. Surprisingly, Indira supported him on the matter. So, the leadership settled for 'social control' of banks. It meant setting up watchdog committees that would monitor credit policies and other operations of private sector banks.

The radicals managed to avenge their defeat over bank nationalization with the issue of privy purses. The rulers of the Princely States falling within India, who were not willing to accede to the Indian Union, were given privy purses, a monetary compensation in perpetuity that would reduce in amount with each succession, and allowed to keep their titles and other such symbolic privileges. Over the years, this arrangement had drawn criticism, but it was continued in the spirit of keeping up commitments made earlier. However, with a rise in radical elements within the party, the mood was shifting. It was decided within the Ten-Point Programme that the privileges would be withdrawn but the privy purses would still continue.

The Young Turks wanted to a take a step forward and do away with the privy purses as well. They were also looking for an opportunity to avenge their defeat over bank nationalization. Late one night, when the attendance at AICC was low and the senior leaders had left, the radicals pushed an amendment to the Ten-Point Programme to abolish privy purses along with the privileges of princes. The amendment sailed through by seventeen votes to four. But since it was ultimately a decision of the AICC, it became a part of the Congress programme. The top leadership gave mixed reactions to the actions of the radicals. Kamraj, who usually endorsed all radical demands, did not comment on the issue. Yashwantrao Chavan, who was the home minister at the time and would have to deal with the problem, did not express any objection to the amendment. Indira also only expressed concern over the means adopted to pass the amendment. On the other hand, S.K. Patil and Desai were furious. They perceived it as a breach of faith with the princes.

The divisions within the party only grew sharper with time. Desai was repeatedly attacked by Indira's supporters. Tensions rose to the point of an open confrontation at an AICC meet in October 1967. The radicals demanded nationalization of banks on an immediate basis. Desai outright refused to acknowledge the demand. Like before, Indira sided with Desai on the issue. She declared that nationalization would only be considered after giving social control of banks a fair chance for at least two years.

The unity of the leadership at the Jabalpur AICC surprised many but it was too good to last. Tempers flared up again when a new Congress President had to be chosen to replace Kamraj. It was decided at the AICC meeting that the search was to be jointly undertaken by Indira and Kamraj himself. After quite a bit of wrangling, they settled on S. Nijalingappa, who was actually an original member of the Syndicate but had no antipathy towards Indira.

Nijalingappa, on his part, tried to be impartial between the two parties. He also appealed for discipline within the ranks but to no avail. The incessant altercations had no end in sight. The animosity between the two camps worsened when Chandra Shekhar, a prominent Young Turk, levelled corruption charges against Morarji's son, Kanti Desai, on the floor of the Parliament. Desai was convinced that Indira was behind these attacks against his integrity. The Congress Parliamentary Party wanted Indira to reprimand him, but she kept herself out of it. This infuriated Desai and his supporters.[3]

Indira further humiliated Desai when he presented the budget in 1968. Desai, as the finance minister, proposed a small indirect tax on the rich Indian farmers. Agricultural income was and has been out of the tax ambit in India as a part of government policy to incentivize farming. When word got out that such a tax was being proposed, the agricultural lobby rose in uproar. Protest marches were organized by farmers in New Delhi. Indira sympathized with them. Evidently, Desai's tax proposal had to be abandoned. He was miffed and blamed Indira for personally humiliating him.[4]

Indira, on her part, felt that the Johnson administration was nudging the pro-American elements in Indian politics to coalesce around Desai so that an alternative node of leadership could develop in India. These beliefs were not unfounded. Within months of becoming deputy prime minister, Desai had taken a trip to the US and had impressed the Americans with his right-of-centre positions on economic and geopolitical issues. Such an atmosphere of distrust and one-upmanship brought Desai close to the Syndicate. By now, they had come to the conclusion that Indira had to be removed from office. They only had to convince Nijalingappa, who believed that ousting Indira would break the party and push the country into chaos.

* * *

Amidst such tumultuous times, where economics was being mainly guided by narrow political gains, a ray of hope emerged from the agricultural sector. Back in the Shastri government, just before his demise, Subramaniam had moved for a market-oriented reform plan for agriculture. The war with Pakistan had brought all such plans to a halt. But two back-to-back drought years brought the demands of self-sufficiency to the forefront. Food shortages, price increases and stagnant agricultural output were becoming the trend. Imports had become the mainstay of India's food requirements. In the three years between 1964 and 1967, imports represented 11.5 per cent of the total foodgrain availability in India. Out of these imports, PL480 grains accounted for two-thirds of the total in 1964 and 1965 and a half of the total in 1967.[5]

However, the humiliation inflicted by the US was getting on Indira's nerves. At one point in December 1966, Indira Gandhi personally called up Johnson to ask for food aid. After the conversation ended, she angrily clenched her fists and told Subramaniam that she never wanted India to beg for food ever again.[6] This put Subramaniam's plans on the fast track. Indira backed his plan on reviving agriculture, even though it meant sounding the death knell on Nehru's dream of bringing about economic transformation through social revolution.

Subramaniam's plan was inspired by the agricultural revolution that had taken place in Mexico. Until the 1940s, Mexico was undergoing a similar agricultural crisis. A scientist, Norman Borlaug, was approached by the Rockefeller Foundation to join on a project that would focus on soil development in Mexico to boost maize and wheat production. Borlaug and his team undertook back-breaking work, walking across fields, trying out different cross-bred varieties of wheat for weather and pest resistance. He had joined the project in 1944, and, over the next nine years, tried out over 6,000 individual crossings of wheat. Soon they had varieties that could withstand a whole range of conditions. By 1963, Mexico's harvest was six times what it had been two decades ago. Borlaug's efforts had not only made the country self-sufficient in wheat but, in fact, a net exporter of the crop.

In March 1963, Borlaug arrived in India on invitation from his friend, Dr M.S. Swaminathan, who was then working at the Indian Agricultural Research Institute (IARI). The two travelled continuously for twenty days across wheat-growing areas in north India, studying the crop in each village. Within a year, a few varieties of Borlaug's seeds were showing promising results. It was around this time that Nehru died and Shastri took over. Fortunately, he appointed C. Subramaniam as the food minister.

Subramaniam organized a round table with scientists from the IARI and asked them for solutions to India's agricultural problems. When it was Swaminathan's turn, he said, 'We have the technology. Permit us to get it tested in farmers' fields so that we can speed up the work.'[7] They immediately got an approval for 500 demonstrations. So, between 1964 and 1966, demonstrations were done, and further research was undertaken.

After Subramaniam received Indira's complete support by the end of 1966, a high-yielding varieties programme for wheat, rice and bajra was approved by the government. The programme was to cover about 32 million hectares. India had to import 18,000 tonnes of two varieties of wheat seeds from Mexico to fulfil the high demand. The logistics of the programme were mind-boggling. The hybrid seeds were transported in hundreds of closed wagons across India in air-tight containers to retain their moisture. Adequate supplies of fertilizers and pesticides along with credit facilities had to be made readily available. Moreover, all of this had to be organized within a limited time frame of 100 days as the slim window of opportunity available to ensure a rich harvest was closing down.

In 1967, the first reports of harvest started to come in. They were mind-boggling. India's wheat harvest stood at 17 million tonnes; 5 million tonnes more than the previous highest yield. The yield had accrued to an extent that schools had to be closed down in Punjab and classrooms had to be used to stock foodgrains. This astounding overhaul of Indian agriculture was placed under the rubric of 'the Green Revolution'. The Indian farmers had silenced the doomsday predictors of the country.[8] Borlaug was awarded the Nobel Peace

Prize in 1970 for his efforts, because, as the committee put it, ' . . .
[M]ore than any other single person of this age, he has helped to
provide bread for a hungry world. We have made this choice in the
hope that providing bread will also give the world peace.'[9]

After the bumper harvest of 1967, Indian agriculture went from
strength to strength. In 1971, India was harvesting over 100 million
tonnes of foodgrains. By that time, almost half of the farmers with
irrigated lands were using high-yielding varieties (HYVs) of seeds.
The new varieties had increased yields of wheat by almost four times
and of rice and maize by about two times. India had finally become
self-sufficient in food. The country was able to build a buffer stock
of foodgrains that could last through several drought seasons and
even managed to become a modest food exporter. Food security
meant that India did not have to face the intimidation of the world
powers in pursuing its own national interests. It would prove to be an
indispensable asset in the oncoming war with Pakistan in 1971 and
fulfilment of India's nuclear ambitions in 1974.

However, the Green Revolution was not without its problems.
Land reforms had not taken place in any meaningful way in India.
Though the Indian landlord had been stripped of his feudal rights,
his position and money allowed him to control the votes in his
village and, thus, only like-minded people found their way into the
government. So, any drastic land reform hardly found support. The
ceiling on agricultural land holdings of about 30 acres per person
imposed in the early 1950s was also bypassed through devious means
to work around the law. The excess land was often transferred to
their children or even fictitious people.

In absence of effective land reforms, the gains from the Green
Revolution mainly accrued to the landed aristocracy. The benefits
from technological and infrastructural advancement failed to reach
even the small farmers. For instance, installation of tubewells to
provide irrigation required operational holdings of at least three
hectares. This was beyond the reach of most cultivators. Thus,
economic disparities only sharpened with the success of the Green
Revolution. Moreover, the Green Revolution only succeeded in the

fertile wheat belt, leaving a large number of states unaffected. So, the disparities between states widened as well.

These accentuating inequalities due to the Green Revolution partly led to the agrarian unrest that gradually began cropping up in certain parts of the country. It is no coincidence that India's first Maoist party, the Communist Party Marxist-Leninist (CPM-L), was formed in West Bengal right around the same time. The Maoists were called Naxalites, after Naxalbari, the village where they had held their first convention. An official study ominously warned that there was a possibility that the 'Green Revolution might turn red'.[10]

The mounting strain of having to deal with such unrest in different parts of the country and the continuous efforts to dislodge her from power finally began to take a toll on Indira Gandhi. She began complaining of disturbed sleep for the first time since she came to power, and at times even found it difficult to sleep at all. Desai, ironically, warned her against using sleeping pills and advised her to overcome insomnia through 'sheer willpower' instead. The latter was something Indira had in abundance. Desai would get a taste of it soon enough.

* * *

Before Indira could finally take down Desai and the Syndicate once and for all, she had to contain a political storm brewing in West Bengal. The United Left Front ministry, which was formed by the militant Communist Party Marxist (CPM) and other smaller constituents, had become increasingly revolutionary. In order to force labour demands on industrial owners and managers, they encouraged a unique coercion technique where thousands of workers would surround the industrialist and prevent him from moving until he succumbed to their will. Even the police were forbidden to intervene. Their excesses were leading people to lose faith in the ability of Indira's own government to control lawlessness around the country.

At first, she allowed the governor to dismiss the Left Front ministry and install a group of ministers who had chosen to break away from the Front and join hands with the Congress. The Marxists cried foul on the Central government's 'constitutional coup' and took to the streets. Their protests were subdued but they made it impossible for the new ministry to function in the legislature. Eventually, President's Rule had to be established in the state. It was decided that fresh elections would take place in February 1969. Indira also decided to use the opportunity to impose President's Rule across several other states like Uttar Pradesh, Bihar and Punjab, where Congress alliances were falling apart in quick succession.

When the elections took place in February for all these states, the only stable government that came into power was in West Bengal where, to Indira's dismay, the Congress was decimated, and the Marxists came into power with an even greater majority. By now, even Nijalingappa was irked by Indira's wont of bypassing him even on matters that concerned him as the party chief. He wrote in his diary on 12 March 1969: 'I am not sure if she deserves to continue as prime minister. Possibly soon there may be a showdown.'[11]

In no time, Nijalingappa launched a scathing attack at Indira and her economic policies during the AICC meet at Faridabad that year. He especially criticized the public sector for its inefficiency and failure to earn profits, calling them criminally wasteful. The delegates at the meet were stunned and some even walked out. Indira, on her part, argued that the primary purpose of the public sector was not to make profits but to ensure self-reliance. This was not entirely true, however. The early planners did intend to make the public sector profitable and utilize the capital gained from these enterprises for further public investment. Nevertheless, she went on to add, amidst applause, that her economic policies would always be guided by what was in the nation's best political and economic interests.

Soon after the stormy session at Faridabad, a renewed test of strength between the two sides came in the form of the sudden death of President Zakir Husain, who had been Indira's candidate but had maintained dignified neutrality in the party's power struggle. As per customary practice, Vice President V.V. Giri should have been the Congress candidate, but both sides had other preferences. The

Syndicate wanted to nominate one of its own members, Sanjiva Reddy, who was then the Speaker of Parliament. Indira knew that Reddy as President would try to dislodge her from office and install Desai instead.

Haksar advised Indira that the best way for her to take on the Syndicate was to convert the struggle for political supremacy into an ideological contest. She immediately put this into practice by intensifying her leftist credentials. When the Congress Working Committee met in July, she cited illness but sent a loyal Cabinet colleague, Fakhruddin Ali Ahmed, to read out 'some stray thoughts' of hers on economic policy. These ideas mainly reiterated the Ten-Point Programme adopted by the party last year, but with one interesting change. She indicated that she was willing to reconsider the long-held demand of the radicals on bank nationalization, even though the two-year period of social control was not over yet.

The issue was evidently not about bank nationalization. Her message was clear. If she was allowed to select a party nominee for the presidential poll as per her wishes, she would allow social control of banks to continue. Otherwise, nationalization of banks would be undertaken across the country. The Syndicate chose to call her bluff and supported Indira's note in 'its entirety'.

The issue of economic policy was shelved for the time being. When the Congress Parliamentary Board met to consider the party's presidential nomination, Indira put forward the name of Jagjivan Ram, a Dalit leader, to fulfil Mahatma Gandhi's dream of placing an untouchable in the highest office of the country. But the Syndicate remained adamant in their support for Sanjiva Reddy and he was chosen by a majority of four votes to two. Back in 1957, even Nehru had been similarly outvoted on the same issue of presidential nomination. But Nehru's political position had stayed as secure as ever and he had respectfully accepted the majority decision. Indira did not have the same luxury. She indignantly left the meeting, making no attempt to maintain her usual calm for the cameras. A press conference was soon hurriedly summoned where she warned the party bosses that their actions would have consequences.

Meanwhile, V.V. Giri announced that he would also run for the presidency. A strong possibility emerged that Indira would support Giri instead of her own party's nominee. But, before any decision was taken on that front, she 'relieved' Desai of the finance portfolio and took it over herself. She explained that since Desai had strong reservations about Indira's economic programme, it would be unfair to 'burden' him with the responsibility of implementing it. Soon after that, quite understandably, Desai also resigned from the post of deputy prime minister.

Before the Syndicate could respond to Desai's sudden dismissal, Indira Gandhi followed up with another stunning move that no one had expected. On 19 July 1969, she nationalized fourteen leading commercial banks of the country. She did so through an ordinance, even though the Parliament was supposed to meet in less than twenty-four hours. This was supposed to highlight the fact that nationalization was Indira's personal effort and, thus, isolate her political opponents. Soon after her announcement on the radio, thousands of people began to gather outside her house shouting slogans in favour of the prime minister. They represented a cross-section of the masses ranging from low-wage government and private employees to taxi and autorickshaw drivers, who had never seen the interior of a bank.

Keeping political motivations aside, nationalization was indeed a commendable step to extend credit facilities to the lower segment of the population that had been left out in the cold. Before nationalization took place, ordinary farmers, small businessmen and entrepreneurs could hardly make any efforts to improve their lot as they lacked access to the banks. So, the public euphoria was understandable. The opinion in the West was also generally favourable. The step was neither perceived as frivolous nor solely politically motivated. Instead, it was seen as a reflection of the determination of a prime minister who was ready to adopt any means necessary to push the Indian economy forward. Nationalization of banks also did not carry the stigma of an ideological upheaval. Countries like France and Italy had also done the same without any effect on the texture of their economies.

It would have been a political and economic masterstroke if Indira had a follow-up action plan in place. But there was none. There was no blueprint as to how and where the sudden spurt of deposits would be invested. This made it clear that the entire operation was undertaken in haste, merely to serve narrow political interests. In fact, within an hour of taking over the finance portfolio, Indira Gandhi asked the Ministry of Finance to draft the bank nationalization ordinance in a day's time. The Finance Secretary at the time, T.P. Singh, was not pleased. He showed Indira a week-old letter of L.K. Jha, who was then the RBI governor, that stated that the nationalization of banks was neither feasible nor desirable. Indira simply chose to ignore the advice. Even the Cabinet ministers took less than five minutes to consider the draft ordinance since it was clear to them that Indira Gandhi would entertain no objections.[12]

The political battle was closely followed by a legal one. Both the ordinance of bank nationalization and the Act passed in Parliament to replace it were struck down by the Supreme Court. The court said that the compensation proposed was quite low and that, even though the government could legally take over the banks, it could not prevent private players from engaging in banking activities that had been left out of the scheme of nationalization. Indira casually solved the problem by taking over the management of the banks without altering their shareholding and gradually passing laws that addressed the objections raised by the Supreme Court. This was the beginning of a growing trend of frequent altercations that the Indira Gandhi government would have with the highest arm of the judiciary in the country.

More drama awaited in the issue of the president's election. Growing anxious about the cacophony of public support for Indira and her policies, Nijalingappa committed the fatal mistake of reaching out to the Jana Sangh and Swatantra to persuade them to cast their second preference votes in favour of the Syndicate's candidate, Sanjiva Reddy. These were two parties that were identified by Indira's supporters as the very antithesis of Congress and everything it represented from socialism to secularism. Nijalingappa's move disillusioned a lot of people, including Congressmen within the workings of the Syndicate.

Indira gained a moral high ground as she had signed the nomination papers for Reddy despite her opposition to his candidature. Her supporters started demanding that they be allowed to vote as per their 'conscience' since Reddy's nomination was tainted. As the day of the election neared, both sides indulged in a hostile exchange of letters that were delivered as close to midnight as possible to meet the deadline for the newspapers, so that each could have the last word when the news reached the public in the morning. The suspense of who would win the race lasted till the very end as it was neck to neck. Eventually, Giri won by a narrow margin. Nevertheless, it was Indira's win all the way. The Syndicate had been vanquished. The people greeted her victory with the same exuberance that they had displayed over bank nationalization.

After such an open conflict, it had become clear that the Congress was headed for a split, but neither side wanted to take the blame for it. Vitriolic exchanges between the two camps became an everyday occurrence. Nijalingappa ultimately wrote a lengthy letter to Indira on 28 October, accusing her of creating a 'personality cult' around her that was 'threatening democracy in the organization'. He added, quite accurately, 'You seem to have made personal loyalty to you the test of loyalty to the Congress and the country.'[13] The statement had quite aptly captured Indira's political stratagem, but, at the time, the support she had was too strong for anyone to recognize its accuracy.

Indira, still sticking to Haksar's advice, responded with an open letter to Congress members on 8 November, claiming the conflict was more than a struggle for power; it was one of ideologies. 'It is a conflict between two outlooks and attitudes in regard to the objectives of the Congress, and the methods in which the Congress itself should function . . . In his last years, my father was greatly concerned that there were people inside the Congress who were offering resistance to change. My own experiences even before the fourth general elections was that the forces of status quo, with close links with powerful economic interests, were ranged against me.'[14]

Four days later, the Syndicate came to the conclusion that a split could no longer be delayed. They expelled Indira from the party. The immediate concern became as to which side the Congress parliamentarians would take. An intense process of lobbying began. When it was beginning to seem that Indira would get majority support, herd mentality took over. Out of a total of 429 Congress members, from both houses of Parliament, 310 sided with Indira. Her Congress initially came to be known as Congress (R), where the (R) stood for Requisitionist, which later evolved into Congress (I), the (I) simply denoting her name. On the other hand, the Syndicate's Congress came to be known as Congress (O), where the (O) was for Organization.

The most significant outcome of the split was that Indira had emerged from the whole affair stronger than ever. She had shed her 'dumb doll' persona for good and transformed herself into a confident, assertive and dominant leader who would not shy away from taking bold steps when needed. After years of meaningless ideological rhetoric by Congress leaders, she was someone who had acted upon it. She always had the support of the masses and now even a significant section of the intellectuals was beginning to rally around her. The tactful fight that she put up against the Syndicate had also won her fresh supporters. Very few had any qualms with the questionable means that she was adopting to get what she wanted. The *New York Times* commented, 'She has proved herself a courageous, tough-minded politician as well as an exceedingly skilful tactician – a Prime Minister in her own right and not a transitional figure, trading on her legacy as the daughter of Nehru.'[15]

CHAPTER 9

THAT WOMAN

The Indian economy by the end of the 1960s had completely closed itself off after a brief attempt at liberalization during the Shastri years. The import premium was back to 30–50 per cent on average and export subsidies had been reinstated. India's share in world exports, which had been 2.6 per cent at the time of Independence, and 1.2 per cent at the start of the decade, had fallen to about 0.7 per cent.

Foreign capital had also become increasingly wary of investing in India—more so after the abrupt nationalization of banks and the split in the Congress party. In fact, a German delegation of bankers and businessmen visited India in 1969 to look for investment opportunities but went back without even considering the prospect seriously. The split in Congress scared them away as their fears of political instability in India were converted into a rude reality.

Meanwhile, industrial production, which had expanded at close to 8 per cent in the Third Plan, almost halved in the second half of the decade due to a recession that had set in during the period. The industrial recession was accentuated by drastic cuts in government expenditure that were undertaken to balance the worsening fiscal situation of the country. Between 1966 and 1970, government capital expenditure fell by about 50 per cent in real terms.

The agriculture sector had also not fared better despite the advent of the Green Revolution. The growth rate of agricultural output had expanded at an annual rate of 3.2 per cent during the Nehru years. This rate falls drastically when the remaining years of 1960s following Nehru's death are included, especially because of the two drought years of the middle of the decade. But even when those years are excluded and the growth from 1949 till 1969 is considered, it turns out to be slightly lower at 2.9 per cent. So, even though the Green Revolution stalled the decline in foodgrain production, it could not eliminate the declining growth trend of the agricultural sector as a whole. This was because the Green Revolution was mainly focused on a few crops, primarily wheat.

Overall, the economic growth hovered around 3.5 per cent during the decade while the population rose at an annual rate of 2.25 per cent. Therefore, the per capita growth came down to barely 1 per cent per annum. So, the economic performance of the country had not been satisfactory by any standards. To make matters worse, economic policy was beginning to be defined more by political considerations in the Indira government. For instance, industry licensing restrictions were not being relaxed as they had become a steady source of revenue for the party.

In 1970, a new Industrial Licensing Policy was enacted along with the Monopolies and Restrictive Trade Practices (MRTP) Act with an aim to prevent the concentration of wealth in the hands of a few and prevent monopolistic practices. Clearance under the MRTP Act was required before a firm would be considered for an industrial licence. However, even though the intent behind the policies was noble, the bureaucratic complexities involved in the process did not allow entrepreneurs to grow at all. New undertakings as well as expansion of existing units that required an investment of less than Rs 1 crore were exempted from licensing requirements. So, firms were effectively incentivized into remaining small. Big businesses were naturally upset. The chairman of the Tata group, J.R.D. Tata, complained that the expansion of state controls was eroding away opportunities for the private sector. He described the government's intervention as 'unprecedented in any country other than those under totalitarian rule'.[1]

Even the licences that were awarded were mired in dubious practices of corruption and favouritism. The most infamous instance is that of a licence awarded in November 1970 for production of low-priced cars made entirely of indigenous materials. The person who won the contract was Indira Gandhi's twenty-four-year-old son, Sanjay Gandhi. There had been discussions among government committees for more than a decade about the production of a cheap, mass-produced 'people's car'. By 1968, fourteen applications had been submitted in addition to Sanjay's, from well-established car manufacturers such as Renault, Mazda, Toyota, Citroen and Morris.[2]

Sanjay was no car manufacturer or businessman. He had opened a car workshop in Delhi with his friend where his dream of an Indian car—called the 'Maruti' after the Hindu god of wind—was kindled. When he was granted the licence despite his inexperience, there was a general outcry against the blatant disingenuity on part of the Indira government. George Fernandes, a Member of Parliament of the Socialist Party, fired accusations at Indira of 'practising nepotism of the worst type'. Atal Bihari Vajpayee, another MP, spoke of 'corruption unlimited'. To all the allegations of corruption and nepotism, Indira could only muster a weakly-worded response: '[My] son has shown enterprise . . . if he is not encouraged, how can I ask other young men to take risks?'[3]

Indira was at such a peak in her career that she could get away with such feeble responses. The mood prevailing at the time in favour of Indira was evident from the case of Jagjivan Ram's unpaid taxes. Ram, who had served as a minister with various portfolios since the first Interim Cabinet was formed under Nehru, had used his long time in office to make a fortune for himself. More importantly, he had failed to file his income tax returns for a period of at least ten years. Desai, as the finance minister, was aware of the fact but kept his silence to use the information at an opportune time since Ram was one of Indira's principal allies. When the Congress split seemed imminent, he made the scandal public. Instead of asking Ram to resign, Indira chose to side with him, arguing that he was a busy man and had merely forgotten to file his returns. Again, the adulation for Indira was so acute that the country accepted the lame explanation.[4]

Despite public support, Indira was aware that she could not continue with a minority government for long and would have to go to polls sooner or later to return to power on her own. For the time being she decided to wait until she could wrest control of the states that were still ruled by ministers who were supportive of the Syndicate. Indira's men went about trying to buy Congress (O) legislators in the states. Further, she even divested the members of the Kitchen Cabinet of their excessive power and influence in the government contrary to expectations. She obviously trusted no one but herself to run the country. She derived such a conviction from a burdened sense of familial legacy, apart from her own personal experiences in power.

But the increasing concentration of power at the top was beginning to have deleterious consequences. The largest democracy in the world was beginning to resemble a Mughal court. Ministers were afraid of overstepping their bounds, so they began to forward all matters to the Prime Minister's Office rather than taking initiative. Bureaucrats began doing the same. The party dynamics were also completely altered. In the words of the historian Sunil Khilnani, '[T]he party . . . degenerated into an unaudited company for winning elections.' It became 'a simple mechanism for collecting funds, distributing tickets or nominations for seats, conducting campaigns.'[5]

* * *

Even after the split, Indira continued to pursue a range of radical measures under Haksar's advice. The most controversial one was the abolition of the privy purses and privileges assured to the Indian princes at Independence. There were 278 princes in 1970 who were annually paid amounts ranging from USD 350,000 for the Maharaja of Mysore to a paltry USD 25 to the Talukdar of Katodia. In September, Indira moved an amendment to the Constitution for the abolition of these privy purses. She argued that the concept of privy purses and special privileges was incompatible with the idea of an 'egalitarian social order'. It sailed through the Lok Sabha with a tally of 339 to 154 votes, but was defeated in Rajya Sabha, by just a single vote. Indira still managed to get her way by convincing V.V. Giri to 'derecognize' the princes. This not only stripped them of their privileges and privy purses but also their titles. The move added over USD 6 million to India's national exchequer. It was no small sum for a poor country. The public welcomed the development with the same enthusiasm they had displayed during the bank nationalization.

The derecognition of princes and the ensuing abolishing of privy purses were eventually challenged in the Supreme Court, which declared the move illegal, as the amendment had not been passed in Parliament. This outcome convinced Haksar that Indira needed to call for early elections as a referendum on her policies. So, on 27 December, Indira declared on air that the elections would be held a year early in February 1971. In the broadcast she dramatically proclaimed that, 'Time will not wait for us . . . the millions who demanded food, shelter and jobs are pressing for action.'[6]

Indira campaigned tirelessly over the next two months, covering over 30,000 miles by air and 3,000 by road and rail. In the process, she addressed 410 election meetings that were attended by approximately 20 million people.[7] The Opposition was a 'Grand Alliance' of the Congress (O), the Jana Sangh, Swatantra and Samyukta Socialist Party. Their alliance was based on a singular goal of removing Indira from power, which was reflected in their campaign slogan: 'Indira Hatao', or 'Remove Indira'. Indira cleverly retaliated with a call of '*Garibi Hatao*', or 'Remove Poverty'.

She managed to spin her entire election campaign around the selfless cause of eradicating poverty and social injustice. At the same time, she also promised stability and economic growth to the growing middle class. Her manifesto vaguely called for the 'advance of socialism . . . [while giving] scope to the private sector to play its proper role in the economy'.[8] She practically managed to appeal to all classes of the society and convince them that she was their only saviour. The poor, who accounted for at least two-fifths of the population at the time,[9] were especially overwhelmed with their belief in Indira.

The strategy worked. The Congress (R) won by a landslide. It won 352 seats in all in 520 constituencies, which was 70 more than what the undivided Congress had captured four years ago. The

Congress (O) and their allies were reduced to insignificance. It was a thumping mandate for Indira. Her communist allies had also bitten the dust. She no longer required their support to either form a majority in Parliament nor for the two-thirds majority she needed to amend the Constitution—an issue that ignited the call for elections in the first place.

After her convincing electoral win, she immediately got down to work on her reform programme, which was dangerously radical in parts. The general insurance and coal industries were nationalized. She also pushed through for the constitutional amendment that finally deprived the princes of their privy purses and privileges. In August and December of that year, the 24th and 25th Amendment were also passed, which restored the authority of the Parliament to amend Fundamental Rights, and to protect such changes from judicial review. Another constitutional amendment made the Parliament, rather than the Supreme Court, the primary arbiter of the compensation that was made on land acquired for public purposes. The checks and balances between the executive and the judiciary that had been enshrined in the Constitution were slowly being eroded.

However, these issues were not of paramount concern in 1971. The whiff of an emerging crisis first began to appear in March from what was then known as East Pakistan, the modern-day Bangladesh. Pakistan had been divided into two blocks, West Pakistan and East Pakistan, at the time of Independence and they were separated by the gargantuan landmass of India. Since the beginning, it was quite clear that there was no bond between the two wings except the common religion of its citizens. The eastern wing was populated by Bengali Muslims while the western one consisted of Muslims who majorly spoke Urdu. So, language became a major cause of divide.

The grievances were aggravated by the fact that despite East Pakistan having a larger share of the population, political power effectively resided with West Pakistan. The eastern segment was practically treated like a colony of the dominant West Pakistan.[10] The revenue earned from the exports of the eastern wing were utilized to build roads, schools, hospitals and universities in the West, while little was done in the East. The army, which was the largest employer of the country, drew almost 90 per cent of its forces from West Pakistan. Similar disparities were true for other government jobs.[11]

Such an outcome could not have arisen had democracy taken root in Pakistan. The eastern wing's numerical superiority would have given it a fair political representation. But since 1958, the country had succumbed to a military rule and the Army's disdain for the Bengalis was higher than that of the West Pakistani civilians. The result was outright repression.

Quite expectedly, a movement of self-determination arose in the late 1960s in East Pakistan led by a charismatic man, Sheikh Mujibur Rahman. He campaigned for almost complete autonomy of the East, except for affairs related to foreign relations and communication. Later, defence was also added to the list but only on the condition of equal representation in the Army. The military chiefs were infuriated and arrested him on charges of sedition.

But in early 1969, Ayub Khan, the military dictator of Pakistan, was ousted from power after a powerful movement that aimed at restoring democracy in the country. The latter failed to materialize, but General Yahya Khan, who succeeded Ayub, was committed to conducting free and fair elections across the country. So elections were held on both sides in December 1970. The results shocked West Pakistan.

Sheikh Mujib and his party, the Awami League, had run an extensive campaign in the East based on the cause for regional autonomy. The Awami League won 160 of the 162 seats that were allotted to the eastern wing in the National Assembly. The western wing, being less populated, accounted for only 138 seats out of which, Zulfiqar Ali Bhutto, the leader of the Pakistan People's Party (PPP), won 81 seats. So, Sheikh Mujib had a clear majority in the National Assembly and was entitled to be the prime minister of the entire country. West Pakistan had not anticipated such an outcome. Yahya Khan had called for elections in the expectation of a hung Parliament so that he could continue to be in power. He collaborated with Bhutto to prevent Sheikh Mujib from taking power. The Awami League launched a civil disobedience movement in response.

Things came to a head when Yahya Khan imposed a brutal crackdown on East Pakistan to repress the ensuing political unrest. In what appeared to be a well-thought-out operation, the Pakistani army descended on East Pakistan and within a few hours slaughtered hundreds of student leaders, writers, poets, journalists and intellectuals who were suspected of dissidence. This was accompanied by looting and burning of homes along with murder of thousands of innocent people. Any person who was seen protesting on the streets was shot at sight.

As the genocide in East Pakistan continued, a deluge of refugees started streaming into India. In a span of just five weeks, from 14 April to 21 May, their count escalated from a little more than 100,000 to over 3.5 million. At its peak, the refugees poured in at a staggering rate of 150,000 per day. The states of West Bengal, Assam, Meghalaya and Tripura, which had to bear most of the brunt of the refugee inflow, were in no condition to manage the crisis. India's entire eastern zone was economically retarded, politically unstable and socially volatile.

Indira visited the hastily built refugee camps a month after the crisis began and was appalled at the condition of the people. P.N. Dhar, the head of Indira's secretariat, who accompanied Indira on her visit, wrote that:

> We had, of course, read the hair-raising reports that had appeared in the world press about the miserable conditions of the refugees and their suffering, but what we saw in the camps defied description. More than the stories of what had happened to them, it was their physical and mental state that assaulted our moral sensibility . . . Indira Gandhi, whom everybody expected would say a few words of solace and sympathy, was so overwhelmed by the scale of human misery that she could hardly speak.[12]

After her harrowing experience, Indira was convinced that India needed to take action. She firmly stated: 'The world must know what is happening here and do something about it. In any case, we cannot let Pakistan continue this holocaust.' On her return to Delhi she decided that India would not absorb the refugees, but Pakistan should ensure that they return home to safety. Until a political solution was found, India needed to make sure that the refugees do not mix with the local population. The sheer numbers made this a Herculean task. By December, the total number of refugees had escalated to 10 million and only 7 million of them could be housed in camps. India had to undertake a massive resource mobilization effort to make arrangements for their housing, feeding and medical needs. The direct expenditure on refugee relief alone cost the exchequer a massive Rs 280 crore until December 1971, when war eventually broke out between India and Pakistan with an added expense of Rs 80 crore until the time they returned home.

To Indira's credit, despite the strenuous conditions imposed upon the Indian economy and all the political clamour surrounding her for a military response, she took no rash or impulsive decisions. Between the months of May and December, she did everything in her power to find a political solution by taking the regional conflict between India and Pakistan to the world stage and highlighting the human rights aspect of the issue. She hoped that global pressure would force a peaceful resolution of the issue.

There was also a strategic reason for not indulging in armed conflict immediately. The Indian Chief of Staff, Sam Manekshaw, had warned Indira that it would be imprudent to go to war until the rainy season was over. Also, China could come to the aid of Pakistan if the conflict began early. Once the winters set in, it would be almost impossible for the Chinese army to cross the snowy Himalayas.

The Indian concerns about a possible Chinese involvement were magnified after the visit of President Nixon's national security adviser, Henry Kissinger, to India in July. In his interactions during the visit, he gave enough indication to Indira that should China intervene in a conflict between India and Pakistan, the Indians should expect no assistance from the Americans. After that he flew to Pakistan and it was announced that he had fallen sick due to Delhi's heat and Indian food. It was later revealed that the Pakistanis had, in fact, put him aboard a military plane and whisked him away to China in the dead of the night where he met Chinese leaders Mao and Zhou En-lai.

In light of the American stance, India decided to reach out to the Soviet Union. The Indo-Soviet Treaty of Peace, Friendship and Cooperation was signed on 9 August, which assured, among other things, that both the countries would abstain from providing any assistance to a third party that was involved in an armed conflict with the other party. A few days after the treaty was signed, Yahya Khan announced a military trial of Sheikh Mujib, the court proceedings of which would remain secret. Indira immediately wrote to world leaders that the trial was only being used as a cover to execute Sheikh Mujibur Rahman and bring an end to the democratic struggle of East Pakistan.

When her plea failed to elicit a response, Indira decided to take up the case personally with the international community. She began with a trip to the Soviet Union in September where she argued that what was happening in Pakistan could not be considered a domestic affair. Now that such a vast magnitude of humanity had been displaced from their homes, it was an international issue. She left with a Soviet promise for aid if India went to war with Pakistan. In October, she undertook a twenty-one-day tour covering Belgium, France, Austria, West Germany, Britain and the United States. She found a sympathetic ear everywhere except in the United States.

It was clear from the start that there was no love lost between Nixon and Indira. Their discussions were steeped in an atmosphere of antipathy and distrust. Kissinger would later describe the talks between them as a 'a classic dialogue of the deaf' and Nixon's comments afterwards 'were not always printable'.[13] Nixon showed no willingness to persuade Khan in opening a dialogue with the leaders of the Awami League. The interactions made Indira completely sure of the American tilt towards Pakistan.

In a typical Indira Gandhi response, she decided to go over Nixon's head and appeal directly to the American citizens. She described the tormented faces of the millions in refugee camps who had been forced out of their homes due to the atrocities inflicted by Pakistani forces. Later, when the question of a meeting between her and Yahya was raised at the National Press Club, she explained that it was impossible to reach any sort of understanding with him as it was impossible to 'shake hands with a clenched fist'. She also pointed out how she had never said a 'rude word' about anybody, but Yahya had been making offensive statements about her, which eliminated all possibilities of a 'friendly conversation'. The room burst into laughter. They were aware that she was referring to Yahya's drunken outburst from a few days ago at a banquet when he had bawled: 'If that woman thinks she is going to cow me down, I refuse to take it.' Quite amusingly, 'That Woman' became the title of one of the numerous biographies written about Indira.[14]

All this while, India had also been assisting the Mukti Bahini (Liberation Army) that was a resistance movement formed by the affected citizens of East Pakistan. Indira assigned the Border Security Force with the task of providing the Mukti Bahini with the necessary training and equipment. As the group began making some successes, a piqued Yahya Khan declared that 'if the Indians imagine they will be able to take one morsel of my territory without provoking a war, they are making a serious mistake. Let me warn you and the world that it would mean war, out and out war'.[15]

General Khan was actually running out of time and war was imminent. He had failed to set up a puppet government in East Pakistan and it was too late to open dialogue with the Awami League. Continuing to fight with the Mukti Bahini was also not an option as a loss to them would have had dangerous repercussions of similar revolts from other parts of the country. So, war with India was the only obvious solution.

The Indian side was very well aware of Khan's precarious situation and decided to let him take the first shot so as not to be termed as the aggressor. The inevitable happened on the night of 3 December 1971, as the Pakistani air force bombed nine Indian air bases on its northern and western borders, including those at Amritsar, Agra and

Srinagar. The Indian forces had been ready in defensive positions for two weeks prior to the attacks. At midnight, Indira broadcast to the nation that India was at war with Pakistan once again, a war that had been 'forced on us'.

On 6 December, Indira announced in Parliament amidst wild acclaim that India formally recognized an independent Bangladesh. She also explained that Indian forces were fighting alongside the Mukti Bahini in East Pakistan. Three days later, Nixon dispatched a military fleet led by a nuclear warship, the *Enterprise*, to the Bay of Bengal. India immediately reached out to the Soviet Union and they sent out a fleet of their own, closely following the Americans. Nixon also denounced the Indian 'aggression' against Pakistan. In response, Indira wrote a carefully worded open letter to Nixon, explaining how India had been seeking a viable political solution for the past nine months with the help of other nations, including the United States, but to no avail. She earnestly asked him to explain 'where precisely we have gone wrong before your representatives or spokesmen deal with us with such harshness of language'.[16]

The war ultimately lasted only fourteen days, ending on 16 December, even before the US forces arrived at Indian shores. The Pakistani army in the eastern wing surrendered unconditionally after being both outnumbered and underequipped. Over 93,000 officers and men laid down their arms. Such a large-scale surrender had not taken place since the Second World War.[17] Indira was in the middle of an interview with a Swedish television team when General Manekshaw called with the news. She politely excused herself and went directly to the Parliament to announce to the assembled ministers:

> The West Pakistan forces have unconditionally surrendered in Bangladesh . . . Dacca is now the free capital of a free country. This House and the entire nation rejoice in this historic event . . . We hope and trust that the Father of this new nation, Sheikh Mujibur Rahman, will take his rightful place among his own people and lead Bangladesh to peace, progress and prosperity.[18]

As the country celebrated the victory, Indira also called for a ceasefire on the western front after careful discussions with Manekshaw. There was a feeling in the country that India should continue the war with West Pakistan and maximize its gains, but Indira was aware that any such attempt would have drawn widespread global criticism.

Nevertheless, Indira had redeemed for India the pride it had lost in the war with China less than a decade ago. It had liberated an entire nation, defeated its arch-enemy and established its dominance in the region. The country was overwhelmed with a sense of pride and joy and Indira was at the centre of it all. She had won immense admiration when she had trumped the Syndicate, but with the victory over Pakistan, that admiration had evolved into adoration. The wave of favourable sentiment towards Indira became evident in the 1972 state assembly elections. In all the states, including the Marxist stronghold, West Bengal, Congress won hands down.

Indira was at the very pinnacle of her career. The *Economist* aptly named her 'the new empress of India'. From this point on, she had nowhere to go but down. However, no one anticipated that her fall from glory would be so abrupt and swift.

CHAPTER 10

POWER PANGS

The war was won but peace had to be restored. This came to fruition six months later. On 18 June 1972, the two countries held a peace summit in the quaint hill station of Shimla. Zulfikar Ali Bhutto had replaced General Khan as the civilian president of Pakistan. Bhutto made no secret of his dislike for Indira. He was very proud of his academic record at Oxford and Berkeley, so much so that he looked down upon Indira's lacklustre academic achievements. Nevertheless, the two managed to come to an agreement with Bhutto, even changing his opinion of Indira by the end.

Bhutto came to Shimla with an objective of getting 93,000 Pakistani prisoners of war (POWs) stuck in Bangladesh and the nearly 5,000 square miles of Pakistani territory that had been lost to India. The talks went on for five days with no resolution in sight. Indira was willing to return a bulk of the Pakistani territory, except that in Kashmir, and the prisoners of war could be returned if Bangladesh consented.

The major issue of contention between the two delegations was that of Kashmir. India demanded that the ceasefire line in Kashmir be transformed into a formal line of control that would later evolve into a recognized international boundary. Bhutto outright refused the proposal. Talks had almost broken down and the Indian Foreign Minister, T.N. Kaul, had even left for Delhi convinced that there could be no resolution when Bhutto asked to meet Indira privately one last time.[1]

But huge concessions were made by the two sides. India agreed to withdraw troops from Pakistani territory. On his part, Bhutto verbally assured that Pakistan would recognize Bangladesh in due course of time and agreed to the Indian demand that both countries would not resort to the use of force in resolving the issue of Kashmir. It was agreed that the issue would only be settled bilaterally without foreign intervention, and especially that of the United Nations. Also, the ceasefire line as of December 1971 was recognized as the 'line of control'—the implication being that it would later evolve into an international boundary.

However, the language of the accord was dubious in stipulating that the line of control 'shall be respected by both sides without prejudice to the recognized position of either side'.[2] It was decided that a more permanent settlement would be reached at a later point in the future. Bhutto would eventually drag his feet on both commitments, of recognizing Bangladesh and hashing out a permanent solution for Kashmir. India would withdraw its troops by December 1972, but since Bhutto persisted in denying recognition to Bangladesh, it would take an entire year for a trilateral agreement to be worked out under which the Pakistani prisoners could be returned with Bangladesh's approval. Also, trade and diplomatic links between India and Pakistan could only be resumed in 1976 and mainly due to Indira's initiative.

The only major bargaining chip that India had was the return of occupied territories. If India had made this conditional on implementing the agreement, the outcome could have been a lot different. Instead, returning the occupied territories became the first step of the implementation process and was done within a month of the agreement coming into force.

P.N. Dhar, who was part of the Indian delegation in Shimla, would later argue that the fatal flaw in the agreement was that 'it was dependent upon a continued occupation of their positions of power by the two leaders who had signed the document. Not only that, there was also a presumption that Bhutto would stand by the verbal assurance he had given Indira Gandhi about implementing the understanding he had reached with her. The possibility that his political will might weaken, or that he might lose power, did not seem to bother the Indian side'.[3]

After Shimla, there was immense criticism that Indira failed to force Bhutto's hand on Kashmir, even though all the chips were stacked in India's favour. However, the Indian stance at Shimla was not impetuous. It was understood that had Bhutto gone back from Shimla having lost both East Pakistan and Kashmir, his political survival would have been impossible, which would have been pernicious to Indian interests. Haksar had argued that India had a vested interest in ensuring that democracy prevailed in Pakistan rather than allowing a return of military rule in the country.[4]

* * *

Trouble came knocking for India and Indira even before the ink had dried on the Shimla agreement. After six successive years of good monsoons, the rains failed in 1972. India dried up. A spectre of famine loomed large as the harvest was abysmal and the government's overflowing granaries had been emptied out to feed the Bangladeshi refugees.

As food became scarce, prices also escalated. The wholesale prices of all commodities, which had been steadily increasing by 3 to 6 per cent since the beginning of the Fourth Plan in 1969, shot up by over 13 per cent between 1972 and 1973, and then escalated further by almost 30 per cent next year.[5] As a result, most of the population experienced an eroding standard of living. The government that was already strapped in finances after dealing with the war and the refugee crisis responded with cuts in expenditure. These moves only accentuated the economic discontent among the masses.

As standard of living dipped due to a crisis in the agricultural sector, no solution for poverty was expected to emerge from the industrial sector as well. In fact, there was a general agreement that 'no foreseeable acceleration in the pace of industrial development in India [was] likely to produce enough jobs to make even a slight dent in rural unemployment and poverty over the next decade.'[6] Instead of an acceleration, the total number of jobs generated by the organized sector stagnated by the mid-1970s at 500,000 per year.[7] In addition, there was a backlog of 18 million persons from the previous decade.[8]

The government was also failing to successfully carry out a planned developmental effort. The growth rates achieved during the 1960s and early 1970s were quite evidently lower than what was achieved in the first years of planning. In the First Plan (1951–56) and the Second Plan (1956–61), the economy grew at an annual rate of 3.4 per cent and 4 per cent, respectively, while it grew at 2.6 per cent during the Third Plan (1961–66), and, after a three-year Plan Holiday, at 3.3 per cent during the Fourth Plan (1969–74).[9]

These growth slowdowns were brought about by a sharp deceleration in both agricultural and industrial production levels. The rapid production gains of the Green Revolution had begun to slow down. After a dramatic spurt in foodgrain production levels till 1970–71, output had begun to decline. This was a result of depletion in soil fertility, shortages and rising prices of fertilizers, and power cutbacks that were affecting irrigation facilities.

The stringent licensing policies imposed in 1970 and the ever-prevalent threat of nationalization were also having an inimical effect on the industrial sector by dampening investment sentiments and the risk appetite for new ventures. The industrial production in the country, which was growing at a rate of over 8 per cent per annum between 1956 and 1961, fell to less than 4 per cent per annum between 1969 and 1974. Corporate profits had also showed a sizeable fall in 1971 over the estimated projections at the beginning of the Fourth Plan.[10] There was, however, one major achievement during this period. In 1972–73, public sector enterprises as a whole broke even for the first time, and even managed to earn modest profits in the subsequent years.

The Indira government would have been better positioned to deal with the economic problems of the country had it not been embroiled under mounting charges of corruption. The phenomenon was nothing new to the Indian economic landscape. The heavy regulatory environment since Independence had given rise to ample opportunities of graft by both politicians and bureaucrats. Both

Nehru and Shastri governments had their share of malpractices. But status quo was not expected under Indira Gandhi's rule, especially after she had come to power promising to be different from the old undivided Congress. On the contrary, within her government, corruption permeated into every level of the government.[11]

The brazen loot that began under Indira Gandhi had a certain precedent to it. During the 1967 elections, she realized to her annoyance that, even though she was the prime minister and the chief campaigner for the party, the funds were tightly regulated by the Syndicate, which disproportionately favoured its own candidates. To avoid facing a similar scenario in the future again, Indira chose to make two changes that engendered an environment of corruption.

First, probably due to a fear that big businesses would heavily support those opposed to her, she banned political donations by joint stock companies. The move had one immediate impact. When legal donations were banned, businesses resorted to under-the-table dealings with political candidates and a dangerous nexus began forming between the two. In the old days, the contributions were made as an investment in the party's goodwill, with no direct link between donations and political favours. Now, a system of quid pro quo developed. Those who expected any favours had to cough up huge sums of cash. This was also the time when black money came into being. The illegal donations were preferred in cash rather than cheque as it left no trail and made it easy to siphon off a part of the collection.

Second, Nehru had made sure he never dealt in fund collections for the party. He assigned the task to other leaders of importance within the party. A typical untrusting Indira decided to keep a tight leash on fund collection and their disbursement. It soon became a talking point of the nation that 'suitcases full of currency notes' were being regularly taken into Indira's house. S.K. Patil commented that she 'did not return even the suitcases'.[12]

Indira's leading fundraiser was a man named Lalit Narayan Mishra, an MP from Bihar. Since the Congress split, he had held various portfolios including defence, production, trade and railways. As Minister of Trade, he had created the system where licences were only awarded in exchange of huge monetary compensation by businessmen and industrialists. Over time, Mishra would come to be associated with a lot of the financial irregularities and political skulduggery within the party.[13]

Another infamous Congressman was Bansi Lal, who was then the chief minister of Haryana, the state that had been carved out of Punjab. He became Sanjay Gandhi's personal benefactor to ingratiate himself with Indira. Two years had passed since Sanjay was awarded the Maruti contract and not a single car had been manufactured yet. Bansi Lal decided to sell Sanjay more than 400 acres of prime farm land in Haryana on the outskirts of Delhi for the Maruti factory at throwaway prices.[14] Apart from the price, the location of the land also raised a few eyebrows as it was situated next to an army ammunition dump. Several prominent businessmen like K.K. Birla also helped Sanjay by investing in his company.

Despite such favouritism, Sanjay's company could not take off. All the prototypes suffered from glaring faults. He, however, continued to make tireless efforts in raising funds for sustaining the business through any means necessary. Even before there was any hope for the first car to roll out, he approached 75 car dealerships and collected Rs 5 lakh from each one of them with a promise to deliver cars within six months. He also managed to obtain an unsecured loan of Rs 75 lakh from the recently nationalized Central Bank of India and Punjab National Bank. Finally, the RBI had to intervene to prevent Maruti from obtaining further loans, citing that it would undermine the very basis of the country's credit policy. Shortly afterwards, the chairman of the central bank was informed that his tenure would not be renewed.[15]

Even though Sanjay's activities were making Indira vulnerable in front of her critics, few around her dared to speak against him. Haksar always had his reservations about the sensibility in awarding a lucrative government contract to Sanjay. He even questioned the Bansi Lal land deal and the feasibility of the Maruti prototypes.

Eventually, he recommended Indira send Sanjay abroad until the murmurs about Maruti died down. This was the first time Haksar had miscalculated Indira. He was aware that Sanjay held immense influence over her mother, but he believed that she would ultimately succumb to her rationality. On the contrary, she remained silent about the matter. However, in September 1973, when Haksar's post as Principal Private Secretary was due for renewal, which had been done automatically since his appointment in 1967, Indira simply allowed it to expire. With Haksar, Indira lost the last person who had the pluck to stand up to her. Now, there was no one—except Sanjay himself.

* * *

As the year 1972 drew to a close, the prestige that Indira had commanded barely a year ago was all but gone. The opposition parties that had been reduced to a rubble in the 1971 general elections were gearing up to exploit the growing discontent with her economic policies. Food, which had become more and more scarce and, when available, costly, was the foremost issue of importance on everyone's minds.

It was also the topic at the top of the agenda when Congress met for its annual session at Bidhan Nagar in December. The temptation to revert to her radical ways must have been high for Indira, for she approved the nationalization of the wholesale trade in foodgrains, making the government the sole buyer of crops from their subsequent harvests. All misgivings regarding the move, especially in a drought year, were summarily brushed aside.

The plan met with immediate resistance. Many private traders managed to operate illegally and since they usually offered much more than the procurement price fixed by the government, farmers chose to sell their produce to them. Some of these wholesalers extended advances to large farmers, who hoarded stocks until they could be smuggled out of the villages. The state governments did not have adequate resources to plug such activities. In fact, many workers of the ruling party, including MLAs and MPs, were complicit in enabling illicit trade of foodgrains for an appropriate sum.

Inevitably, supplies began to decline dramatically from the public distribution system. Consumers who were unable to get their hands on foodgrains began to panic. The government could do little to protect them. Adequate arrangements were not made for imports as well. Indira did not want to go back on her rhetoric of self-sufficiency, especially for food, made during her election campaigns. Food riots began to spring up across cities like Nagpur, Bombay and Mysore. In Kerala, schools and colleges had to be shut down after students began looting food trucks.

The government had no option but to retreat. All proposals for state trading of foodgrains were abandoned by September 1973 and the return of private trading was announced by March 1974. But since inflationary pressures had strengthened as a result of the policy misadventure, the poorest sections of society, which were the intended beneficiaries, suffered most from the failures of implementation. By now, Indira's campaign slogan 'Garibi Hatao!' (Remove Poverty!) was becoming a subject of ridicule as her critics argued that she was not removing poverty but the poor themselves.

The price rises were also accentuated by the 'first oil shock' in 1973 when the members of the Organization of Arab Petroleum Exporting Countries decided to collectively cut the production of oil to achieve certain economic and political objectives in the Middle East. The balance of payments started to deteriorate from October 1973 due to an escalating import bill triggered by the oil price rise. The current account deficit almost doubled between 1972-73 and 1975-76.[16]

As the rise in prices in India was beginning to threaten the entire developmental effort, the government was convinced that some drastic action was needed to contain inflation. Indira Gandhi was also now wary of taking the advice of her closest economic advisers after the failure of the state takeover of trading in foodgrains.

Amidst all the economic mayhem, the long-simmering confrontation between the Indira government and the highest judiciary of the country came to the forefront in the spring of 1973. After her electoral win in 1971, Indira had enacted a law that gave the Parliament untrammelled rights to amend the Fundamental Rights without any judicial review. It had been immediately challenged in the Supreme Court.

Opinions were so strongly divided on the constitutional amendment that Chief Justice S.M. Sikri decided to appoint a special bench consisting of all thirteen judges to consider it. They delivered their judgment in February 1973. Six judges, led by Chief Justice Sikri, ruled against the government while six others, of whom A.N. Ray was the most senior, pronounced their judgment in favour of the government. Justice H.R. Khanna provided the verdict to break the deadlock, although he agreed with the first six on some issues and the rest on other points.

The end result of the narrow seven-to-six judgment was that the Parliament was given the power to freely amend the Constitution as long as it did not interfere with its 'essential features'—namely that India was a democratic, republican, federal state. This implied that any legislation affecting the basic structure of the Constitution would be subject to judicial review. The interpretation of what exactly constituted the essential features of the Constitution was left for the courts to decide.

The judgment was majorly seen as a defeat for Indira, and her supporters painted it as an attack on the Parliament, and the prime minister in particular. The opposition parties were hailing the verdict as a necessary move to contain Indira's authoritarian tendencies. In an interesting happenstance, Justice Sikri was due to retire on the very next day after the verdict was delivered. Since the time of Nehru, convention dictated that the senior-most member on the bench of the Supreme Court would replace the Chief Justice. This was done to avoid the slightest suspicion from arising that the government was interfering in the workings of the judiciary. As per the established norms, the next Chief Justice should have been J.M. Shelat. But he was one of the six judges who had outright ruled against the Indira government.

The most senior judge who had delivered a verdict in favour of the government was A.N. Ray, who was three positions down on the seniority list. Indira chose to bypass all the three judges who had joined Sikri in rejecting the government's case and appointed Ray as the next Chief Justice. The move came as a shock to the nation. It enraged her opponents but also alarmed many who were not particularly hostile to her until then. All the three superseded judges resigned.

Amidst all the humdrum surrounding the appointment of the Chief Justice, a judicial proceeding was taking place in a dingy room at the Allahabad High Court, almost unnoticed by the public eye because of the sheer triviality of the issue. Raj Narain, the electoral candidate from Raebareli who had lost to Indira in the 1971 general elections, had filed a petition challenging her candidacy. As was customary of the Indian judicial system, the hearing was taking place at a snail's pace. Two judges had retired while still hearing the petition and the third, Jagmohan Lal Sinha, was still recording evidence.

For now, the slow-moving judicial proceedings at the Allahabad High Court was the least of Indira's worries. The economic crisis was escalating as the drought extended into its second year in 1973, affecting almost 180 million people. The government policy on state trading of foodgrains was not helping matters either. Prices continued to rise and, by mid-1973, they had risen by almost 22 per cent more than they had been in the beginning of 1972. By August, the budgetary deficit, trade deficit and foreign exchange reserve had all reached precarious levels.[17] Indira had to set aside all her bold plans of being self-reliant and reach out to the IMF and World Bank for help.

But there was rising pressure from the IMF to carry out a 'stabilization programme' that would help bring inflation under control as a precondition for extending credit to cover India's growing balance of payment deficit. It recommended that India follow a path of stringent fiscal discipline to reduce money supply and enforce complementary policies to freeze wages, promote exports and incentivize private investment across sectors. The World

Bank pressed even harder on the need to completely overhaul the economy by opening up the economy along Western lines.

Accepting these conditions would imply backtracking on the economic strategy pursued since 1971. But Indira realized that she had to do the needful. A series of ordinances were passed in July 1974 to combat the inflationary pressures within the economy. These ordinances mandated compulsory savings on part of the earnings of all salaried employees and a ceiling on the dividends that could be distributed from the after-tax profits of companies. Simultaneously, the RBI announced a sharp rise in lending rates and also the interest rates of various savings instruments. Shortly thereafter, the government took measures to rapidly issue industrial licences that had been in limbo since 1970. Steps were also taken to clamp down on hoarding and smuggling activities. All of these steps did begin to display a downward pressure on inflation by late 1974. However, this outcome was achieved at the expense of the urban lower-middle and middle classes, who bore most of the brunt of the anti-inflationary measures.

The country was soon gripped by a growing wave of industrial and social unrest and even the grants from IMF and World Bank could not bring it to an end. In January 1974, a major upheaval erupted in Gujarat to protest against the rising prices of even the most basic commodities. The unrest began with students but quickly spread to the entire population, reducing the state to near anarchy. Burning of buses and government property, looting of shops and attacks on the police became routine. Corruption charges against the state's chief minister, Chimanbhai Patel, also became a point of disaffection. There were demands for him to resign and the state assembly to be dissolved.

Patel was one of the few chief ministers who was not of Indira's choosing. So she had no qualms about letting him go when he was forced to resign in February. But, she was unwilling to dissolve the state assembly where her party held a two-thirds majority. However, she ultimately gave in and imposed President's Rule in February. Even though she had conceded to the demands, Indira was convinced that the unrest was part of a bigger conspiracy backed by hostile foreign elements—namely the CIA. Indira was always fearful of an American attempt to topple her government as had been the case with many countries around the world, more so because the Nixon administration had no affinity towards her.

But the situation in Gujarat was only part of a larger malaise. The Jana Sangh president, L.K. Advani, commented, 'The Gujarat happenings were the result of inflation, corruption and youth frustration. It was the explosion of the people's anger, not so much against a situation as against a system under which the collusion of corrupt politicians and hoarders was starving them of food . . . And such collusion and allied practices were by no means confined to Gujarat.'[18]

Against this backdrop of chaos and discontent, a figure emerged to coalesce all the independent protests against Indira and her style of governance into a powerful movement on a national scale. The man in question was a former freedom fighter and a long-standing friend of the Nehru family, Jayaprakash Narayan, or J.P. as he was popularly known.

J.P. had retired from mainstream politics quite a while ago, but he had grown increasingly appalled at how drastically-awry things were going under Indira. When Indira had superseded three Supreme Court judges to appoint A.N. Ray, he had written to her expressing his fear that the very foundations of Indian democracy were being destroyed.

The J.P. movement managed to draw under its umbrella a wide range of groups from across the political spectrum. On one hand, it included the right-wing Hindu party, the Jana Sangh and its militant wing, the Rashtriya Swayamsevak Sangh (RSS), and on the other hand, the far left-wing organizations such as the Naxalites. Morarji Desai had also joined the grand alliance of these non-Congress parties. Together they were known as the Janata Morcha, or People's Front. The only shared objective of all these disparate groups was to overthrow the Indira government.

The movement began in Narayan's home state of Bihar in early 1974. Just like in Gujarat, the demands were to remove the chief minister and dissolve the state assembly to hold fresh elections. But that was where the similarity ended. Unlike in Gujarat where the protests were spontaneous, and the political parties only joined in later, the protests in Bihar were orchestrated by the Opposition. Moreover, in Gujarat, it was students who had taken up the mantle of leading the unrest, while in Bihar J.P. tapped into the discontent of the poorer sections of society and tried to bring farmers and landless labourers into the movement. He called for a week-long strike and used a unique tactic of protest, where the agitators would simply encircle the Parliament, which Indira refused to dissolve, and prevent it from functioning.

While the Bihar situation was climaxing, the socialist trade union leader George Fernandes launched a country-wide railway strike in May. The railway workers at the time were 1.4 million in number, accounting for 10 per cent of the total number of public sector workers in the country. Their demands included an eight-hour working day and a wage hike of 75 per cent to bring them in line with salaries of workers in nationalized industries. This was a time when the country was still reeling from an economic crisis and food availability was still low. A railway strike would have brought about large-scale starvation and also its success would have given rise to similar demands from other industries. So, Indira decided to put an end to it at all costs.

The sheer brutality with which the strike was crushed had never been witnessed before. Over 20,000 railwaymen were arrested and families of those who were absent from work were thrown out of railway quarters. Strikers were also beaten up, sometimes fatally.[19] Indira managed to crush the strike within twenty days. Even though there were a lot who were appalled at the brutality of the crackdown on protesters, most of the country's middle and upper class praised Indira for her firmness in dealing with the situation. This section of society had its reservations about Indira's authoritarianism but also wanted that the trains in the country run on time and not be held ransom to some aggressive trade unionists. Nevertheless, even though Indira may have won this round, the brutal suppression of the railway strike acted as the uniting force for her Opposition. It would soon return with a vengeance.

In the midst of the railway strike, a temporary moment of pride swept across the nation when, in a place called Pokhran in the Rajasthan, India successfully detonated a nuclear device underground, unknown to the entire world, and became the sixth nuclear nation in history after the United States, Soviet Union, United Kingdom, France and China. Indira and her government would continue to insist that it was only a peaceful nuclear experiment and India had no aims of building nuclear weapons. She remained true to her word until the end. The stance was believable since India had no means to deliver the nuclear device via a missile or a plane yet.

Nevertheless, there was considerable global criticism for India's actions, especially from Pakistan and the established nuclear powers. Indira powerfully responded to such criticism in Parliament: 'No technology is evil in itself: It is the use that nations make of technology which determines its character. India does not accept the principle of apartheid in any matter and technology is no exception.'[20]

However, the fervour over India's achievement was more short-lived than the one following the Bangladesh war. The J.P. movement was nearing its pinnacle after breaking out of the confines of Bihar and engulfing the entire country. He had made it a crusade against the widespread corruption in the Indira government and the sheer disregard it had for democratic processes. When the movement began, J.P. had vowed to take on Indira in the 1976 elections. But now he expressed fears that Indira was destroying democracy so quickly that elections might not be held altogether. He called not just for Indira's removal, but for a much wider 'total revolution'—spanning political, social, economic, cultural, intellectual, educational and spiritual spheres. He had an idealistic notion of a society, which was never fully defined. But the opinion against Indira was so hostile that when J.P. travelled across the nation sharing his message, huge crowds gathered to hear him, and most viewed him as their saviour.

J.P. was, thus, becoming a real threat to Indira. Many within Congress held him in high respect and felt that Indira should try and reconcile with him instead of confronting him. She came under their pressure and reluctantly agreed to meet him. The meeting that took place in November 1974 turned out to be a disaster. J.P. was under the impression that he would meet Indira alone, but when he turned up for the meeting he was infuriated to find out that she was flanked by Chavan and Jagjivan Ram. From then onwards, conversations between the two remained curt and acrimonious. She alleged that his movement was backed and financed by the United States through the CIA. He, in turn, retorted by saying that she was turning India into a Soviet-backed dictatorship.[21]

After the unfruitful meeting, the confrontation between the two became a fight to the finish. He called upon the armed forces and the police to disobey her orders and even appealed to Jagjivan Ram and Chavan to join him in the struggle to overthrow her. Indira had to watch from the sidelines as a march to the Parliament, led by J.P. on 6 March, turned into one of the biggest demonstrations the Indian capital had ever seen.

Meanwhile, to add to Indira's miseries, in April 1975, Morarji Desai began protesting the unfair delay of elections in Gujarat where the assembly had been dissolved in January 1974. He declared that he would fast unto death unless the elections were held immediately. Indira argued that polls could not be held until the drought was over, since it would hamper relief efforts. Desai alleged that the real reason for the delay was Indira's fear that she would lose, as had been the trend in a number of by-elections held across various parts of the country.

Desai, who was seventy-nine at this point, did not have the strength to survive much longer on a fast unto death. Still, egged on by J.P., he enthusiastically played his part as Indira weighed the pros and cons of letting a respected national leader fast unto death for a whole week. Eventually, she gave in on the seventh day and called for elections in Gujarat. Her opponents went wild with excitement.

The elections in Gujarat were slated for early June. Later that month, Indira was supposed to attend the first-ever UN Conference on Women, to be held in Mexico, and she was the star speaker at the event. Pupul Jayakar, who was a close friend of Indira's and one of the members of Indira's delegation, was leaving for New York a month early and came to bid her farewell. 'See you in Mexico,' Jayakar said as she was about to leave. Indira smiled and replied, 'You know, there is that judgement yet to come.' Jayakar did not grasp the importance of that remark until much later.

CHAPTER 11

DEMOCRACY INTERRUPTED

June is a particularly crucial month for most of India. It is that time of the year when the monsoon begins to set in from the south and the farming community gets its first hint of the kind of harvests they should be expecting. After two successive drought years, the June of 1975 held a lot of fates in balance. Everyone and everything seemed to be on the edge.

Within the political corridors of Delhi as well, a sense of unease prevailed. Amidst vigorous campaigning for the Gujarat elections and the bitter J.P.–Indira conflict, tensions were at a tipping point. In a curious happenstance, it all climaxed on 12 June. On that day, in Gujarat, the votes that had been cast a day ago were being counted, and in Allahabad, Justice Jagmohan Lal Sinha was readying himself to deliver the verdict on the petition that Raj Narain had filed against Indira's alleged electoral malpractices in the 1971 elections. The outcome of both events would strike Indira like a bolt of lightning.

At 9.55 a.m., Justice Sinha walked into Room 24 of the Allahabad High Court, a decrepit building dating back to the British times. When the judge had seated himself, the court aide addressed a crowded courtroom: 'Listen gentlemen, no clapping when the Judge *Sahib* announces judgment on the poll petition of Raj Narain.' But all eyes of the room were on the 255-page document resting in front of Justice Sinha carrying his decision on the case. He said: 'I shall read out only my findings on the various issues involved in the case.' He took a dramatic pause, then added: 'The petition is allowed.'[1]

The audience gasped in surprise, and then broke into applause in blatant disregard of what was just asked of them. Hundreds of miles away, a teleprinter typed away in a New Delhi bungalow of the prime minister's private secretary: 'Mrs Gandhi Unseated.'

The judge had found Indira guilty on two charges. Both were trivial but still illegal. All candidates are prohibited to use 'a government servant for the furtherance of [their] prospects'. It was found that Indira's former private secretary, Yashpal Kapoor, had submitted his resignation papers a week after he had begun working for Indira on the election campaign. Also, the Court found that Indira had employed officials of the Uttar Pradesh state government to make logistical arrangements for her campaign rallies. There is no possibility that Raj Narain lost to Indira by a margin of over 100,000 votes merely due to these improprieties, but the law was the law, and the High Court saw it fit to unseat Indira. As the *Times* in London put it, '[I]t was like dismissing a prime minister for a traffic offense.'[2]

Within a few hours of the judgment, elections results from Gujarat also started coming in. It was clear that Indira had lost to the amorphous coalition of opposition parties led by J.P., the Janata Front. The state of affairs was at its worst for Indira. However, the election results were a non-issue for now. Hectic discussions were taking place on how to proceed with the court verdict.

Like any other citizen, she had the option of appealing in the Supreme Court. But it could take a long time for the Supreme Court to reach a decision and, until then, she could only stay in office if it gave her an unconditional stay on the judgment. This had not been the case in all the past instances. The court usually gave a conditional stay to a minister in a similar situation where they could participate in parliamentary proceedings but not vote. A prime minister without voting powers was a ludicrous proposition.

There was a brief moment when it seemed that Indira would step down. But most of her colleagues and supporters advised her to stay in office and fight. It was ultimately decided that she would ask the Supreme Court for an unconditional stay. There was mass hysteria among people on both sides of the issue. The prime minister's propaganda machine resorted to organizing massive pro-Indira demonstrations by diverting Delhi's notoriously inadequate transport services to amass people from neighbouring states. J.P. and his supporters demanding Indira's resignation responded not only with equally massive rallies but also with daily sit-ins at Rashtrapati Bhavan, the presidential palace.

Finally, on 24 June, Supreme Court Justice Krishna Iyer gave his ruling on Indira's appeal for a stay order. In an unnecessarily long order, he awarded Indira only a conditional stay on the Allahabad High Court verdict, taking away her voting powers in Parliament. She had been reduced to a lame-duck prime minister. The stay order made the cries for her resignation from the Opposition louder and more determined. J.P. called for a mass rally to be held in Delhi's Ramlila Grounds the next day.[3]

Indira was informed by her intelligence advisers that Narayan planned to appeal to the police and the army to mutiny from the rally. Moreover, Morarji Desai told a foreign journalist on the eve of the rally that they planned to 'overthrow' Indira by camping outside her house day and night until she resigned. Unwittingly, by threatening to unleash chaos and stage a coup, Narayan and Desai had given Indira legitimate reason to impose a state of Emergency across the nation.

In the utmost secrecy, Indira was considering the possibility of imposing an Emergency under Article 352 of the Indian Constitution with the help of her closest advisers and aides. On 25 June, she summoned the chief minister of West Bengal, Siddhartha Shankar Ray, who was a prominent lawyer and an acquaintance of Indira's since her childhood. She shared with him the findings of the intelligence reports regarding Narayan's plans. The reports had implicated the CIA, igniting Indira's fears of an American effort to oust her in the same way Chile's Salvador Allende had been replaced in 1973.[4]

She was, however, not seeking advice from Ray, but only his approval for the course of action that she had already set in motion a day before. In fact, while Indira was meeting Ray, Sanjay Gandhi, Bansi Lal and Om Mehta, the second-in-command at the home ministry, were drawing up a preliminary list of people to be arrested once the Emergency was enforced. Once Ray approved that a case could be made for the imposition of an Emergency due to internal disturbance in the country, she made up her mind to go through with it.

At around 5.30 p.m., she left with Ray for Rashtrapati Bhavan to inform President Fakhruddin Ali Ahmed that, in light of recent events, her government had decided to impose a State of Internal Emergency (an External Emergency had already been in place since the 1971 war). When he asked if the Cabinet had been consulted, Ray explained that it was not legally necessary for the Cabinet to give their endorsement in advance and, since the matter was so urgent, it could be done retrospectively. The proclamation, thus, received the president's assent.

India immediately went into Emergency rule. The world's largest democracy was now a virtual dictatorship. Mass arrests were made in the dead of the night. J.P. and Desai were among the first to go. At midnight, the power supply was cut to Delhi's Bahadur Shah Zafar Marg, where most of the capital's newspaper offices were located. When the breakdown lasted throughout the night, plans to publish the morning papers had to be abandoned. It was a deliberate move to prevent reporting of the events that had transpired in the night.

A Cabinet meeting was called at six in the morning. Most of those present were dumbstruck by the news of the Emergency and the long list of detainees. No one dared to ask a question except the defence minister, Swaran Singh, who queried under which law the arrests were made. Indira gave him a laconic reply. Singh would later be relieved of his position for his reservations about the Emergency. Nothing else was discussed in the Cabinet meeting and the Emergency Proclamation was ratified in less than half an hour. The country first learnt of it from the BBC World Service broadcast at 7.30 in the morning on 26 June.

Half an hour later, Indira addressed the nation on the radio: 'The President has declared a state of Emergency. There is no need to panic.' She explained how there was a 'deep and widespread conspiracy' that had been brewing against her since she began to 'introduce certain progressive measures of benefit to the common man and woman of India'. So the Emergency was necessary to restore stability, peace and order in the country and also, ironically, to safeguard democracy.[5]

Immediately after claiming that she was saving democracy, Indira went on to consolidate her position and safeguard herself from any threats. A series of bills were passed to amend the Constitution and safeguard her from the judiciary. With most of the Opposition behind bars, passing bills through Parliament was a cakewalk. The 38th Amendment made the declaration of Emergency final and conclusive by putting it beyond the reach of the courts. Any ordinances passed by the president and laws violating Fundamental Rights were also barred from judicial review. The 39th Amendment invalidated the judgment of the Allahabad High Court against Indira by retroactively nullifying all the corrupt practices in election law for which she had been found guilty.

The most alarming of all the amendments that took place during the Emergency period that would last for twenty-one months was the 42nd Amendment that was made in November 1976. A clause in the Amendment gave the government power to even amend the basic structure of the Constitution, thus authorizing the Parliament to change any feature of the Constitution—including that of India being a democratic, republican, federal state.

* * *

Despite the nefarious nature of the imposition of the Emergency, in its initial months, it turned out to be very popular with the people at large. Most common men were tired of the incessant protests, strikes, sit-ins and clashes with the police. A return to orderly life once the Emergency was enforced was quite a welcome change. Government officials, notorious for their lackadaisical attitude, started to arrive at work on time and took fewer tea breaks as they were unsure of what would happen to them otherwise. Taxis and autorickshaws were seen driving on the correct side of the road. People queued to board buses. Trains ran on time. The *New York Times* carried a front-page story with the headline: 'Authoritarian Rule Gains Wide Acceptance in India.'[6]

Coincidently, the weather also worked in Indira's favour. The rains were bountiful that year—the 'best distributed rainfall' reported over the past thirty-five years—and the economy picked up.[7] As a result, the 1975 harvests reached an all-time record. A peak of 118 million tonnes of foodgrains was achieved that year against an average of 104 million from 1969 to 1971 and 100 million from 1972 to 1974. It was also the first year in almost a decade when agricultural growth exceeded the population growth rate. Between 1964 and 1974, agricultural production grew at a paltry 1.3 per cent per annum against a population growth of 2–2.5 per cent per annum. This was despite the period encompassing the much-celebrated 'Green Revolution' that is now mostly understood to be a 'wheat revolution'.[8]

The improved performance of the agricultural sector was only due to favourable weather conditions and had hardly anything to do with government policy or the Emergency. In fact, the government attributed a lot of economic gains made during this period to the imposition of the Emergency, but most of it was either good fortune or due to policy moves adopted before the Emergency.

The rapid reduction in prices soon after the imposition of the Emergency bolstered their claim. In the first six months immediately following the Emergency, the wholesale prices of all commodities fell by around 7 per cent. But this halt in inflation that had become a major cause of discontent over the last two years was brought about by a combination of various factors that had been initiated much before the Emergency began.

Since July 1974, the government had been operating a restrictive monetary policy that had propped up the interest rates in the economy disincentivizing spending. The government's income policy of compulsory deposits and freezing of bonus payments also lowered consumer demand, especially for foodgrains, thereby lowering prices. Finally, the crackdown on hoarders and speculators after the ordinance was issued in 1974 reduced the difference between prices of goods in the official and black markets. Therefore, all the factors inducing inflationary tendencies in the economy had been negated with measures that had little to do with the Emergency.

The industrial sector was the only significant aspect of the economy that did make substantial gains out of the Emergency, after witnessing a dramatic reduction in the number of man-days lost in strikes and lock-outs. Between the months of July and September 1974, India lost a total of 6 million man-days. The corresponding figure for 1975 was just 1.56 million, with a progressive decline in each successive month. Overall, industrial production grew at a brisk 6 per cent, which was more than double what it had been in the previous year, while the economy as a whole recorded its most impressive growth in a few years of over 8 per cent. It had last grown at a comparable rate in 1967 when economic recovery was yet again achieved through a record crop harvest following two successive drought years.

But since no structural changes took place during the Emergency period, the high economic growth could not be sustained. Poor weather conditions the next year led to a dip in foodgrain output by 5–6 per cent. The overall economic growth immediately slumped to less than 2 per cent. The industry did grow at an impressive 10 per cent in 1976, but it was largely driven by public sector enterprises and could not be sustained without the excessive public investment that was being undertaken. Moreover, the old problems came rushing back in 1976. Inflation began rising again, majorly due to price increases of food and industrial raw materials. Unemployment was still growing as job creation in the organized sector was stable at 500,000 per year.[9]

It becomes increasingly evident throughout Indian history that the country's leaders failed to develop and follow a comprehensive economic strategy, except perhaps for the first few years after Independence. Since then the economy has mainly been used as a battleground for the fulfilment of narrow political agendas. The Emergency was no different.

Indira Gandhi justified her decision to suspend constitutional procedures as a means to undertake economic reforms. Within five days of the imposition of the Emergency, a Twenty-Point Economic Programme was announced, promising implementation of long-standing policies for basic social change. The programme intended to abolish bonded labour, implement agricultural land ceilings, liquidate rural debt, increase agricultural wages, bring prices down, step up agricultural and industrial production, prevent tax evasion, confiscate the properties of smugglers, and enlarge overall employment. The Congress party portrayed these promises as the 'beginning of a renewed and vigorous battle against poverty, for laying the foundation of a new social order'.[10]

The Twenty-Point Programme was clearly inspired by the forgotten Ten-Point Programme of 1967, especially in terms of agricultural reforms. But the new programme lost momentum more quickly than the last one. Even though the Emergency had provided the Central government with unlimited powers, the implementation of the programme suffered because it required direct administrative apparatus down to the village level. But the Indira government completely lacked support at the grassroots level, mostly because centralization of power had been the norm for almost a decade now. Problems of implementation affected the success of the programme at every level.

The abolition of bonded labour is a case in point. The Centre was entirely dependent on the states for the identification of such cases, and, at the state level, the district collector was responsible for ensuring their rehabilitation. But the district collector was usually ill-equipped to carry out these directives without the help of village communities that were mostly non-existent or hardly active.

Some real gains were achieved, but they were mostly in the campaigns against income tax evasion and smuggling. When a voluntary disclosure scheme was introduced during the Emergency, around 250,000 people came forward and reported their wealth, resulting in an additional income tax collection of Rs 249 crore rupees. The efforts against smuggling that had been enforced well before the Emergency were reinforced and over 2,000 smugglers were arrested and illegal goods worth tens of crore of rupees were confiscated in 60,000 raids.[11] But this was where the success of Indira's economic programme ended. Indira's claim of the necessity of suppressing constitutional procedures to administer economic reform did not hold water in the light of such minuscule gains.

* * *

Even though Indira's Twenty-Point Programme failed, her plan to make a political heir out of Sanjay Gandhi met with incredible success. The Emergency proved to be the heyday of his career. More than Indira's complex Twenty-Point Programme, it was Sanjay's Five-Point Programme that captured public imagination. His five goals were to increase public literacy, abolish bride dowry, end the caste system, 'beautify' the environment (through slum clearance and tree plantations) and, finally, to introduce a radical programme of family planning.

Even though Sanjay had stepped into politics through the back door with no experience, authority or electoral mandate, no one dared to question his role in directing government policy. On the contrary, the government spent Rs 8 lakh on publicizing his plan, and it caught on like wildfire. The excitement about his plans lasted until the excesses that accompanied their enactment were realized.

The most controversial of the five points of Sanjay's programme was the one on family planning. It was a desirable objective and the fact was that Sanjay had done his homework on demography. He had consulted various international agencies and local family-planning experts. The officials at United Nations Fund for Population Activities (UNFPA) had told him that the world population had been growing at an alarming rate. By 1980, the world population was expected to double from where it had stood just three decades ago. Also, the poorer nations were adding considerably more people to the planet than the advanced ones. The 127 Third World countries added more than 1 million people every day against an annual increment of only about 8 million by the industrialized nations.

India could ill afford such galloping population growth rates given its inadequate social and economic systems. The country's population was growing at an annual rate of 2.1 per cent and life expectancy had improved from 32 years at Independence to 55 by 1975. With more and more people living longer, the population base was expanding fast. The UN officials told Sanjay that due to such alarming growth rates of population, the Third World would be required to create a billion jobs—more than what existed in the entire industrialized world.

It did not help matters that India had a sketchy record on population control. In the early 1950s, India became the first Third World country to adopt family planning as a part of its national policy. A population planning committee was formed under the first Plan and the third Plan even claimed that 'stabilizing the growth of population over a reasonable period must be the very centre of planned development'.[12]

So in the 1960s, genuine efforts were made to stem the population growth. But these efforts were met with multiple practical and cultural obstacles. The pill was mostly unavailable, and diaphragms were impossible to be used in close-knit Indian villages that utterly lacked privacy. Condoms were the best bet, but their level of acceptability is best explained in Dom Moraes's book on family planning, *A Matter of People*. He describes how in the late sixties, elephants used to roam around Indian villages, carrying a load of condoms that were meant to be distributed freely. Only children saw the practical value of the condoms who blew them up into small balloons that were then attached to sticks. So, the condom-dispensing elephants failed to have any impact on the birth rate.

The most efficient method of population control was sterilization. But in a society where fertility was perceived as an asset and a means to ensure a source of income in the form of children, sterilization was hardly embraced willingly. The Emergency gave Sanjay the perfect opportunity to force it upon people. In April 1976, the government initiated the 'National Population Policy' with an aim to lower the annual birth rate from 35 to 25 per 1,000 by 1984. The policy incentivized people to limit their family size to three children by withholding certain benefits to people who did not undergo sterilization after the birth of the third child. But when these measures failed to produce significant results, Sanjay adopted harsher ones.

Vasectomy tents were opened up in cities and sterilization vans roamed the countryside. There were reports of forced sterilization from across the country. Tens of thousands of homeless people who lived on the streets were arrested and taken off to sterilization camps where they had to undergo vasectomies. Moreover, government employees such as teachers, doctors and policemen had to meet certain sterilization quotas to get their salaries. Official sterilization certificates were issued to people who had undergone the process and it was made mandatory to produce these certificates in a variety of situations. For instance, motor rickshaw drivers had to produce these certificates to get their licence renewed.

All of this was done independently on Sanjay's orders and Indira was mostly unaware of the matter. She usually shrugged off reports of such excesses as rumours. But when P.N. Dhar produced irrefutable evidence that schoolteachers were physically assaulted when they failed to produce their quota of vasectomy volunteers, she immediately sent out a stern message to all chief ministers to curb such nefarious activities. The order, however, came too late in the day. In just six months between April and September 1976, more than 2 million Indians had been sterilized. The programme not only proved harmful to its victims but also to Indira. It undermined her credibility even among her strongest supporters and would prove to be her undoing in the 1977 elections after the end of the Emergency.[13]

The other major controversial aspect of Sanjay's plan came in the form of a slum clearance drive. The poor in Delhi bore most of the brunt of the excesses that were unleashed under this initiative. In April 1976 when the Delhi Development Agency's slum clearance and beautification efforts were in full swing, Sanjay visited Old Delhi, which was then, as it is now, a congested warren of lanes and alleys lined with ancient houses and broken-down shacks. Sanjay stopped at the entrance of the old city, Turkman Gate, and demanded that he should be able to see the Jama Masjid from there, which was at least two kilometres away. Everything that obstructed the view of the mosque had to be demolished.

In a few days, it was declared that the tens of thousands who were inhabiting the area would be relocated to the outskirts of the city and, on 13 April, demolition teams arrived with bulldozers to level their shops and houses. The shop owners were given forty-five minutes to vacate while the householders were given slightly longer to gather their belongings. Eventually, an uprising broke out on 19 April, as the mob began pelting stones and bricks at the demolition squads. The police arrived immediately and dispersed the crowds with tear gas and bullets. Somewhere between 6 to 150 people died, depending on the source of the information. A curfew had to be imposed in the area until May so that the demolitions could continue. At the end, 150,000 structures had to be demolished and 70,000 people were relocated, often at gunpoint.

Turkman Gate and other areas in Delhi were not the only ones that witnessed 'beautification' drives during the Emergency. Other cities like Bombay, Agra and Varanasi were also targeted for similar urban improvement drives. Again, Indira was mostly unaware of the extent of Sanjay's excesses. When Pupul Jayakar visited Varanasi and took photographs of the devastation that 'looked as if a bomb had fallen on it', and showed it to Indira, she was shocked beyond her wits. She immediately called the chief minister of Uttar Pradesh and 'exploded' at him. He panicked and promised to investigate the demolition.[14] Again, it was too little too late. The biggest victims of the Emergency, thus, were the very sections of the population that Indira claimed to protect and represent—the urban and rural poor.

* * *

Sanjay's antics did not stop there. He had revived the previously defunct Youth Congress, which ultimately degenerated into an umbrella organization for thugs and criminals under his leadership. This coterie of men under Sanjay would go around Delhi harassing shopkeepers and extorting donations from them for non-existent adult literacy programmes or family planning centres. They also levied heavy fines on commercial establishments for violating one or the other Emergency regulation and pocketed most of the money collected through such extortions.[15]

Indira could never find the courage to confront Sanjay for his damning activities. This was probably because Sanjay was the last intimate relationship that was left in her life after most of her confidantes had either distanced themselves over time or passed away. P.N. Dhar noted that she was in some ways 'afraid of her son, at least to the extent of fearing his displeasure'. He could never decipher whether she was simply unwilling or just unable to restrain him.[16]

Whatever be the reason for Indira's inability to manage Sanjay, the nation suffered grievously for it. He convinced Indira to postpone the general elections that were slated for February 1976 and extend the Emergency. Thus, democracy remained suspended because, as Indira explained, the government needed more time 'to consolidate the gains' made during the Emergency.

By this time the fear among the people had subsided and was being replaced with anger. Even though the press remained constrained, the government's misdeeds were beginning to spread through word of mouth beyond the privacy of people's homes. The number of arrests made during the Emergency was shocking in itself and difficult to hide. As per Amnesty International, over 140,000 Indians were detained without any trial in 1975-76. Even during the Quit India Movement of 1942 against the British, less than half the people were thrown into jails in the entire subcontinent!

In November 1976, Indira postponed the elections again and this time for a period of twelve months. Both the postponements would prove to be grave errors in judgement for Indira. Had elections taken place in February when the Emergency still had some supporters, she would have probably won the election. But Sanjay had convinced her otherwise. When P.N. Dhar expressed reservations about the move, Indira said that she was uncomfortable about the postponement as well because it made it seem like she was afraid to face the people.

Quite unexpectedly, on 18 January 1977, she announced that the nations would go to polls in two months' time and not in November as she had declared earlier. This was the first time Indira had defied Sanjay. Furthermore, she released all the political prisoners and lifted press censorship. At this point Indira sincerely believed that the masses would be pleased with the government's heavy-handed approach in combating crime, corruption and inflation and that they would forgive the minor violations of personal liberty that she had deemed as a necessary cost. She told a journalist several years later, 'I was by no means sure that I would win. I was sure that we would not get a big majority. I thought that we would just get through perhaps.'[17] Her assessment could not have been more wrong.

She again campaigned vigorously, visiting each state and speaking at a total of 224 public meetings. But the crowds that came to her rallies were fewer in number compared to her previous election campaigns and even hostile at times. Meanwhile, support for the Janata Front was stronger than ever. Realizing the inevitability of a defeat, Sanjay urged his mother to cancel the election, but she did not budge. When it was clear that the election would take place no matter what, Sanjay decided to run for Parliament for the first time from a Congress stronghold, Amethi, which was next to Indira's constituency of Raebareli.

India's sixth general elections took place on 16 March 1977. About 194 million people voted in five days of polling, accounting for 60 per cent of the electorate. In a sharp contrast to the 1971 elections, when 43 per cent of the votes polled had been for Congress, in 1977, it fell to a little more than 35 per cent. In terms of number of seats, it had been reduced from 352 out of 518 seats in 1971 to 153 out of 540 seats in 1977.

Indira's party had been decimated. She herself was convincingly defeated by her nemesis, Raj Narain. Sanjay suffered a similar fate. In fact, Congress failed to win a single seat in the state of Uttar Pradesh, the party's stronghold since Independence. By contrast, the Janata Party had managed to garner 43 per cent of the popular vote, numbering a total of 270 seats. Together with its allies, it had enough numbers in Parliament to reverse all of Indira's constitutional amendments that it intended to repeal.

On the night of 20 March, as Indira had a quiet dinner with her older son Rajiv and his wife Sonia, India rejoiced on the streets with drums and fireworks. Such scenes had not been seen since the Independence Day celebrations over three decades ago. At midnight, Indira called a Cabinet meeting. It had been twenty-one months since the Emergency had been enforced. Twenty-one months ago, she had acted independently without consulting the Cabinet. This time she did so before going to the president. At four in the morning, she left for the home of the acting president, B.D. Jatti, who had been appointed after President Ahmed had unexpectedly died in office a month ago. She instructed him to end the Emergency and herself resigned.

A week after that, the External Emergency that had been in force since the 1971 war with Pakistan was also revoked. On 24 March, Morarji Desai finally achieved his personal ambition of becoming India's prime minister at the age of eighty-one. Jayaprakash Narayan, who had taken ill during his imprisonment in the Emergency, retired from political life, having achieved his goal of ousting Indira Gandhi from office.

India clearly showed in the 1977 elections that it found totalitarianism completely unacceptable even if it were seemingly practised in its name. It was pragmatic enough not to blindly follow anyone into an abyss, not even the daughter of Jawaharlal Nehru.

CHAPTER 12

UNITED WE FALL

For the first time in India's three decades of Independence, a non-Congress government was in power. They had come into power, promising a dramatic shift from the gross misconduct of the previous regime and to set the nation on the path of development and progress. After all, under the Congress rule since Independence, India had become an unproductive and inefficient economy. The country was growing at an average rate of 3.5 per cent a year, which economist Raj Krishna scathingly termed the 'Hindu rate of growth' as the rate was close to India's population growth during the period. Such low levels of growth paled even more in comparison to India's South East Asian neighbours that had averaged growth rates of 8 to 15 per cent per annum. India was an extremely poor nation when the Britishers had left, and three decades had not made much of a difference. So a lot of hopes were riding on the Janata Party when they came to power in 1977.

The Indian correspondent of *Guardian* had pitted the survival of democracy itself on the introduction of 'economic progress and reform' by the Janata government. 'Already, the new government faces an economic crisis; inflation rampant again, an explosion of wage demands, and a wave of strikes. If it is overwhelmed by protest, the cycle of repression could start all over again.'[1]

Unfortunately, the party was set up for failure from the start. The Congress, at least until Nehru, had been driven by a singular ideological force, which defined its political, economic and social goals. On the other hand, the only cohesive factor that was holding the Janata Party together was the removal of Indira Gandhi from office. Once that was achieved, it was only a group of hastily cobbled-up parties and individuals that espoused independent beliefs and conflicting personal ambitions.

The metamorphosis of Chimanbhai Patel portrays the extent to which the Janata Party had sunk just to garner enough support to oust Indira. Patel was the chief minister of Gujarat when protests swept the state in early 1974 against the corruption in his government, among other things. These protests had inspired J.P. to begin his movement against Indira. But when Patel was expelled from Congress, he formed the Kisan Mazdoor Lok Paksh, which eventually went on to become a constituent of the Janata Party itself!

Even J.P. was not convinced that Janata's win could solve the inadequacies of the Congress rule. While he was in detention during the Emergency, he wondered in his personal diary: 'The question is, can the picture be fundamentally altered through the ordinary democratic process? Even if the Opposition wins, will the picture change? I fear no. Laws will be passed and applied, monies will be spent—even if all this is done, possibly without corruption creeping in, will the structure, the system, the "order" of our society change? I think no.'[2]

P.N. Dhar wrote about J.P. that he eventually realized that in his relentless effort to gather support for his revolution, a lot of people had merely used him for their own agenda. The political support that the protesting students in Gujarat received was only aimed at bringing the government down, and nothing more.[3]

As the Janata government spent a few months in office, the divergent social and political interests of factions within the party began to hinder consensus on an economic strategy. The leadership ultimately chose to adopt a familiar approach in the 'Janata Statement on Economic Policy' by stressing on 'the need to develop an alternative both to capitalism and communism'.[4] The alternative that they put forward was 'treading the path of Gandhian socialism based on political and economic decentralization'.[5]

The idea was to move away from Nehru's policy focus on heavy industries and mechanization to the development of small-scale and cottage industries using labour-intensive techniques of production and indigenous technology, wherever possible. The statement strongly opposed 'any system which is based on exploitation' and aimed to shift development focus to 'the jobless and the homeless, the small and marginal farmers and labourers'.[6] The policy statement also famously imposed rigid restrictions on foreign investments.

It had been becoming increasingly difficult for foreign companies to survive in India. Since 1974, the Foreign Exchange Regulation Act (FERA) had come into force. Under the Act, foreign equity participation in India was limited to 40 per cent. Such a company would be treated on a par with Indian firms. But the policy statement of the Janata government made it mandatory for foreign firms in India to find domestic partners.

The soft drink manufacturer Coca-Cola, which refused to share its secret recipe, chose to quit the country. IBM, Mobil and Kodak soon followed suit. The Janata leadership gave little regard to the signal that such a move sent out to the rest of the world that was hoping for a more welcoming investment environment after a change in government. Instead, 'the Janata ministers chose to celebrate the departures of these multinationals as a further triumph for socialism and anti-imperialistic self-reliance'.[7]

Coca-Cola's exit was followed up with setting up of Double Seven, India's first government-manufactured soda, which took its name from the year that Janata Party came into power. It was marketed and manufactured by the government-owned Modern Food Industries but found it difficult to compete with private players in the soft drinks market and wound up production in 1980.[8]

A positive outcome of the whole affair was the birth of domestic firms like soft drink manufacturers Campa Cola and Thums Up, and information technology (IT) companies like Wipro and Infosys. But since the manufacturing was largely done for domestic consumers without any foreign competition, the incentive to innovate died down. As India was closing itself down during the Janata period, a nation with comparable population and economic size was beginning to adopt market reforms. China, under Deng Xiaoping, gave up on socialism and decided to become more market-friendly. The country would go on to leave India far behind from this point onwards.

In macroeconomic terms, the Janata government was fortunate to have come into power when the economic situation was pretty benign. Prices had been stable since before the Emergency. Inflation did rise in 1977-78 owing to poor foodgrain production in the previous monsoons, but the rains were back to being normal in 1977, leading to a fall in prices in 1978-79. The balance of payments remained largely under control. In fact, India experienced large current account surpluses in 1976-77 and 1977-78. It went into deficit again in 1978-79, but the country's overall balance of payments still remained at comfortable levels. The calamity would come after.

* * *

Despite stable economic conditions, the tumultuous political environment during the Janata rule would prevent any structural changes from taking place. The government found itself mired in a complex internal strife. Even the planning process suffered as a lot of time was wasted in scrapping the Fifth Plan, which was supposed to go on until 1979, and formulating a new Sixth Five-Year Plan. Bureaucrats were left to themselves to run the economy with no clear political leadership, which was necessary if any radical reforms were to be introduced. Expectedly, no one took initiative.

Meanwhile, the leadership was focused on a matter that was far disassociated from developmental concerns. It was the only issue that inspired consensus among the party's leaders. All prominent members in Desai's Cabinet, including the new deputy prime minister, Charan Singh; the foreign minister, Atal Bihari Vajpayee; and Jagjivan Ram, who was given the defence portfolio, agreed that the task that demanded primacy was hunting Indira down and bringing her to justice, along with her son Sanjay. Instead of trying to determine what to do about India, the Janata Party was focused on what to do about Indira.[9]

Everyone in the Indira household was followed wherever they went and their telephones at home were bugged. Their passports were impounded, and house raided. The media did not spare them either. Indira was the hot topic of discussion on the airwaves and fresh exposes on her time in office were vied for by media houses. Anti-Indira books started to flood the market. Amidst writings by the intelligentsia that had interacted with Indira up close came a masterpiece by an obscure novelist by the name of Salman Rushdie. His *Midnight's Children*, even though a work of fiction, demonized Indira as a monstrous widow in a manner that invited legal action from his subject. Nevertheless, Rushdie went on to win the Booker Prize for his work in 1981.[10]

However, these were only minor inconveniences for Indira. The real predicament began with the appointment of a commission headed by Chief Justice J.C. Shah in the last week of May for an enquiry into the 'subversion of lawful processes and practices, abuse of authority, misuse of powers, excesses and/or malpractices committed during' the Emergency period.[11] Sanjay's activities during the period also fell under the purview of the Shah Commission. In addition, the Khanna Commission was set up to specifically investigate the activities of Maruti Limited and the Reddy Commission was established to review the activities of Bansi Lal.

Indira managed to fly under the radar and keep a low profile through the entire summer of 1977 and prepared for her Shah Commission inquiry with her lawyers. Her first opportunity for revival came very soon in July when a group of upper-caste landowners massacred numerous Dalits in the remote village of Belchi in Bihar. Janata was indifferent in its response to the incident, but Indira immediately swung into action. She resolved to visit the village, even though it was hardly accessible. She initially began her journey in a Jeep, but soon the rains forced her to change her mode of transport to a tractor. When she was close to her destination, she even had to travel on an elephant to cross a river. The locals, upon recognizing her, gave her a hero's welcome. Some even threw themselves at her feet. Probably even Indira wouldn't have imagined that the doors to her political comeback would crack open so soon.

On her way back to Delhi, she decided to meet J.P. in Patna, the capital of Bihar, where the old man was slowly dying. Narayan held no grudges against Indira now that she was down and out. The two talked for almost an hour and posed for photographs afterwards. Getting forgiveness from J.P. was a major win for Indira. It absolved her of all the misdeeds committed in office in the public eye to a considerable extent. This could be seen on her first visit to her constituency, Raebareli, after her electoral loss. She was welcomed even more enthusiastically than she had been at Belchi. In England, the *Guardian* reported that her constituents forgave her 'in ten minutes flat'.[12]

The Shah Commission hearings began on 29 September 1977. Four days later, in the late afternoon of 3 October 1977, an unmarked car drove up to Indira's house while Sanjay and his wife Maneka were playing badminton on the front lawn. Two officers from the Central Bureau of Investigation got out of the car and, after Indira emerged from the house, informed her that she was under arrest. She asked them for some time to pack, and in the time she got ready to leave, the media was informed. A throng of supporters gathered outside and showered her with garlands as she left.

She spent the night in jail and was produced before a magistrate the next morning. The Janata government had charged her with selling Jeeps that to the army were donated to the Congress in the 1977 elections and favouring a French company with an oil contract when an American company had placed a higher bid. But the magistrate observed that there were no grounds for believing that either accusation was well-founded and released her unconditionally. The Janata government was left red-faced. Instead of bringing Indira down, they had made a martyr out of her and aided her on the road to political recovery.

Indira's popularity soared after the incident. Soon, she was confident enough to re-enter the political scene. Most of the Congress leadership had distanced themselves from Indira. So, on the very first day of 1978, the Congress was split for a second time. Indira formed the Congress (I) party, where the 'I' stood for her name. Over the year, enough MPs would defect the parent party for Congress (I) to become the official Opposition. The old-rump party headed by Swaran Singh would come to be known as Congress (S). There would be a tussle between the two parties over the original party symbol of a cow and her calf. Indira's party eventually adopted the present symbol of the Congress party: a raised, open palm.

Meanwhile, the Shah Commission hearings were trying hard to nail Indira down. J.C. Shah wanted to question Indira on eleven specific points, which included certain questionable appointments, the series of events that took place between 12 and 22 June 1975, and the arrests made on the night that the Emergency was declared. She was called to appear before the Commission on 9 January 1978. She did so, but under protest. She refused to be questioned or make a written statement citing that she was not constitutionally bound to do so. In the month of January, Indira was called to appear before Shah four times, but she maintained her stance of non-cooperation every time. The hearings drew to a close on 20 February 1978.

The Commission came out with three reports in the months of March, April and August. The reports declared that the proclamation of the Emergency was unconstitutional because there was no 'evidence of any breakdown of law and order in any part of the country'. It went on to state that Indira had resorted to declaring Emergency in 'a desperate endeavour to save herself from the legitimate compulsion of a judicial verdict against her'.[13]

The reports were an overarching indictment on both Indira and Sanjay. Every matter, big or small, was discussed comprehensively. Yet, it proved to be a pointless exercise in the end. The proceeding had been entirely investigatory in nature and had no legal authority. All actions that the report termed illegal had to be proved to be so in a court of law. In India's slow-paced judicial system, that could take years.

It did not seem like the Janata Party had time on its side. The loosely-held coalition was quickly falling apart. Since multiple power centres had unnaturally combined to form the party, a struggle for the top post was always simmering. The prime minister, Desai, and his deputy prime minister, Charan Singh, were usually at loggerheads for this reason and J.P. was too frail and old to hold the party together. The tussle climaxed in June 1978 when Charan Singh accused the prime minister and his Cabinet to be 'a collection of impotent men' for failing to bring Indira to justice.[14] In response, Desai dropped Charan Singh from the Cabinet along with his disciple Raj Narain, who was heading the health ministry. Desai was inevitably forced to take Singh back into the Cabinet, but the fissures in the Janata Party were becoming clearer.

Indira, on the other hand, was consolidating her gains. She had travelled throughout the country and had been received with immense enthusiasm, especially from the rural poor. She clarified her position on the Emergency as a necessity to save the country from chaos. She also apologized for certain aspects of it like the arrests and the censorship of the press.

When she was assured that she had regained enough trust among her voters, she decided to run for Parliament once again in November through a by-election in the rural constituency of Chikmaglur in Karnataka. It was the ideal constituency for Indira. It was a Congress stronghold with nearly half the population below the poverty line.

Janata sent their Minister of Industry, George Fernandes, to campaign for Indira's opponent, Veerendra Patil. Fernandes was a popular leader, with strong left-wing credentials, who had led the railway strike throughout the country just before the Emergency. He campaigned vigorously against Indira. Everyone expected Patil to win. But, against all odds and predictions, Indira won by a convincing margin of 70,000 votes. Less than two years after everyone had written her off the Indian political scene, Indira was back with an irrefutable mandate.

The Janata Party, however, continued with its efforts to bring Indira down. In December 1978, the Privileges Committee in Parliament found her guilty of obstructing the investigation into Maruti. A resolution was passed in the Parliament demanding that she be expelled from the House. Indira responded with a dignified display of anger on the floor of the Lok Sabha. 'I am a small person, but I have stood for certain values and objectives. Every insult hurled at me will rebound, every punishment inflicted on me will be a source of strength to me . . . My voice will not be hushed for it is not a lone voice.' As she was leaving the House, she dramatically turned back and declared, 'I will be back.'[15]

She would be back, but not before a last-ditch effort by Desai who put up a special court in place to try Indira and Sanjay. The whole situation played out like before. Indira was arrested and taken to Tihar Jail. A week later, on 26 December, she had to be released due to nationwide protests by her supporters who were claiming that the arrest had no grounds. An Air India plane was also hijacked in the process by two friends, Bholanath and Devendra Pandey, who demanded her immediate release. However, they eventually surrendered a few hours later.[16]

After her release, Indira became an impossible juggernaut for the Janata to stop. By early 1979, they had also lost all capability to do so. The infighting was beginning to destroy the party from within. Desai and Charan Singh had a falling-out again. The latter wanted to investigate Desai's son Kanti, who had been accused of multiple corruption charges. It seemed hypocritical on Janata's part not to act against Kanti and level charges against Sanjay. They had filed a total of thirty-five criminal cases against Sanjay in their two and a half years in power. These ultimately led to Sanjay being sentenced to two years' imprisonment on 27 February 1979. He was soon released on bail.

On 11 July, the internal strife within Janata imploded. A no-confidence motion was moved against Desai and he could not prove a majority. The government fell. Desai resigned on 15 July and was replaced by Charan Singh. In an odd turn of events, he managed to assume power with the support of Congress (I). But before he could be appointed as the prime minister, he had to submit to a vote of confidence. Indira agreed to support his government only if the legislation that Desai had enacted to try Indira for her actions during the Emergency—the Special Courts Act—was withdrawn. Charan Singh refused and the Janata's reign was done for good this time.

The President dissolved the Parliament and called for elections in the first week of January 1980. The cards were stacked in Indira's favour. Her return to office was inevitable.

* * *

The Janata Party's luck on the economy front also ran out in 1979. The last two years in office had been marked with good harvest and stable prices. The only problem was a deteriorating trade balance, which was in surplus during Indira's final year in office but widened by about USD 2.5 billion during the Janata period. However, the country's fortunate improvement in foreign exchange reserves through higher remittances from workers in the Gulf kept the balance of payments in check.[17]

The troubles began in February 1979 when prices began to rise. This time, food prices were not a major reason for the growing inflation forces. The primary contributors turned out to be manufactured goods and fuel. In fact, the inflation rose by 17 per cent in 1979-80, but food prices went up only by 8 per cent.[18] The second oil shock took place in 1979 following a drastic reduction in supply due to the Iranian Revolution. World oil prices rose, and India's trade balance took a further hit.

As if on cue, the rains failed that year. Even though foodgrain production fell more than 17 per cent, it did not affect food prices as noted due to a comfortable food-stock position. But the supply of industry raw materials was severely affected due to the drought, and their prices rose steeply.

All of this could be attributed to forces that were mostly beyond government control. But certain bad decisions were taken by the Janata government as well. During the budget of 1979, Charan Singh, as the finance minister, went against Desai's advice and doubled the subsidies of farmers, which he planned to finance through higher taxation. However, the new taxes could not account for the new largesse. For the first time in India's planned history, a deficit of over Rs 1,000 crore was left uncovered to be financed by printing of notes. The plan was bound to end in disaster. And, coming in a year that was already inflationary, it only added fuel to the fire. Such were the circumstances when India stepped into the 1980s.

CHAPTER 13

CRASH AND BURN

A remarkable fact about India is its inclusive and accommodating nature of democracy that its founders inscribed into the very fabric of its society. Religious tolerance and cultural pluralism were intended to be the defining hallmarks of the Indian democracy. This myth survived to a certain extent in the first three decades in an independent India. But, by the beginning of the 1980s, it was beginning to fall apart.

Communal violence had been flaring up across the country. Hindus were turning on Muslims, Sikhs on Hindus, upper castes on Dalits, and almost everyone on the tribals.[1] The states of Punjab, Assam and Kashmir were the worst affected. These issues were a direct result of the manner in which Indira Gandhi had severely undermined state and local autonomy in a bid to centralize power. She had an unflattering history of disposing unfriendly chief ministers by imposing President's Rule, which allowed her direct control at the regional level.[2] Such actions had fuelled discontent on regional and communal lines. As the seventies drew to a close, the anguished regional and religious minorities across the country were demanding more power and self-determination.

But it is often realized that the attention span of the Indian electorate is very short. Indira had been forgiven for all her fallacies and the voters truly believed that she was their sole saviour. On her part, Indira was campaigning hard for her comeback. She travelled over 40,000 miles in her 62-day campaign, addressing an average of up to twenty meetings per day. In the end, the Congress captured 351 seats out of a total of 542 Lok Sabha seats.

Sanjay Gandhi, who ran from the Amethi constituency in Uttar Pradesh, was also among the elected MPs. Indira Gandhi stood for her old constituency of Raebareli and also from Medak in Andhra Pradesh. She won both seats by a comfortable majority. So she resigned from Raebareli and instated a family member, Arun Nehru, in her place.

While the electorate had forgiven Indira for her previous transgressions in office, her spell in the wilderness after the 1977 defeat was also erased from history. Soon after she came to power, the special courts that had been appointed to investigate her actions during the Emergency were dissolved. Cases pending against Sanjay were also conveniently dropped. The Janata government, which was in power in nine states, were also dissolved one by one and President's Rule was imposed.

Everything seemed to be working out for Indira until tragedy struck soon after she took office. On the morning of 23 June 1980, Sanjay Gandhi left for the Delhi Flying Club to take his new Pitts S-2A for a joyride. He invited one of the flying instructors at the club, Captain Subhash Saxena, to accompany him. Since he was aware of Sanjay's inexperience in flying the plane, he initially refused to do so. However, he relented after some persuasion. When they were up in the air, Sanjay made a steep dive, probably with an intention to pull up in an aerobatic loop. But he lost control and the plane crashed nose first into the ground. Both Sanjay and Saxena were instantly killed.[3]

It was a wrenching loss for Indira. Despite all his imperfections, Sanjay was the closest person to her heart. He was also her prodigal child whom she had groomed to carry on her legacy. She later confided in Pupul Jayakar that, 'No one can take Sanjay's place, he was my son but like an elder brother in his support.'[4] She began to lose her confidence in public life as well. Usually sure-footed and decisive about her actions, she became more and more desperate and reactionary in her responses. In the rest of her term, she would play various communities, castes and religions against each other in a futile attempt to secure her position with disastrous consequences.[5]

* * *

Indira developed a different side to herself in terms of economic policy as well during her second stint in office. In the pre-Emergency period, Indira was heavily populist. She also carried a loud rhetoric of *Garibi Hatao* (Remove Poverty), although it hardly materialized into real policy. When she returned to power, she gave up on populism and dropped even the rhetoric of poverty alleviation. She had a different approach to the country's economic problems, an approach that can unequivocally be termed 'right' of her previous terms in office.[6]

The first hint of her right-ward shift in economic policy was evidenced in her approach to the economic crisis that India had imported from the oil-starved world. Oil prices had increased from USD 13 in 1978 to USD 34 by March 1981. As a result, the current account deficit expanded from 0.3 per cent of GDP to 2 per cent of GDP during the same period. The remittances that were still growing strongly could not suffice to contain the deficit. India's balance of payments was in a precarious state.[7]

In a significant departure from the past when international institutions like the World Bank and IMF were seen as extensions of the colonial agenda in the post-War era, India approached the latter for a loan of Rs 5,000 crore (in 1980 prices). As always, the loan was approved subject to certain conditions. It was the largest loan awarded to any country at the time and was to be disbursed over a period of three years, beginning in November 1981.

There was undoubtedly considerable furore across the country, especially among left-wing economists and politicians, who felt that the move was a blatant 'sell-out' of national interests to the vested interests of the Western powers. The then West Bengal finance minister, Ashok Mitra, furiously told an audience at the Delhi School of Economics that, 'The capital of India has shifted from Delhi to Washington.'[8] The Parliament sessions of the time were also marked with loud protests and walkouts. Nevertheless, despite all the voices of discontent, Gandhi stood her ground and the loan was ratified.

The second evident shift in her policy stance was making an improvement in production levels her top priority. A *Times of*

India editorial noted, within a year of her coming into power, that, 'A change of considerable significance is taking place in India . . . the emphasis has shifted from distributive justice to growth.'[9] In a similar vein, *Economic and Political Weekly* noted that the prime minister has clarified in various meetings with industrialists that 'what the government was most concerned about just now was higher production'.

Commensurate economic policy decisions were taken in 1981-82: manufactured imports were liberalized; prices of steel and cement were decontrolled; and the competition-inhibiting controls on both entry and expansion of firms were relaxed. The Sixth Five-Year Plan, which was implemented in 1980, also aimed at undertaking a slew of measures like fiscal reforms, restructuring of public sector undertakings, reduction in import duties and delicensing. This also allowed Indira Gandhi to save face by arguing that the IMF loan conditions were exactly what the government had intended to do anyway.

As a result of the government's gradual shift towards liberalization, four times as many applications for expansion and establishment were sanctioned in 1981 as compared to any of the five preceding years. Moreover, following the recommendations given by the L.K. Jha Commission on Economic and Administrative Reforms, the government gave up complete control on expansion and new production of twenty important industries by placing them under 'automatic licensing'.[10]

Indira's right-ward shift started to become evident in other aspects of her political leadership as well. Now, her political speeches had a communal ring to it and carried themes of Hindu hegemony meant to appeal to India's Hindi-speaking majority.[11] In India's political landscape, Hindu chauvinism has gone hand in hand with pro-business policies, while secularism found itself tied up with socialism. There is no particular logic behind these two sets of political alternatives apart from that of political mobilization. India's founding fathers understood that if a multi-ethnic polity like India had to survive, appealing along caste or communal lines would be fatal. Therefore, their go-to tactic was to appeal across economic lines by calling for a need to uplift the poor and the downtrodden. This was how socialism came to be tied up with secularism.

On the other hand, the ones who favoured pro-business policies found themselves in a fix as the majority of the Indian population was poor. The only solution for them to build a political base was to appeal to a different majority mix and the religious majority of Hindus seemed like the best bet. Therefore, just as the economically downtrodden were the champions for the socialists, Hindus became the champions for the political parties that were on the right of the ideological spectrum. Indira Gandhi adopted a similar strategy when she wanted to pursue a pro-business approach. Nevertheless, the shift in her stance was not abrupt. The rhetoric of socialism and nationalism was still maintained, but the poor as the erstwhile champions were sacrificed.

Such a shift was not surprising on Indira's part. After the ignominious rout of Congress in the 1977 elections, especially in the Hindi-speaking north, Indira had to regain their support. She also had to appease the business community, which had been quick to support the Desai government. Indira had always been mostly pragmatic when it came to her policy choices. Unlike Nehru, she was hardly fettered to ideologies throughout her career. Thus began India's gradual shift towards liberalization. Unlike popular opinion that the economic crisis of 1991 was the trigger for India's liberal reforms, the process had already begun in the early 1980s. In fact, India's first major reform took place in 1982 after the Indira government partially decontrolled the cement industry.

However, it must be noted that India's move towards liberalization during these years was more pro-business than pro-market. It is important to understand the distinction between the two as both vary in terms of policy choices, implementation and outcomes. A pro-market strategy is one which supports new entrants and consumers while a pro-business strategy is one that supports expansion of existing producers. The former is based on the idea that market forces lead to an efficient allocation of resources and help boost productivity and growth. It is also the idea advanced by the World Bank and the IMF.

Neoclassical economists who were dominant in the field of economics during the time argued that an economy which followed a pro-market strategy would have beneficial developmental outcomes. As the 'invisible hand' of the markets would drive production, economic growth would be efficient in the sense that the same amount of investment would lead to higher rates of economic growth. For developing countries, comparative advantage would result in creation of labour-intensive industries. Also, as capital migrates into areas where it is scarce in order to find higher returns, regional inequality would fall. The only pitfall of the pro-market approach was the short-term shock a state-driven economy would receive in the transition.

On the other hand, pro-business strategy was more politically appealing since it was inspired by real-world growth experiences, especially that of the East Asian economies. These countries had shown that economic growth had been the best when the goals of the private sector and those of the state had aligned. By bending state policies to aid efficient operations of established corporations, these economies had managed to achieve unprecedented growth rates. The state had a single-minded focus on boosting growth and most policy measures were aimed at dismantling supply and demand constraints that were faced by private entrepreneurs.

The Indian move away from its classic statist, import-substituting model of development was more pro-business. But, considering that it was a democracy, the repressive East Asian models could not be completely emulated. Their progressive education and health outcomes also could not be replicated in India simply due to lack of political intent. The Indian approach was only akin to the East Asian models in its prioritization of economic growth and its proximity to industrialists.

Among the new pro-business policies, the first was the government's withdrawal of several constraints on expansion of big businesses and also allowing them to enter areas previously reserved for the public sector. The infamous Monopolies and Restrictive Trade Practices (MRTP) Act which inhibited the growth of big businesses was diluted, removing licence restrictions and allowing businesses to venture into core industries such as chemicals, drugs and cement. These developments were enthusiastically welcomed by big businesses. Small ones, which did not have the resources to enter these sectors, were not particularly welcoming of these changes.

Second, finance was made easily available to big businesses. Credit was liberalized for big borrowers and tax breaks were also given to them to encourage investment. Finally, incentives were provided to boost household savings which were channelled into productive investments. According to Pranab Mukherjee, who was the finance minister from 1982, the total amount of capital raised by the private sector expanded by 170 per cent in the first three financial years of the decade from merely Rs 300 crore in 1980-81 to Rs 809 crore in 1983-84.[12]

Finally, there was general consensus between the national government and the business community that for faster industrial development, labour activism had to be controlled. This was a particularly tough ask from Indira Gandhi who had been the erstwhile champion of the poor and a leader of the masses. Despite this challenge, she put labour on notice and criticized worker strikes in popular media as 'anti-social demonstrations'. In fact, special legislations were passed to discourage such strikes.[13]

Anyhow, the pro-business shift of the government managed to extricate the economy from its rut. Economic growth revived, exports rose, and foreign exchange earnings improved from 1982 onwards. By the time Pranab Mukherjee rose to present the budget in 1984, India had written back to the IMF that it no longer required the final instalment of the loan and would instead pay back the entire amount in due course. It was the first time in IMF's history that a borrowing country had not taken the entire loan amount.

* * *

Indira managed to weather the economic crisis that she had inherited from the previous decade. But the pent-up social discord at the regional level across India would prove much more difficult to handle. Punjab and Kashmir would prove highly problematic for Indira throughout her tenure, but it was Assam that was of primary concern in her first two years back in office.

The problem in Assam rose from the excessive influx of Bengali immigrants—mostly Muslims—who had settled in the state since the 1971 war. Their numbers had been so huge that they threatened to reduce the indigenous Assamese population to a minority. Anti-Bengali demonstrations began to take place in the state demanding their deportation or dispersion into other states. The violence reached critical levels in April 1980 and the state was declared a 'disturbed area'.

The unrest in Punjab originated much further back than the one in Assam. Soon after Indira came into power in 1966, she acceded to the long-standing demand of the Sikh community for the creation of a separate Punjabi-speaking state. So, Haryana and Himachal Pradesh were carved out of the larger state of Punjab. However, since the formation of a mutilated Punjab, the issues of land distribution, river access and a shared capital city of Chandigarh with Haryana remained unresolved. In 1973, Akali Dal, a Sikh party, met in Anandpur Sahib and formalized their demands in what came to be known as the Anandpur Sahib Resolution. They wanted sole possession of the state capital, complete control over rivers that met its agricultural needs and wanted to retain Hindu Punjabi-speaking regions as well.

Delhi did not accept these terms. Over time, the Akali Dal gained popularity in the state and posed a legitimate political threat to Congress. The latter was eventually defeated in the 1977 elections. Sanjay began looking for options to undermine the dominance of the Akali Dal in the state. A Sikh Congressman who had been the former chief minister of Punjab, Zail Singh, suggested that he should attempt to split the Sikh voter base by backing a newcomer who could prove to be a viable alternative to the Akali leadership.

Such potential was found in a fundamentalist named Jarnail Singh Bhindranwale, who wanted to 'purify' Sikhism and had gained a huge follower base. Sanjay and Zail Singh supported him quietly. He campaigned heavily for Congress in the 1980 elections. But soon after the elections, he refused to do the bidding of Congress and parted ways. As his strength and followers grew with time, so did his demands. He became increasingly vocal and violent about the creation of a sovereign Sikh state of 'Khalistan'.

Hindus were murdered randomly throughout the state. Cows were decapitated, and their heads were thrown in temples. Sikhs who were critical of the activities of Bhindranwale and his army were also killed, and journalists who wrote against the movement were assassinated.[14] As panic spread, Hindus began leaving the state. Indira made little effort to stem the violence.[15] Meanwhile, Bhindranwale and his followers settled into the Golden Temple in Amritsar, the holiest of Sikh shrines. This was the scenario in Punjab throughout 1982.

The situation was no better elsewhere in the country. Communal violence and riots were flaring up across all major cities. It was announced in Parliament in 1982 that in the span of two years, 960 Dalits had been killed. There were also reports of forced conversions of Dalits to Islam or Christianity. There were demands for a ban on conversions but Indira insisted that doing so would go against the idea of a secular India.

Meanwhile, in September 1982, Sheikh Abdullah, the chief minister of Jammu and Kashmir died in office. His son, Farooq, was sworn in as the new chief minister within ninety minutes of Abdullah's death. Even though Farooq was an unlikely candidate who led a flamboyant lifestyle that revolved around parties, discos and girls, he took his new responsibility in stride.[16] He immediately got down to addressing the charges of corruption and incompetency within the government by removing suspect individuals from the Cabinet. He also reached out to the Governor of Kashmir and Indira's cousin, B.K. Nehru, for guidance and counsel.

However, when the elections were called for in the following year, he refused the proposition of an alliance from Indira. This was unacceptable to her. She had perfected the art of running states from the Centre, and with a state like Jammu and Kashmir that shared a border with Pakistan, it was even more important that the reins were in her hands. Indira was even more annoyed when he visited Amritsar in November and met with Akali leaders and Bhindranwale himself.

She began denouncing him publicly after that. With elections slated for June 1983, Indira herself descended on Kashmir to campaign for Congress. In the end, her party won in the Hindu-dominated Jammu region but lost heavily in Kashmir. Since the election was lost, Indira tried desperately to discredit it by calling it rigged. But no one in Kashmir bought into her claims.[17]

All this time, the violence in Punjab showed no sign of relenting. On 23 April, the Amritsar police chief, A.S. Atwal, was shot dead. He was himself a Sikh, but he did not support the Khalistan movement. The chief minister of Punjab, Darbara Singh, begged Indira to allow him to send police into the Golden Temple and arrest Bhindranwale and his army. Indira was still reluctant, which her biographer, Katherine Frank, attributes to her intent of still keeping the Sikhs divided and gaining as much support as possible from the Hindu majority across India.[18] This was probably the last opportunity to try and resolve the Punjab crisis because, after that, the situation reached a point of no return.

Bhindranwale moved his outpost into an internal shrine called the Akal Takht. Arms began to be smuggled into the temple and fortifications began being built. He sent out terror squads with the sole purpose of murdering Hindus. On 5 October, they stopped a bus on the Grand Trunk Road, forced six Hindus to get off, lined them on the road and shot them to death. The incident sparked a national furore and Indira imposed President's Rule in the state. Two weeks later, a train passing through the state was derailed, killing nineteen, and soon after that, another bus was hijacked, and four Hindus were shot dead.

By early 1984, Indira was battling on two fronts, Kashmir and Punjab. She was aided by her elder son, Rajiv Gandhi, who had reluctantly entered the world of politics after his brother's death. Rajiv was everything Sanjay was not. He was quite competent, intelligent and efficient. He belonged to the new generation with immense faith in the wonders of technology, statistics and computers.[19] Unlike Sanjay's coterie of thugs and goons, Rajiv remained in the company of his friends from the elite Doon School and Cambridge University, who were more comfortable conversing in English than in Hindi. They were a group of young men who had no time to spare for the baser instincts of religion, ideology or superstition.

In order to counter the Punjab threat, Rajiv hatched a contingency plan for a military routing of Bhindranwale and his followers from the Golden Temple. Indira was aware of 'Operation Blue Star', as it would be popularly known, but was hoping for a solution to materialize so that the invasion of the temple could be avoided. Repeated negotiations had been tried and failed in January and February. The violence kept on escalating. In March and April alone, over eighty people were murdered.

Indira made a last-ditch effort at negotiations by sending her foreign affairs minister, Narsimha Rao, to meet the Akali leader Longowal, and Bhindranwale. The Akalis were ready to meet the Indian government half-way, but Bhindranwale demanded that all of the demands of the Anandpur Sahib Resolution be met. Since this was impossible, talks broke down and Rajiv's contingency plan seemed inevitable. Punjab was sealed on 3 June and civilians asked to exit the temple complex on the evening of 5 June. Everyone was expecting the invasion. Bhindranwale even issued threats to the 'throne of Indira' if authorities entered the premises.

The assault began on the morning of 6 June. Since Bhindranwale's men had taken vantage points more than a hundred soldiers died in the initial attempt. The army had to eventually call in the tanks in the afternoon. As Bhindranwale and his men were inside the Akal Takth, the holy shrine had to be fired at directly. When the Army finally managed to enter the shrine in the night, Bhindranwale's body was found along with thirty-one of his followers'.

Bhindranwale was dead. But the cost of Operation Blue Star had been too high. Thousand soldiers had been sent into the Golden

Temple and somewhere in the range of 300 to 700 had been killed. More civilians were dead. The library, which contained hand-written manuscripts of Sikh Gurus, had gone up in flames and the Akal Takth, which was a shrine built by the Fifth Guru himself, was severely damaged. There was only one person who would pay the ultimate cost of the carnage—Indira Gandhi.[20]

During these months, Indira was also working the Kashmir angle. She was pressuring B.K. Nehru to dismiss Farooq Abdullah and impose Governor's Rule—the Kashmiri equivalent of President's Rule. But Nehru refused to do so without valid grounds, which Indira was unable to provide. The plan was to replace Farooq with his brother-in-law, G.M. Shah, who was more loyal to Indira. Nehru argued that a vote of no-confidence against Farooq in the state assembly was the only constitutional means of instating Indira's candidate.

When it was clear that Nehru would not budge, she replaced him with Jagmohan, an old acquaintance of Sanjay's. Indira then accused Farooq of anti-national activities and asked Jagmohan to get rid of him and replace him with Shah. Members of Farooq's party were bribed to defect and support Shah.[21] When sufficient numbers were gained, Shah was sworn in as the chief minister with the defectors as members of his Cabinet. A similar coup was forced in Andhra Pradesh as well. There was a public outcry against these blatant violations of democratic norms. Indira's popularity was dipping to an all-time low. With elections around the corner, there were murmurs of the possibility of Indira introducing a constitutional amendment to postpone elections. A familiar sense of Emergency was spreading across the nation.

But all such fears were brought to a nought in a cruel turn of events on the morning of 31 October 1984. Indira had an interview with Peter Ustinov from the BBC who was making a documentary on her. As Indira left her house to walk to her office, she saw her bodyguard, Beant Singh, a Sikh from Punjab, and a new constable named Satwant Singh. There had been considerable concern about Indira keeping Sikh bodyguards in employment after Operation Blue

Star. But when she was asked merely two months earlier if they could be trusted, she glanced at Beant Singh and said, 'When I have Sikhs like this around me, then I don't believe I have anything to fear.'[22] Her trust only took her as far as that fateful October morning. As she folded her hands to greet him, Beant Singh pulled out his revolver and fired at her. Satwant Singh followed to do the same. The two men managed to spray thirty bullets into the prime minister. The assault on the Golden Temple was avenged. Indira Gandhi was dead.

* * *

When Indira Gandhi took to the highest office of the country almost two decades ago, she was written off as a non-starter. But it is irrefutable that, since that time, she went on to become the most dominant figure in the Indian political scene. This remained true even when she was briefly out of power. The initial ridicule she faced made her suspicious of everybody and the later adulation she received convinced her that only she could save the nation. These two factors led to her extensive inclination towards centralization of power even at the cost of democratic norms.

The body blow to Indian democracy during Indira Gandhi's time in office was the most glaring discrepancy in her tenure when compared to the days of her father. Nehru, who was usually no less impatient than her, always put the democratic path up on a pedestal even if his power was under threat. Indira had no qualms about bypassing or temporarily suspending democratic norms to secure her position.

As for the economy, her failings were many. It merely became a tool to consolidate her political position. She was too pragmatic to let ideological constraints define her economic policy, unlike her father. When the poor needed to be appeased, she was populist and when she needed the support of businesses, she was a liberal. All economic policy initiatives, right from minor liberalization efforts at the start to completely closing down the economy to finally opening it up again ever so slightly towards the end, were guided by immediate political motives. For a major part of her tenure, the state control of the economy increased exponentially, and the domestic markets closed down even more while the rest of the world, especially in the East, moved in the opposite direction. Probably the only major achievement on the economic front that can be attributed to Indira Gandhi is the end of India's dependence on aid from other countries for food. The Green Revolution, despite all its limitations, was a leading factor in ensuring India's self-sufficiency of agricultural goods.

She had some successes in advancing India's stature on the world stage as well. During her time in office, India achieved the distinction of building the third largest reservoir of skilled manpower in the world, building the fifth largest military, became the sixth entrant into the nuclear club, became the seventh to join the space race and became the tenth industrial power.[23] She also led India to victory in the Bangladesh war, which ensured India's prominence in the region.

Due to such a chequered political career, Indira will always remain a controversial and compelling figure in Indian history. She has been usually at the receiving end of intense criticism from the intelligentsia, but despite all her excesses and failings, the hold she commanded over the Indian masses was of enviable proportions. Everywhere she went, millions would come to listen to her speak, even if most of what she talked about was beyond their understanding.

Even though she failed to deliver most of what she promised, the poor in India never ceased to believe that Indira cared for them. The faith that the electorate restored in her merely three years after the end of the Emergency and the unprecedented victory of her son soon after her death stand testament to the fact. Since then, no leader has been able to captivate the Indian electorate for such a prolonged period. If Indira is guilty of undermining the foundations of democracy during her time in office, it must also be remembered that it was the same institution of democracy that kept ensuring her survival. Like Indira's complex personality, a judgement on her tenure will always remain complex.

CHAPTER 14

PANGS OF CHANGE

When Indira suffered the fatal shots within the confines of her own home in Delhi on 31 October 1984, Rajiv Gandhi was addressing a meeting in West Bengal. He had been touring the state for a few days with an agenda to revamp the faction-ridden party organization. The murder of Indira Gandhi was the first major political killing since the assassination of Mahatma Gandhi. As evening fell over a shocked Delhi that day, Rajiv was sworn in as the prime minister of India at a ceremony hastily organized in the Ashoka Hall of Rashtrapati Bhavan.

Even as the swearing-in ceremony was taking place, anti-Sikh riots were taking place across India in response to Indira's assassination by her Sikh bodyguards. Delhi was the worst-affected. In the days between her death and her funeral on 3 November, mobs determinedly hunted down Sikhs from their homes and burned or beat them to death. The official estimates put the death toll of the Sikh community close to 3,000. In response to the situation, Rajiv Gandhi remarked, quite insensitively, that 'once a mighty tree falls, it is only natural that the earth around it shakes'.[1] It was only on the evening before Indira's funeral that Rajiv appealed for the violence to stop and called in the Army to make sure that it did.

A month later, another tragedy claimed even more lives than the anti-Sikh riots. In the wee hours of 3 December, white smoke began enveloping the city of Bhopal. People woke up in their beds coughing and vomiting with a burning sensation in their eyes. Most of those who rushed out to the streets in panic, fainted after being overcome with dizziness and exhaustion.

The smoke was a deadly gas known as methyl isocyanate that came from a pesticide plant of an American firm, Union Carbide. The gas was stored in underground tanks and usually rendered harmless using a scrubber before being released into the air. However, that night, an unexpected chemical reaction led to the release of 30 tonnes of the gas in its toxic form. It eventually led to the death of at least 5,000 people, leaving thousands more with life-long illness or injury due to exposure to the gas. About 600,000 people were affected in total. The incident is still considered the worst industrial accident in human history.[2]

Even though Rajiv's stint in office got off to a tragic start, it had no impact on the eighth general elections slated for the end of December. The election campaign centred on the death of Indira Gandhi and Rajiv was presented as the logical heir to her legacy. The results were declared on 24 December. Congress swept the polls with 404 seats out of 514, far more than the party had ever won under Nehru or Indira. At the age of forty, Rajiv Gandhi became the youngest elected head of the country.

There is no doubt that the electoral victory was more due to sympathy for Indira than Rajiv's personal appeal. But it would be unfair to believe that the latter aspect did not play a role. Rajiv represented a generational change in Indian politics, with a fresh mind that was not weighed down by ideologies or the past. He was full of promise of a better future for India with an efficient government and state-of-the-art technologies. He vowed to 'propel the country into the twenty-first century'—straight from the age of the bullock cart to the age of the personal computer. Naturally, the middle class and especially the younger generation of Indians, who were tired of numbing regulations and controls, were excited at the prospect of change.

Rajiv also discarded most of the advisers and Cabinet members that served under his mother and chose to rely on his friends, who were equally disassociated with politics until a few years ago. His main advisers were Arun Singh and Arun Nehru, who were from the corporate sector and, like him, young and at ease with modern technology. Rajiv Gandhi was often compared with John F. Kennedy, who like his Indian counterpart 'symbolized youth and the hope of a new generation' and had assembled a 'team of the best and the brightest' to lead his nation into a promising future.[3]

* * *

When Rajiv was voted into power, the economy was in a comfortable position. A record foodgrain production of 151 million tonnes in 1983-84 had resulted in a high growth momentum in 1984. The industrial growth in the first half of 1984-85 was 7 per cent. Also, inflation in the first week of December had come down to 6.3 per cent compared to 10 per cent a year ago. So, Rajiv had the electoral mandate as well as the right economic conditions to introduce the economic reforms that he promised.[4]

Unlike Indira Gandhi, who had been calculating and subtle about her transforming ideology, Rajiv was never shy of displaying his enthusiasm for a liberal mode of development. He made it clear within a few weeks of coming into power that his government's economic approach would involve a 'judicious combination of deregulation, import liberalization and easier access to foreign technology'.[5] The sharp contrast in Rajiv's approach from the yesteryears of Nehru and Indira, when the political rhetoric was high on socialism and self-reliance, was hard to miss.

The contrast was evident in Rajiv Gandhi's choice of economic advisers as well. While Nehru had kept company with a group of left-leaning nationalists, Rajiv chose the likes of Manmohan Singh, Montek Singh Ahluwalia and Bimal Jalan, who had career backgrounds in institutions like World Bank that were popular proponents of free-market policies. In fact, the first budget that the Rajiv Gandhi government presented in March 1985 did not mention the word 'socialism' even once.

The budget was presented by Rajiv's finance minister, Vishwanath Pratap Singh, a low-key politician from Uttar Pradesh with a formidable reputation for integrity. Keeping in line with the economic agenda of his prime minister, he announced liberal tax concessions for businesses and the upper middle class. The onerous licensing regulations were drastically reduced, and imports were further liberalized across various sectors.

Most importantly, the private sector was allowed to venture into areas that were previously off limits. This came as a welcome move for many businesses that were vying to expand into sectors that had been reserved for the public sector. For instance, Tata, an Indian business group since the British era, had plans to manufacture wristwatches under its brand Titan. But, as Xerxes Desai, who had been trying to obtain a licence for Tata since a decade, said, 'Our entry into watches was attempted to be blocked by various lobbies— the anti-business lobby, the smugglers lobby, Indian manufacturers like HMT, bureaucrats, etc. It was only after Rajiv Gandhi became Prime Minister that the situation changed and we were given the go-ahead.'[6]

Naturally, such a drastic shift in the government policy stance raised a few eyebrows but the initial response to it was positive. The fact that the new government represented a break from the past resonated quite well with the masses, and even more so with the business community and the urban middle class. Rajen Kilachand of the Dodsal Group pointed out after the budget that 'for the first time in India, after thirty-eight years of independence, there is a realization that creation of wealth, not just personal accumulation of money, is not a crime'.[7] The Opposition in the Parliament was also minimal at this stage since Rajiv Gandhi commanded the lion's share of the parliamentary seats. The voices of dissent were only strong among the left-leaning and opposition parties, but they were tuned out in the widespread sense of euphoria for change under the new government.

Expectedly, business groups were generally favourable towards the government's liberalization efforts. However, some areas received mixed reactions. A major issue of concern was the extent to which the economy should be opened up. There was a general consensus among the political and business classes that foreign borrowing and foreign capital were undesirable.[8] The debate was a bit more complex on the issues of trade. Liberalization of technological imports was beneficial for most industries, but the domestic manufacturers of those technologies naturally saw it as a threat to their existence.

The government obliged in such cases and chose to retain the import-substitution bias of Indian industries. This became apparent in the government's approach to the automobile sector. In 1985, the government had shown an inclination towards expansion of automobile production across the country and even allowed foreign collaboration. The plan had been underway when the government backtracked completely in early 1986 and postponed the idea indefinitely, citing India's worsening balance of payment situation as the reason. Even after global oil prices dipped in mid-1986 and India's balance of payment situation improved, the automobile policy was left untouched. Clearly, the government had succumbed to pressure from domestic manufacturers who feared foreign competition.

Therefore, in some respects, the Rajiv Gandhi government chose to stay in line with Indira Gandhi's pro-business approach rather than moving on to a pro-market one. The political feasibility of sacrificing business interests at the altar of free markets was still non-existent, despite the government's liberal proclivities.

The Indian middle class was completely on board with the government's initial growth push. This segment of population had become quite large in India, numbering as high as 100 million by the mid-1980s. They derived huge benefits from a reduction in their taxes, along with other measures that the government took to encourage consumption as a part of its early economic policy. This was probably part of an economic strategy to drive demand for goods that would be additionally produced in the economy as government-stipulated controls were lifted. The growing supply would be easily soaked up by growing income levels of households. The strategy worked. In 1984-85, the number of two-wheelers sold in India increased by 25 per cent while the number of cars sold shot up by over 50 per cent.[9]

As consumer spending increased, the housing and real estate markets witnessed a boom and there was a sudden rise in the number of restaurants and shopping malls that opened up in cities.

Moreover, the middle class was also beginning to invest in the stock markets, creating a structural link between big businesses and them. Therefore, they were gradually becoming invested in the functioning of the private sector. In such a scenario, any policy that was pro-business was enthusiastically welcomed.

Business was not the sole focus of the government. The new prime minister realized the benefits of creating an educated workforce, something which had been grossly neglected in independent India. In September 1985, Rajiv Gandhi called upon Narasimha Rao, one of the rare members of the old guard that he had retained in his Cabinet, and asked him to take over the education ministry that would now be renamed the 'Human Resource Development ministry'.

Rao, who had previously held defence, home and foreign affairs portfolios in the Indira government, took up the responsibility with an equal enthusiasm. He framed the National Policy on Education within a year, which most significantly launched 'Operation Blackboard' to ensure the bare minimum facilities for students in primary schools. Rao also ensured the creation of the Navodaya school system, a brainchild of Rajiv Gandhi, which finds talented children from rural areas and provides them with quality education in residential schools.

The Rajiv Gandhi government also introduced two disruptive reforms that sparked the future growth process of Indian IT and telecom industries. Within a month of coming to power, he announced the 'New Computer Policy', which eliminated licensing for manufacture of small and microcomputers, allowed import of technological know-how and ancillary units, and also withdrew any ceilings on capacity. Import duties on components were also drastically reduced.

This came as a welcome relief for industry and computer users who had been languishing under the inefficient bureaucratic regulations that impeded the use and manufacture of computers in the country. The duty structure that was applicable to computers was so skewed that indigenous manufacturing was simply uneconomical. Import duties on components were as high as 200 per cent and excise duty added another 30 per cent on the retail price of the finished product. The import of computers was also a Herculean task. An application for import took as long as two years to pass through various committees before it was accepted or rejected.

Even after the advent of integrated circuits, when computers became smaller in size and their assembly became possible in India, the final product ended up being four to five times costlier than its foreign counterparts due to the exorbitant duty structure. All of these impediments were eliminated almost completely by Rajiv Gandhi, setting the ground for the development of a fledging IT industry.

The second major reform was introduced in the telecom sector with the establishment of the Centre for Development of Telematics (C-DOT) in 1984. The body was set up with an aim to develop telecommunication technology in India under the leadership of Sam Pitroda. C-DOT laid down a nationwide telecom network with Pitroda's idea of coin-dropping public call offices (PCOs), making calling accessible to the masses from every nook and corner of the country.

Pitroda had been in the process of implementing his plan even under Indira Gandhi, but after her death, he was unsure of the future of his plan. But Rajiv Gandhi gave him the needed push with the establishment of C-DOT. It is sometimes argued that the actual telecom revolution was brought about much later as teledensity saw an exponential growth only in the first decade of the twenty-first century, but it cannot be denied that Rajiv Gandhi foresaw the importance of the technology for the country and showed no reluctance in introducing it to India. Accelerated liberalization and technocratic reforms were, thus, the two highlights of the Rajiv Gandhi government.

However, opposition to these moves began to appear soon enough. To the surprise of the party leadership, the first major opposition came from within the party itself. Reports indicate that when Rajiv Gandhi made an attempt to pass a resolution to get his party's backing for the new economic policies that he had introduced since the budget, he met with an unexpected level of opposition.[10]

The resolution was eventually passed, but not without recommitting Rajiv Gandhi and the party to socialism. The party, therefore, made it clear that it would not deviate so radically from the ideological left. Socialism was still the limit within which any new policies had to be fit. Definite boundaries were set for Rajiv Gandhi and his advisers, who had to slow down the pace of reforms from then onwards.

In an attempt to balance reform with continuity, however, the policy over the next few years became slightly muddled. Piecemeal reforms were undertaken while assuring that the government was still committed to the idea of socialism. The conflicted nature of the governmental discourse came out in the open quite often. For instance, in November 1985 while discussing the Seventh Five-Year Plan, Rajiv Gandhi said that its industrial policy will remain unchanged. A few days later, he argued that India could encourage imports in areas where import substitutes were not cost-effective. This was supplemented with the release of the Abid Hussain Committee report on trade policy reforms which stressed on an outward-looking industrial policy in the form of growth-led export. Soon, however, as if to balance out the incessant talk of reforms, the government reassured that whatever liberalization took place, the public sector would continue to retain the 'commanding heights' of the economy.

A similar back and forth was visible in policy implementation as well. Since vocal narratives of change had begun to backfire, the government began making quiet policy changes to carry on with their reforms without making waves. In December 1985, soon after Rajiv Gandhi himself assured that there would be 'no shift from socialism' in government policy,[11] the government quietly passed a new textile policy that removed the age-old restriction on capacity of the mill sector. This was a significant policy change that the first-generation nationalist leaders would have found blasphemous. The textile mills of the British had destroyed India's famed handloom sector by dumping their machine-generated products into the world and Indian markets. Now, Indian policymakers had given a free rein to the same technology which would ensure a similar decline of the traditional manufacturers. Nevertheless, Rajiv Gandhi had now learnt the art of flying under the radar while making such radical changes.

The budget of 1986 made it clearer that Rajiv Gandhi intended to stick to his plan of liberalization, albeit in a restrained manner. The government continued the strategy followed in its first budget by cutting taxes, liberalizing imports, reducing tariffs and pumping in more money into the economy. The latter was being funded by excessive government borrowings, for which India would go on to pay a high price later.

This was being done in spite of a commendable fiscal policy that the Rajiv Gandhi government had adopted in 1985 known as the 'Long-Term Fiscal Policy', which aimed to place government revenue and expenditure in a longer-term perspective. It was meant to bring about stability in the government's economic and fiscal policies by setting long-term goals. But, given the excessive spending of the government, it failed to stick to the new fiscal policy and, as we shall note, public finances ultimately spiralled out of control.

Government spending was on the rise for a couple of reasons. The leading cause was the defence sector. As per the Seventh Plan (1985–90), defence expenditure was supposed to rise from 3.3 per cent in its first year to 3.8 per cent in its final year. However, that limit was already breached by the end of its second year. V.P. Singh merely told Parliament, 'I need not elaborate on the compulsions of the geo-political climate which have made the increase in defence expenditure inescapable.'[12]

Second, the implementation of the Fourth Pay Commission, which awarded higher wages to government employees, had also burdened the government coffers. Finally, the government had failed to reduce its subsidy expenditure despite admitting in the Long-Term Fiscal Policy that 'if subsidies continue to grow at the present rate, they will either be at the expense of developmental expenditure or they will lead to higher budget deficits.'[13] Due to political constraints, it was almost impossible for the government to reduce food and fertilizer subsidies, which formed a bulk of its subsidy bill.

In the third budget of the government in 1987, imports were further liberalized by relaxing excise and custom duties. But the budget did not account for the loss of revenue due to these policies and left an uncovered deficit of nearly Rs 6,000 crore. This was in addition to a deficit of similar magnitude that had been accumulated over the last two years. To put things in perspective, the overall deficit of Rs 12,000 crore for these three years was higher than the combined deficit for the time period 1970–84.

* * *

It was also around this time, in early 1987, that the first signs of trouble began to appear within the Rajiv Gandhi government for completely different reasons. V.P. Singh in his capacity as finance minister had conducted a series of raids on industrial houses that were suspected of tax evasion. These actions were perceived to be beyond his domain and he was shifted from the finance ministry to defence, and Rajiv himself took over from Singh. Barely four months later, in April 1987, Singh was dropped from the Cabinet altogether.

Four days after V.P. Singh was ousted as the defence minister, the ministry was shaken by a corruption scandal of a magnitude that India had never seen before in its independent history. On 16 April 1987, Swedish Radio alleged that a number of top Indian politicians and defence officials had received kickbacks for a USD 285 million deal between the Indian government and a Swedish company, Bofors, for the purchase of artillery guns made a year ago. This revelation was the undoing of the Rajiv Gandhi government.

For the rest of the term, the press and opposition parties pressed the government to reveal the names of the offenders. But the government chose to maintain silence, which gave way to suspicion that the prime minister himself was somehow involved. Rajiv Gandhi quickly lost his squeaky-clean image. In public eyes, he was relegated to the company of the familiar old Congress clan that had gained a nauseating reputation for corruption. On the contrary, V.P. Singh was looked upon as the rare unblemished politician since his departure from the Cabinet was largely seen as linked to the Bofors scandal.

The government received massive criticism from the press due to the corruption charges and, to make matters worse, Rajiv Gandhi introduced a defamation bill in the Parliament under which editors and proprietors of newspapers could be imprisoned for publishing 'scurrilous material', whose definitions were left to the state to decide. The bill naturally invited widespread criticism and Rajiv Gandhi had to make a hasty retreat.

Bofors was not the only mistake that Rajiv would be remembered for. Another came in the form of a petition to the Supreme Court by a man named Mohammed Ahmed Khan, who had been directed by a lower court to pay monthly maintenance to his wife, Shah Bano. Khan argued that as per Islamic law, he was only obligated to pay an allowance for three months, which he had already done. The Supreme Court rejected his appeal on grounds that Section 125 of the Criminal Procedure Code entitled a divorced wife to claim allowance if she could not support herself, which was the case with Shah Bano. Three months after the judgment, a bill was passed in Parliament to exempt Muslims from the purview of Section 125. Congress, with the support of Rajiv Gandhi, voted against it.

But the debate continued among discontented Muslim clergy and Congress began losing numerous by-elections in 1985. The 'Shah Bano factor' was believed to have initiated these losses.[14] In a bid of desperation to please the Muslim vote-bank, the Congress introduced the 'Muslim Women's Bill' in February 1986, which looked to overturn the Supreme Court verdict and keep Muslim law out of the purview of the Criminal Procedure Code. The bill placed the burden of supporting a divorced wife on her own relatives. It became a law in May.

On the other hand, so as not to alienate the Hindu voters, a controversial judgment was passed by a district judge in Uttar Pradesh just before the 'Muslim Women's Bill' was introduced. He ordered the opening up of locks for a small Hindu shrine that was placed within the confines of the Babri Masjid, a large mosque in Ayodhya that was built by Mughal Emperor Babar. The site of the mosque is believed to be the birthplace of Ram, the mythological character in the Hindu epic Ramayana, even though there is no evidence of its veracity.[15] When clashes were taking place in the nineteenth century between rival groups for possession of that piece of land, the British had effected a compromise, whereby the Muslims could continue worshipping within the mosque and the Hindus could make offerings to a raised platform outside.

However, since Independence, Hindu bodies like the Vishwa Hindu Parishad had called for the freedom of their god from 'a Muslim jail'.[16] A lawyer had filed an appeal seeking public worship of the idol within Babri Masjid. It was in response to this suit that the district judge had ordered for the locks to be opened up. Given the rapid pace in which the order was implemented and its suspicious timing, it was popularly believed to have come from Rajiv Gandhi himself.[17] Quite expectedly, this upset the Muslims.

Later, when the general elections were nearing, Rajiv decided to win over the Muslims by banning Salman Rushdie's *Satanic Verses* for hurting Islamic beliefs. In fact, India was the first country in the world to ban the book, much before even the Muslim-dominated countries considered such injunctions. The actual intent behind such appeasement of communal sentiments on both sides was not lost in the public eye. It was clear that the Congress had given up on its idea of secularism and was playing religious politics.[18]

Another controversial mistake that Rajiv Gandhi committed during his tenure, for which he would go on to pay a heavy price, was an ambitious attempt to quell an ethnic strife beyond India's borders. The neighbouring country of Sri Lanka was caught in a bloody civil war between the Sinhala majority and the Tamil minority. The conflict began when Sinhala was imposed as the official language of the nation, leaving the Tamilians isolated in their own country. Over time, the protests by the minority group escalated into armed struggle, which was led by the Liberation Tigers of Tamil Eelam (LTTE). In the summer of 1987, the President of Sri Lanka J.R. Jayawardene asked Rajiv to mediate the conflict. An agreement was signed by the two nations wherein an Indian Peace Keeping Force (IPKF) would be sent to Sri Lanka and the Sri Lankan army would retreat while the LTTE would be persuaded to disarm.[19]

However, as Indian troops were being stationed in Sri Lanka from July 1987, the Sinhala faction saw their presence as an infringement on their sovereignty. The Tamilians initially set certain conditions to give up their arms but became equally averse to the Indian forces once they resorted to using force against them. As bodies of soldiers returned home, the opinion at home also turned in favour of India's withdrawal. This began in 1989, but not before more than a thousand soldiers lost their lives in a fruitless venture. Sri Lanka proved to be India's Vietnam.

As things began going south for Rajiv Gandhi since the Bofors scandal, he dropped his outward-looking, growth-oriented policies, as he realized that he had little political capacity left to expend on bold reforms. His shift in outlook was first seen in May 1987, when the Planning Commission circulated a document that called for a larger role of the private sector in industrialization. It was quietly shelved. The reform process was slowed down, if not halted, from then onwards.[20]

On the contrary, Rajiv decided to turn populist towards the end of his term. The government's final budget in 1989 generously increased allocation to pro-farmer and poverty alleviation programmes. He increased taxes on consumer durables and levied fresh surcharges on airfares and luxury hotel bookings. He also confessed in his rallies that for every rupee allocated for the welfare of the poor, only 15 paisa reached the intended beneficiary. The rest was siphoned off in between. He promised to improve that if he returned to power.[21]

However, the final damage came in the form of a report by the Comptroller and Auditor General of India, who strongly criticized the government's handling of the Bofors scandal. The opposition parties escalated their attack on the prime minister and resigned from the Lok Sabha en masse on 24 June 1989. They were now united under

V.P. Singh, who had formed the Jan Morcha after leaving Congress and won a parliamentary by-election from Allahabad in June 1988. In October, his Jan Morcha combined with the Janata Party to form the Janata Dal.

Fresh elections were to be held in November 1989. Despite waning popularity, Rajiv Gandhi tried hard to secure his position. He addressed 170 rallies across India and, picking up on his mother's antics, claimed a threat to the country's unity, which only the Congress could preserve. He even appealed to the Hindu majority like Indira had done in her final stint.[22]

But the die was cast. Congress could not escape the ghost of Bofors. It managed to win only 197 seats, down 218 seats from the last election and losing power in the Centre. In spite of such a brutal drubbing for Congress, the Opposition fared no better. The Janata Dal only managed to win 142 seats, while the right-wing Bharatiya Janata Party had won 86 and the Left a few more than 50. Just like 1977, the Opposition running on a mandate of ousting Congress formed a coalition government with equally shaky foundations. V.P. Singh was sworn in as the prime minister of the National Front coalition government.

* * *

The 1980s was an inflexion point in Indian economic history. It was a decade dominated by two dynamic leaders who gave India its first whiff of being more market-driven. Liberalization as an idea was not pursued at its fullest, but it nudged India towards considering it as a viable economic alternative—more evidently in the second half of the decade.

The decade also gave India a welcome break from the infamous Hindu rate of growth, with the economy clocking a decadal average of 5.8 per cent. Rajiv Gandhi had only taken baby steps towards liberalization, but the economy was underperforming so much that even a slight shift in policy led to rapid economic growth. It was a good time for Indian businesses. In the latter half of the decade, the industry grew at 5.5 per cent per year, with the manufacturing sector growing even faster at 8.9 per cent per annum.

The exceptional growth of Indian businesses through the decade is epitomized in the spectacular growth story of Reliance Industries. The company's assets grew at an astounding 60 per cent per annum, its sales at more than 30 per cent every year, and its profits at around 50 per cent.[23] Even though Dhirubhai Ambani, the founder of Reliance Industries, was a man with great business acumen, a lot of arguments have been made to highlight other factors that may have contributed to his company's rise. The *New York Times* famously documented in 2008 that 'the company routinely engages in political lobbying and covert monitoring to gain a leg up on its rivals'. When Mukesh Ambani was interviewed by the newspaper, he did not deny exerting influence when necessary but also played down its importance when compared to the other strengths that the company possessed.[24]

Apart from Reliance, other business groups like Adani and Mahindra have also been the subject of similar controversial claims. The close nexus between the government and businesses in India and its ill-effects on the economy have been well documented.[25] As the former central bank head Raghuram Rajan put it, '[T]oo many people have gotten too rich based on their proximity to the government.'[26] And the phenomenon had its origins in the pro-business policies of Indira and Rajiv Gandhi. The quid pro quo system also led to a profound transformation in the lifestyle of Indian politicians, who used to be associated with austerity and simple lifestyles, but now lived in large, well-furnished houses and drove flashy cars.[27]

There were other serious blemishes in the high-growth phase of the 1980s. The sudden growth spurt was heavily driven by excessive public expenditure, which was inadvisable and unsustainable in the long run, as deficits continued to rise. Defence spending, interest payments and subsidies, combined with the implementation of the Fourth Pay Commission, drove these expenditures upward.

In the first half of the decade, government expenditure averaged 18.6 per cent of the GDP, after which it rose to 23 per cent in the second half. These high levels of public expenditures naturally resulted in widening fiscal deficits, averaging 8 per cent for the first half of the decade and 10 per cent for the second half. Public debt levels and interest payments rose, and the economic situation worsened by the day.

On the external front, as the markets were slightly opened up, exports rose through the decade, but the gap between exports and imports remained large. According to RBI data, the total imports to GDP ratio exceeded the total exports to GDP ratio by 2.5 to 3 percentage points throughout the decade. These high levels of imports were partially financed through external borrowing.

Foreign borrowing was also used to finance investment throughout the decade. In the period 1985–90, savings and investments stood at 20.4 and 22.7 per cent of the GDP respectively. Since foreign investments were low at the time, the only explanation for higher investments remains foreign borrowing. In the process, India's external debt to GDP ratio rose from 17.7 per cent in 1984-85 to 24.5 per cent in 1989-90.

V.P. Singh had inherited an economic mess. To make matters worse, he was leading a minority government that could fall as soon as any party withdrew its support. The country was bound for a crisis.

* * *

The National Front government did not have the political appetite or the unity to undertake any major reforms after they came into power. The business class and foreign investors eyed the approach of the new government towards the economy with understandable concern as most of the members of the Janata Dal were from the erstwhile Janata Party. Their fears were reinforced when the new railway minister, George Fernandes, made remarks in foreign media about throwing out Pepsi from India, which had been allowed entry in 1988 after much debate and deliberations.[28]

Soon after Fernandes's remarks, three heavy-duty tractors that had been imported by Pepsi to increase tomato output in its demonstration farms in Punjab were stalled. Then, the import of a tomato-processing line was delayed by customs authorities citing capacity violations at the Pepsi plant. As a result, the launch of Pepsi suffered a delay of two to three weeks. Other foreign companies began to have second thoughts about coming to India.

In May 1990, V.P. Singh visited Kuala Lumpur for a meeting of the Group of 15, an international forum of cooperation among developing countries. He was surprised at the rapid progress Malaysia had made since his last visit to the country in 1985 when he was in Rajiv Gandhi's Cabinet. Montek Singh Ahluwalia, a renowned economist from Oxford who had accompanied Singh on the trip, told him that India had not achieved the same level of development as its East Asian peers 'because they were seriously engaged in economic reforms, whereas we were hesitant to make changes'.[29] So, Singh urged Ahluwalia to write a strategy paper on reforms that would enable India to catch up with them.

The report—later dubbed as the 'M-document'—discussed the trade and exchange policy changes that India needed to undertake and the impact of tariff changes, among other reform recommendations that were far bolder than anything that previous government documents had ever discussed. Somehow the press got hold of the document and released it to the public. A huge controversy was created in the process. V.P. Singh immediately distanced himself from it.

Luckily for Ahluwalia, a bigger issue took precedence soon after his document leaked. Back in 1977, the Janata government had appointed the Backward Classes Commission, which would later be popularly known as the Mandal Commission, named after its proactive chairman. The body was to identify the socially and educationally backward classes in India and to consider the possibility of reservation for these sections of society so as to redress caste discrimination.

The Indian caste system was a historical system of social stratification generally based on occupation. The 'backward castes' were the intermediate groups between the Schedules Castes (SC) and Tribes (ST) at the bottom, for whom there was a reservation of 22.5 per cent in all Central government jobs, and the Brahmins and Rajputs at the top. The Mandal Commission found that 'Other Backward Castes' (OBCs), as these groups were legally known, comprised more than half the Indian population, but were not adequately represented in administrative posts. As of 1980, the OBCs filled only 12.55 per cent of Central government jobs.

The Commission recommended that 27 per cent of the posts in the Central government be reserved for this section of the population in addition to the seats reserved for SCs and STs. However, by the time the report was submitted, the Janata government had fallen, and Congress chose to bury it after coming to power. V.P. Singh, either due to his vulnerability in a minority government or sensing the rising political power of the backward castes with time or both, issued the basic recommendation of the Mandal Commission on 13 August 1990.

A lively debate ensued. Some argued that the criterion for reservations should have been income while others lamented the effect this policy would have on the quality and efficiency of the public sector. Meanwhile, those in support of it pointed out that states in south India always had two-thirds of their jobs reserved on the basis of caste hierarchies, which had no effect on the efficiency of the administration. Nevertheless, the constitutional validity of the Mandal Commission's recommendations was contested in the Supreme Court in September.

As the proceedings took place in the Supreme Court, the disagreements over the policy spilled into the streets. Upper-caste students resorted to self-immolation, resulting in sixty-two deaths. Rallies and demonstrations were held across north India, which often ended in police firing. More than fifty lives were lost in this manner.[30] The protests were mostly concentrated in north India as affirmative action programmes were already prevalent in the south and the region also had a thriving industrial sector, which left their youth less dependent on government jobs. The upper-caste population was also much lower in south India.[31]

The Supreme Court would eventually give the verdict on 16 November 1992. Seven of the ten judges on the bench chose to uphold the constitutional validity of the Mandal Commission, and only added caveats that the overall reservation should not exceed 50 per cent and should be applied only in recruitments and not in promotions.

Meanwhile, back in 1990, as V.P. Singh was pursuing his political agenda with the Mandal Commission, the Bharatiya Janata Party, which was a part of the National Front, decided to move forward with its own agenda. The party president of the BJP, Lal Krishna Advani, revived the old Babri Masjid debate, vowing to begin construction of the temple at Ayodhya on 30 October.[32] He began a tour across northern states appealing for support wherever he went, intending to reach Ayodhya on the promised date.

But the government denounced the campaign as it was spreading tensions and violence across the country. V.P. Singh declared that he would not allow the mosque to be touched, knowing fully well that his government could not afford to lose the support of the BJP. He stated on national television that now 'it is not a question of saving the government but of saving the country'.[33] On his orders, Advani was arrested when his entourage reached Bihar.

The BJP withdrew its support and V.P. Singh faced a vote of no-confidence in Parliament, which he lost 142 to 346. He finally resigned on 7 November 1990. Chandra Shekhar, a socialist leader who had played an instrumental role in the nationalization of banks and the abolition of the privy purses under Indira Gandhi, but would ultimately go on to criticize her for the Emergency and become the president of the Janata Party, seized the opportunity and left the V.P. Singh government with sixty-four MPs. He convinced Rajiv Gandhi to support him and became the eighth prime minister of the country, three days after Singh's resignation.

But his timing could not have been worse. The Indian economy, which had accumulated massive amounts of debt since the Rajiv Gandhi era, finally came undone by the end of 1990. Between 1984-85 and 1990-91, the country's external debt doubled from

USD 35 billion to USD 69 billion. For an economy that was under USD 290 billion in size, the burden was considerably huge. Foreign reserves were abysmally low by the end of the year and export earnings were overshadowed by India's import bill.[34]

India's current account deficit, the difference between its exports and imports, worsened further by the end of 1990 for two reasons. First, the Gulf War had begun with the invasion of Kuwait by Iraq in August 1990. This had led to a sharp escalation in crude oil prices, leading to a doubling of the petroleum import bill from USD 2 billion to USD 5.7 billion. The Middle East crisis also led to a decline in workers' remittances and narrowed a major source of funding for the current account. Exports to Iraq and Kuwait had to be halted as well, resulting in a loss of USD 500 million for India.

The second reason that led to a deterioration of the current account was the slow growth of India's major trading partners. Between 1988 and 1991, global economic growth declined steadily from 4.5 per cent to 2.5 per cent. In the United States, which was India's largest single export destination, the decline was even greater as growth fell from 3.9 per cent to -1 per cent during the same time period. India's exports took a hit in the process and the growth of the country's export volume slowed down to 4 per cent in 1990-91.

As the current account deficit reached USD 9.7 billion in 1990-91, which was 3.1 per cent of India's GDP, the only way to finance it was by drawing down reserves. However, the foreign currency reserves with the RBI stood at USD 1.1 billion in early 1991, which could cover merely five weeks of imports when the minimum safe limit is considered to be twelve weeks. The low level of reserves triggered a number of consequences. Credit-rating agencies downgraded India and commercial bank financing became hard to obtain. To make matters worse, an outflow of NRI deposits began since investors lost confidence.

There was no other option but to approach the IMF for assistance or face a possibility of defaulting on its interest payments. This outcome was to be avoided at all costs. Mexico had defaulted on its external obligation in 1982. Over the next six years, the country suffered capital flight, inflation and unemployment. By 1989, the real wages in the country had halved.[35]

Nevertheless, Yashwant Sinha, the Minister of Finance in the Chandra Shekhar Cabinet, was of the view that a temporary relief from the IMF would help the country avoid a full-blown crisis. He presented a mini-budget in December 1990, which introduced some new indirect tax levies to show the world that the Indian government was serious about raising resources. The IMF rewarded the government with a loan of USD 1.8 billion in January 1991 with assurances of more loans after a reform-oriented budget was presented.

Although it is not popularly known, Yashwant Sinha did go on to prepare a reform budget that was, by some accounts, more revolutionary and radical than the budget that was famously presented later that year by Dr Manmohan Singh.[36] However, the Congress was not completely on board with the idea, as any credit for reforms would go to the Chandra Shekhar government and any failures due to it would be alluded to them as they were supporting the government from the outside.[37] In the end, a watered-down version of the original budget was presented.

Such disagreements between the Chandra Shekhar government and Congress over a range of matters resulted in the withdrawal of support by Rajiv Gandhi, and the minority government fell on 6 March 1991. Fresh elections were announced, to be conducted in phases. President R. Venkataraman requested Chandra Shekhar to continue as the prime minister until a new government could be elected into power.

Over the snext few months, the caretaker government of Chandra Shekhar had to ensure that the country did not default, especially on its short-term debt of over USD 5 billion, which was equal to the reserves that India had at the best of times. To begin with, the government severely limited its spending to curb the fiscal deficit. Also, even though the IMF and World Bank were disappointed with India's failure to present a reform-oriented budget, their member nations were approached for more loans. Japan, Germany and

Netherlands obliged. Thus, crisis was averted for the time being. Chandra Shekhar had managed to save India from defaulting on its payments, an effort that has largely gone unnoticed in the pages of history.

Meanwhile, the time for electing a new government into power had finally arrived. On 21 May, a day after the first phase of elections was held, Rajiv Gandhi was campaigning in Tamil Nadu. At around 10 p.m., he arrived for a public meeting in Sriperumbudur.

A young Sri Lankan Tamil woman was waiting in the crowd among his supporters. She was a member of the LTTE, which now feared that Rajiv might send Indian troops into Sri Lanka again if he came back into power. When Rajiv Gandhi reached near her, she put a garland around his neck and bent down to touch his feet. As Rajiv leaned forward to lift her up, she detonated a jacket of explosives strapped under her dress. Rajiv's body blew to pieces. The Gandhi family lost a third member in the span of a little more than a decade.

CHAPTER 15

THE PERFECT CRISIS

The pundits had predicted a hung assembly in the 1991 elections with no party anywhere near majority. Rajiv Gandhi's death changed the outcome in favour of Congress, but only slightly. The party won 244 seats, which was still nearly 30 seats short of majority. However, it did manage to come into power with the support of independents and the Jharkhand Mukti Morcha. This coalition was formed relatively smoothly when compared to previous non-Congress coalition governments and would also prove to be more stable in terms of its survival for the entire five-year period.

The election of a new Congress President to replace Rajiv Gandhi, on the other hand, was a more dramatic event. Rajiv's wife, Sonia Gandhi, was disinterested in taking up the role, even though she was beckoned by her party workers to do so. She detested the political life and had, in fact, been against Rajiv Gandhi becoming the prime minister as well. With anyone else from the Gandhi family being out of question, a lot of candidates began eyeing the position. Sonia Gandhi was ultimately left with the job of choosing her husband's successor. P.N Haksar, Indira Gandhi's principal secretary, was summoned for advice.

Haksar first suggested Shankar Dayal Sharma, who was then the vice president of India and the most senior Congress leader alive. However, Sharma politely declined the offer, citing his old age. The second suggestion that Haksar gave was Pamulaparti Venkata Narasimha Rao, a southern Brahmin, who had served in the Cabinet of both Indira and Rajiv Gandhi. Haksar was of the view that Rao was an intellectual who lacked enemies and had been extremely loyal to the Gandhi family.[1] Such traits were rare in most Congressmen and would help keep the party united.

It was under these circumstances that P.V. Narasimha Rao was elected as the president of the Congress on 29 May 1991. Less than a month later, Congress emerged as the single largest party in Parliament and Rao was sworn in as the tenth prime minister on 21 June.

In a time when India was facing its worst economic crisis, a prime minister who had never dealt with economic affairs was placed into power. In his twenty-year career, he had never held a finance post. But Rao had displayed an exceptional ability to adapt to the needs of his environment. When he was in Rajiv Gandhi's Cabinet and overheard the prime minister complain about how the 'old guard' would not understand his programme of technology and modernization, he asked his son to send him a computer prototype from the United States. He soon became quite familiar with the machine and over time would even master two computer languages, COBOL and BASIC.[2] Rao was thus adept at adjusting to the situation in which he found himself. And in 1991, the economy needed him to be proactive with reforms, failing which the country risked defaulting on its debt obligations for the first time in its independent history.

His limited experiences with the economy at a personal level had prepared him for the same. As a foreign minister under Rajiv Gandhi, he visited Singapore in 1989 and was awestruck by the technological advancements the city-state had made. When he brought back a laptop and some electronic gadgets with him, customs officials at the Delhi airport levied heavy duties on them. This irritated him deeply and he developed a strong aversion to the barriers imposed on technological imports to India.[3]

Nevertheless, Rao's intellectual understanding of economy was severely deficient and he was quite aware of this limitation. He admitted as much to Jairam Ramesh, an economist who had earlier worked with the World Bank, with the Planning Commission and, most recently, in the election campaign of Rajiv Gandhi. Rao's ignorance ended a day before being sworn in as the prime minister when the Cabinet Secretary, Naresh Chandra, handed him an eight-page document detailing the abysmal state in which the economy found itself. Initially, Rao put off reading the document, but when

Chandra insisted that he do so, he took an hour to read it. His first response was to ask Chandra, 'Is the economic situation that bad?' The Cabinet Secretary replied ominously, 'No, sir. It is actually much worse.'[4]

* * *

The economic crisis of 1991 was the culmination of the economic policy choices of the previous decade. In the aftermath of the second oil shock that took place in 1979-80, Indian exports faltered as the exchange rate appreciated. As foreign exchange earnings dipped, and the current account deficit widened, India rapidly accumulated domestic and foreign debt. By the time Rajiv Gandhi came into power, the country's macroeconomic situation was precarious.

The Rajiv Gandhi government did make some good policy choices in the second half of the decade. There were policy shifts towards industrial deregulation and trade liberation, at least until the Bofors scandal made it impossible to maintain a radical stance. Nevertheless, industrial growth escalated during this period and trade picked up. The only mistake was that the worsening fiscal situation was completely ignored, and, to the contrary, higher spending was used to fuel growth. As debt rose to dangerous levels, any minor shock was enough to introduce a full-blown economic crisis.

The Gulf War provided the trigger. It did not help matters that the political situation was unstable. Since the V.P. Singh government came into power, investors lost confidence in the economy and began withdrawing money. In the last three months of 1990, USD 200 million went out of the country. This flight of capital accelerated to almost USD 950 million in the months of April and June, right around the time Narasimha Rao took over as the prime minister.[5] The foreign exchange reserves in June had dipped so low that they could cover only two weeks of imports when the safe limit was considered to be six times that amount.

India had even lost the option of borrowing to fulfil its debt obligations. The short-term borrowings that India had accumulated during the Rajiv Gandhi era were taken in a period when interests rates were low. As international confidence dipped with respect to Indian finances, the interest rates rose, and the cost of credit escalated. So India could not afford to borrow any more to roll over its short-term debts.

Inflation levels had also gone through the roof. During the second half of the previous decade, inflation had averaged at around 6.7 per cent. But in the financial year 1990-91, it had escalated to double digits. India's higher inflation rates in comparison to its trading partners meant that Indian exports were now costlier for them. The economy was taking a hit at every level.

The only option left for India to avoid defaulting on its loans was to approach the IMF and the World Bank for loans. The short-lived Chandra Shekhar government had already done so just before they lost power. Confidence in India's ability to repay the loan had been so low that the IMF had asked the country to pledge her gold in return. The loan was exhausted by mid-1991 without making any impact on the economy's worsening balance of payments situation. India needed a second tranche, but the IMF refused. Narasimha Rao explained that 'consultations were held with both the IMF and the World Bank [in April 1990]. The report of the discussions was that no fresh commitments of aid would be forthcoming until basic reforms were undertaken'.[6]

Since then, talks of possible reforms began to be heard in political corridors. On 20 June, Pranab Mukherjee, who had been the finance minister in the Indira Gandhi government between 1982 and 1984 and was widely expected to hold the same post in the new government, gave a detailed interview in the *Times of India*. To a question about how India's planning will be balanced with the IMF demands of liberalization, he argued, 'We want planning and liberalization. We must give room for play to the private sector. The public sector must vacate the areas in which the private sector has the capability to come in. The public sector must move into the difficult areas of advanced technology.'[7]

Soon after, Narasimha Rao delivered his first speech as prime minister on 22 June. He warned the nation that, 'The economy is in a crisis. The balance of payments situation is exceedingly difficult. Inflationary pressures on the price level are considerable. There is no time to lose. The government and the country keep living beyond their means and there are no soft options left.' As a step forward, he did not hold back on suggesting the path of reforms and promised that his government will be 'committed to remove the cobwebs that come in the way of rapid industrialization'. He went on to add some unimaginable promises:

> We will work towards making India internationally competitive . . . We also welcome foreign direct investment, so as to accelerate the tempo of development, upgrade our technologies and to promote our exports. Obstacles that come in the way of allocating foreign investment on a sizeable scale will be removed. A time-bound programme will be worked out to streamline our industrial policies and programmes to achieve the goal of a vibrant economy that rewards creativity, enterprise and innovativeness.[8]

Such a bold rhetoric was Rao's alone. He had drafted the speech himself with the help of some bureaucrats.[9] His finance minister, Manmohan Singh, the man who would soon be at the centre-stage directing the biggest reform measures India had adopted yet, had been sworn into the Cabinet merely a day ago and, thus, had little to do with Rao's first speech. However, it is hard to deny that pressure from the IMF had a major role to play in the genesis of these views.

* * *

When Rao was deciding who would be a part of his new Cabinet, he was aware that the decision of the post of finance minister had to be taken with utmost care, considering India's economic plight at the time. P.C. Alexander, who had been the principal secretary to both Indira and Rajiv Gandhi, was helping Rao narrow down the names. Rao's first instinct was to reject Congress leaders who were eyeing the finance ministry for themselves. Pranab Mukherjee, thus, lost out immediately. Rao asked Alexander to suggest names of apolitical economists who were capable of dealing with the West.

In their discussions, two names came up: one was Dr I.G. Patel and the other was that of Dr Manmohan Singh. When the former declined, Alexander approached Manmohan Singh for the position. The unenviable job of handling an economy in crisis was, thus, entrusted with the bespectacled, blue-turbaned man, who would soon become the face of Indian reforms. Singh was a Cambridge-trained economist, who had previously held various crucial financial positions, including that of the governor of the Reserve Bank of India, when Pranab Mukherjee was the finance minister. Later, he had served as the secretary general of the South Commission, an independent economic think tank in Geneva. This experience gave him the additional qualification of having the ability to deal with Western institutions, something that Rao had specifically demanded since it would come in handy during negotiations with the IMF.

In terms of economic matters, Singh had often been critical of the numbing system of controls that had been imposed upon the economy in the name of socialism. For instance, in 1972 he reviewed the book *India: Planning for Industrialization*, the first empirically robust critique of India's early economic policies, written by eminent economists Jagdish Bhagwati and Padma Desai. In his review, he argued that there is a need 'to recognize that the knowledge available to civil servants is not necessarily superior to that of entrepreneurs'. However, Singh also knew how not to irk his political masters. He added in the same review that 'it would be too presumptuous to claim that modern neoclassical economics has answers to all the economic problems in all parts of the world'.[10]

Rao also drew Montek Singh Ahluwalia, the author of the M-document, and Jairam Ramesh, Rajiv Gandhi's go-to man on the economy, into his inner circle. Both were staunch advocates of liberalizing the economy, and both had worked with the World Bank at some point in their career. As his commerce minister, he chose P. Chidambaram, a young lawyer from Tamil Nadu who also held liberal economic leanings. Thus, Rao had a clear intent in his mind on what needed to be done to bring the economy back from the brink of disaster and he had found the perfect men for the job. The time to act had come.

* * *

A major obstacle that Rao had to face was having a minority in Parliament. No Congress leader before him had to ever face such a scenario and it could not have come at a more challenging time. In fact, globally, no other leader had ever undertaken reforms from such a position of weakness. In China, Deng Xiaoping was firmly in control of the Communist Party of China when he introduced reforms more than a decade before India. Margaret Thatcher and Ronald Reagan had also come to power with clear majorities.

So, Rao had to take the opposition leaders into confidence for his radical policy measures. On 25 June, five days after formally becoming the prime minister, Rao called for an all-party meeting where he urged Manmohan Singh to explain India's economic situation to the audience. Most of them were taken aback as they had not realized the gravity of the situation. However, Rao did not disclose two crucial policy decisions that were about to be taken in response to the crisis. One was the devaluation of the rupee and the other was the move to mortgage India's gold in return of foreign loans. Both would have generated furore across parties and become difficult to pursue thereafter.

Devaluation was a particularly awkward issue to consider after the disastrous experience of 1966 when Indira Gandhi devalued the rupee and endured a barrage of criticism for her decision. It was also complicated by the fact that the West failed to hold up its end of the bargain then and the promised aid did not materialize. Due to the bitter aftertaste of the devaluation episode, even Rao was in a dilemma about going through with the move. But it was deemed absolutely necessary, especially by his finance minister. After the consistently worsening macroeconomic situation in the previous decade, the Indian rupee was grossly overvalued against the dollar, which discouraged foreign investments and hurt exports. So an adjustment was long overdue.

Rao was even more uncomfortable with his finance minister's insistence on adopting a 'two-step devaluation' approach. It was necessary to devalue the rupee in two phases, because the first one was needed to test the waters while the second was required to introduce the actual change. For Rao, however, one stroke of devaluation was bad enough, but two in a row was preposterous.

Nevertheless, Rao decided to back his finance minister and, on 1 July 1991, the value of the rupee was lowered against major currencies by about 7 to 9 per cent. Opposition members were furious. So were the Congress ministers who were kept in the dark. In the early hours of 3 July, the day the second devaluation had to take place, Rao got cold feet and called Manmohan Singh not to go through with it. Singh immediately called the deputy governor of the Reserve Bank of India, C. Rangarajan, at around 9.30 a.m. and asked him to hold back on the announcement of the second phase of devaluation. But Rangarajan informed him that the devaluation had already been carried out half an hour ago.

The markets and the media reacted quite positively to the two announcements. The same could not be said for the Parliament. Manmohan Singh had to face much of the flak from across the political spectrum. He would insist in the media and in the Parliament that the exchange rate is merely a price and its downward revision is wrongly perceived as immoral or anti-national in India. In the Rajya Sabha, during a heated exchange about devaluation, he reminded his adversaries:

If you look at the whole history of India's independence struggle before 1947, our national leaders were fighting against the British against keeping the exchange rate of the rupee unduly high. Why did the British keep the exchange rate of the rupee unduly high? It was because they wanted this country to remain backward and they did not want this country to industrialize.[11]

All through, Rao backed his finance minister. Singh, aware of the support, decided to take India further on the path of reforms. He asked Montek Singh Ahluwalia to brief P. Chidambaram, the commerce minister, on abolition of export subsidies. Since the Indian rupee had been overvalued, the Indian government provided exporters with subsidies to encourage trade. With the devaluation, such a subsidy was now unnecessary. However, Chidambaram was worried that dismantling the subsidy cut would generate discontent among exporters and so it was decided that another sop would be announced simultaneously, which would allow them to import restricted items. Manmohan Singh immediately agreed to the proposal and got Rao's consent to go ahead. All of this was achieved in a short span of twelve hours. Rao faced any backlash with a matter-of-fact approach. 'Desperate maladies call for drastic remedies,' he argued.[12]

Another decision that was met with widespread criticism from not only the Opposition but also from the public was that of mortgaging India's gold in return for dollars, so that the country did not default on its outstanding loans. The process of using gold to tide over a crisis was nothing out of the ordinary. In fact, the Reserve Bank of India Act, 1934, allowed the central bank to keep 15 per cent of its gold outside India. But, again, the country's gold was symbolic of its pride and pawning it to incur daily expenses seemed blasphemous to the public eye.

Also, Rao was not the one who initiated it as well. The Chandra Shekhar government decided to dip into the country's gold reserves to raise foreign loans in May 1991. About 20 metric tonnes of confiscated gold was leased to the country's largest bank, the State Bank of India, which used it to raise a loan of USD 200 million in a repurchase option with the United Bank of Switzerland.

But this proved insufficient for the new government and two weeks after it came into power, about 46.9 tonnes of gold were taken out of the vaults of the Reserve Bank of India and airlifted to London over a period of four days. The Bank of England gave India a total sum of USD 405 million in return. But when the news of the transaction leaked, there was public outcry. The matter rocked the Parliament and even Congress MPs were miffed. The finance minister argued that this step was the best possible decision after taking everything into consideration. Nevertheless, after this endeavour, everyone in the country realized the extent of the crisis. This prepared them for the drastic reforms that were yet to be introduced.

* * *

India's infamous licence raj that had introduced a nauseating web of controls across the economy was still very much in place. For years, the system of licensing and legislative restrictions was monitoring and controlling the expansion of private businesses in India. These controls were the major contributors to the painful 'Hindu rate of growth' phase.

To understand the extent of problems inherent in the system, the amount of clearances that an entrepreneur was required to obtain are noteworthy. First, an 'in-principle approval' was required from the Ministry of Industry. Once the approval was granted, a Letter of Intent was issued, which was necessary for obtaining further clearances. In case funds were required or equity had to be raised, a clearance of the controller of capital issues in the Ministry of Finance was needed. Next, if raw materials or machinery had to be imported, a visit was required to the chief controller of imports and exports in the Ministry of Commerce. In case a foreign collaborator was in play, an approval was needed from a committee of the Ministry of Industry, which was also chaired by a secretary of the Ministry of Finance. After all approvals were obtained, the entrepreneur had to return to the Ministry of Industry to obtain a formal licence.

Such a maze of bureaucratic processes naturally disincentivized private investment and deflated any prospects of growth. It also had a detrimental impact on the competitive spirit of the economy. A Letter of Intent once issued by the Ministry of Industry remained valid for six months and, during that period, no other applications in the specific area were accepted. So a lot of businesses applied for licences merely to eliminate competition. An interim report on licensing revealed that a group had applied for 375 licences, out of which merely a third were eventually used for creation of capacity. The rest were just allowed to lapse.[13]

Seeing how existing Indian entrepreneurs had learnt to game the system to their advantage, Milton Friedman, the eminent free-marketeer once commented, 'One gets the impression, depending on whom one talks with, either the government runs business, or that two or three large businesses run the government.'[14]

By the 1980s, economists and policymakers were aware that these structural issues had to be resolved to stimulate economic growth. The time for industrial reforms had come. The 1991 economic crisis only highlighted the urgency of such corrections and provided the necessary political motivation to adopt a radical path. So, after resolving the short-term currency and debt problems, the Narasimha Rao government got down to changing India's industrial policy.

The process of industrial reforms had been set into motion much before the crisis of 1991 ensued. Soon after the Bofors scandal hit and Rajiv Gandhi shunned his reformist ways, another economist who had briefly worked with the World Bank, Rakesh Mohan, joined the Ministry of Industry as an economic adviser in 1988. He soon began working on a new industrial policy, but then the government fell.

In the V.P. Singh–led National Front government, Ajit Singh was made the Minister of Industries. Ajit Singh had just quit his job in IBM and understood the inefficiencies that pervaded India's corporate culture. He set up a team comprising Amar Nath Varma, who was then the secretary in the Ministry of Commerce and Industries, and Rakesh Mohan, who was the Chief Economic Adviser. The two of them drafted India's new industrial policy, which aimed at dismantling the licence raj.

Throughout the process of the formulation of policy, Ajit Singh enthusiastically consulted economists and businessmen for their inputs. He even had discussions with the prime minister, but the government was dependent on the support of the left and the BJP for survival, and such radical reforms were not politically feasible. So, the draft was unfortunately put on the back burner.

When Rao came into power, he gave the draft a new lease of life and empowered Varma to convert it into policy. By 7 July, Varma, along with Rakesh Mohan and Jairam Ramesh, had moulded the old draft into a new industrial policy. Rao asked for a summary of the policy, which was promptly forwarded to him the next day by Jairam Ramesh. On 9 July, as the Parliament session was about to begin, Rao told the Congress MPs that the government would soon announce a comprehensive package of industrial reforms.

On 12 July, before any official announcement was made, the *Hindustan Times* carried a headline on the front page—'Industrial Licensing to Go'—which carried the contents of the note that Jairam Ramesh had written for Narasimha Rao a few days ago. 'Abolition of all industrial licences except for a short negative list, automatic permission for foreign direct investment up to 51 per cent and increase in foreign equity limit up to 51 per cent . . . are some of the bold and innovative measures contemplated in the new industrial policy,' it read.[15]

Jairam Ramesh frantically rushed to the Prime Minister's Office to clarify that the leak had not originated from him, only to be nonchalantly told to remain calm. He understood that the leak had come from Rao himself as he was testing the waters before taking matters forward.[16]

The final step before introducing the policy in Parliament was to present it before the Cabinet. The meeting for the same was held on 19 July. The outcome was disastrous. The ministers were critical of both the style and the substance of the policy document. Some argued that the Congress ideology was left behind while others felt there was not a strong case for such colossal changes. Manmohan Singh ferociously defended the reform proposals, but eventually it was decided that it was necessary to revisit the policy.

After some deliberations, Jairam Ramesh realized that the political packaging of the reforms proposal was not proper. The policy proposed a significant break from the past without providing any historical context. This had created a disconnect between the economic and political nature of the reforms. So, he added a long preamble to the Cabinet note without making any changes to its original content. The preamble talked about how industrial policy had evolved with time under Nehru and Indira and described how this was an extension of their efforts. 'The major objectives of the new industrial policy package will be to build on the gains already made, correct the distortions or weaknesses that may have crept in, maintain a sustained growth in productivity and gainful employment, and attain international competitiveness,' it stated. Rao liked it and so did the Cabinet, which met on 23 July and approved the revised document with the preamble.[17]

Leaving nothing to chance, the prime minister also called a meeting of the Congress Working Committee in an unusual move, seeking their nod for what the Cabinet had already approved. He portrayed the new policy as merely a step back from the sharp left-ward tilt that Indira Gandhi took in 1969 and into Nehru's industry policy resolution of 1956, which was more flexible in nature. This was not entirely true, but Rao had understood that the only policy-packaging that would help implement the reforms was one that gave a sense of continuity from the past.

Manmohan Singh was also learning from his boss. He specified how this policy was just a reflection of the 1991 election manifesto of Congress. The ploy worked. The party was satisfied with the industrial reforms. The next day, 24 July 1991, was the day when the budget was to be presented in the Parliament. As the new industrial policy was being prepared, Manmohan Singh was simultaneously working tirelessly to frame a reformist budget to complement it. While the industrial policy was supposed to end the licence raj, the budget was aimed at ending India's isolation from the rest of the world. The final draft of the budget was ready by 21 July. The import–export policy was revamped, subsidies were slashed, and foreign investment rules were made easier.

Everything was finally in place for the budget day. The only issue of contention on the penultimate day was the manner in which the industrial policy and the budget were to be delivered. Manmohan Singh was of the view that they should be presented as a combined whole to the world to signal India's commitment to both internal and external liberalization. But bureaucrats in the Ministry of Industry who had worked hard on the new policy wanted a separate announcement by Rao, who was the industry minister at the time, so that their efforts were adequately recognized.

Narasimha Rao managed to broker a compromise. He allowed for separate announcements but both to be made on the same day. So, on 24 July, India's new industrial policy was announced in the afternoon followed by the budget speech. Some commentators argue that the idea of separate announcements and their placement were deliberate as, in a time when people did not get real-time news updates, the next day's newspapers would be filled with the announcements made in the budget speech and the earlier policy changes, which were more politically sensitive, would end up getting sidelined.

The potentially explosive and historic industrial policy was also delivered in the blandest manner possible. At around 12.50 p.m. on the day of the budget, instead of the industry minister, the Minister of State for Industry, P.J. Kurien, got up to make an announcement in the Lok Sabha, 'Sir, I beg to lay on the table a statement on Industrial Policy.' And that was it. The four-decade-old licence raj had been brought down with a soft blow.[18]

The statement that carried the greatest significance in the entire declaration was that 'industrial licensing will henceforth be abolished for all industries, except those specified, irrespective of levels of investment'.[19] The specified exemptions were a total of eighteen industries, which were left for security or environmental purposes. The sectors reserved for the public sector were also reduced from seventeen to eight. Another major change was the easing of the anti-monopoly laws, which had been made severely restrictive with the Monopolistic and Restrictive Trade Practices (MRTP) Act under the Indira Gandhi regime. And lastly, 51 per cent foreign investment was allowed in 34 industries with 'automatic approval'. These announcements were the single-most radical reforms undertaken in India's independent history and they were introduced without much fanfare.

A few hours later, Manmohan Singh stood up in Parliament to deliver his landmark budget. He began by claiming to take forward the work that Rajiv Gandhi had initiated in his last term and then, over the next few hours, went on to declare that India was open to the world. He gave exports a push, brought the policy of import licensing to an end and slashed tariffs. Later, he also stressed on the changes in the industrial policy that were announced earlier in the day. Singh dramatically ended the speech with a quote from Victor Hugo: 'No power on earth can stop an idea whose time has come.' He added that 'the emergence of India as a major economic power in the world happens to be one such idea'.[20]

While turning India's industrial policy on its head, Singh ironically made sure that Nehru, Indira and Rajiv were credited for ensuring that India develop a robust industrial structure. The way the announcements of a complete overhaul of the system were made during these days is an interesting case study on balancing political and economic goals within a democratic society. Rao had been in this game for a long time now and was wary not to claim credit for these changes. He refused to announce the industrial policy and he sat disinterested beside Manmohan Singh as he delivered his budget. Sure enough, Manmohan Singh was the face that every media outlet carried the next day as the main orchestrator of India's historic reforms.

* * *

The criticism soon came barrelling down from all corners. Rao consistently found crafty ways to appease his critics. His usual approach was to play up the crisis surrounding the need for such drastic reforms. But he also had specific responses up his sleeves to nullify his opposition. When he was accused of pandering to the interest of the West, he would cite examples of the pro-business policies of the East Asian economies. When National Front leaders questioned him, he simply argued that he was only carrying forward what Chandra Shekhar and V.P. Singh began. When it came to BJP, he leveraged on his knowledge of Sanskrit and poetry to assuage them.[21]

The business groups were also terrified that foreign competition might prove fatal to their existence. So, he met some of them to allay their fears and asked Varma to do the same. He even awarded J.R.D. Tata with the country's highest civilian honour, the Bharat Ratna, which was conferred for the first time to an industrialist. This was a symbolic gesture by Rao to the business community that the government was not working against their interests.

But, Rao also knew when to back down. When it became difficult to defend the elimination of subsidies and protests against it threatened the destruction of the entire reform agenda, Rao asked Manmohan Singh to reduce the hike in fertilizer prices from 40 to 30 per cent. The dissenting voices, some of which were coming from within Congress itself, quickly subsided.

As the initial reactionary forces were neutralized one by one, the Rao–Singh duo kept introducing further reforms, bit by bit. Controls were further eliminated, and tariffs reduced. In the 1992 budget, foreign investment into India was made even easier. By mid-1992, the foreign exchange reserves of India—which had kickstarted the reform process—were finally back to normal. In April itself, the reserves were enough to buy twelve weeks of imports, which was deemed to be the safe limit for a country.

In a speech to the industry lobby, FICCI, in September 1992, Rao declared, 'The balance of payments crisis is now under control and we have been reasonably successful in reducing the fiscal deficit . . .'[22] It had taken more than a year, but he had extricated India from the worst economic crisis it has yet faced with deft political and economic manoeuvring.

As for the Indian economy, it was probably the perfect crisis— one that was necessary to stimulate change and just enough so as not to reduce it to ruins. It could be said that in India, it always takes a crisis to bring about revolutionary change. This was at least true for the Green Revolution of the late 1960s and the economic reforms of 1991.

CHAPTER 16

GOING THE DISTANCE

The economic reforms of 1991 had three crucial aspects—devaluation, delicensing and trade liberalization. But even after the crisis had subsided by 1992, a lot was left wanting. State control over banks, capital markets, infrastructure development, media houses and so on were still complications that had to be ironed out.

Each sector had its own set of critics against liberalization. The banking sector, for instance, was a legacy of Indira Gandhi, and any privatization efforts would imply an abrupt deviation from the past. Bank unions were also adamant against any such moves as it threatened the status quo of indolence and inefficiency. By 1992, Rao had also lost the excuse of crisis to push through any significant reforms.

The political parties, including Congress, had their own reservations with liberalization reforms. The nationalist BJP was in favour of delicensing but did not support the entry of foreign firms into India. On the other hand, the communists were against both of these ideas. Finally, Congress was concerned about losing touch with Nehruvian socialism.

This was the background against which the 79th Session of the Congress party was held in Tirupati, the famous temple-town of Andhra Pradesh in April 1992. The previous session was held in 1985 to commemorate 100 years of the Congress party. It was the first platform where Rao was meeting his party workers en masse after the crisis and, thus, was expected to explain his liberalization policies introduced in the course of the previous year.

This was a complex task, which even Rajiv Gandhi had refrained from doing in the previous session where he had intended to announce his economic vision of liberalization. But when it was presented to party leaders, the ideas were bitterly opposed, and he quickly decided to drop all references to economic reform.[1]

So, Rao spent days perfecting his speech and trying to find the simplest means to explain complex economic jargon. He spoke on the final day of the session and argued that there was a need to find a middle ground between free-market economics and state-sponsored socialism. He used his usual tactic of quoting Nehru, Indira and Rajiv to substantiate his claims.[2] He explained that the radical actions were necessary as the country's fiscal situation had deteriorated, which he likened to a person using a small blanket to cover himself. When the head was covered, the feet were exposed; and when the feet were covered, the head was bare. 'It is only to meet that extra length, so to say, and to fill the gap that we are taking the help of private sector.'[3]

Despite this lesson in liberalization, the next set of major reforms again came out of a crisis. Soon after Rao spoke at Tirupati, a scandal broke out on a scale that India had not seen before. Harshad Mehta, a prominent name in the Indian stock market and someone who presented India with a fascinating rags-to-riches story, was accused of fraud. Over the previous decade, Mehta had made thousands of crores off the stock market and everything he touched was believed to turn into gold. The media and the investors followed his every move.

However, in 1992, the financial journalist Sucheta Dalal got a tip that he was exploiting the loopholes in the banking system to game the markets. She broke the story in April that Mehta was fraudulently drawing money from banks using worthless bank receipts, forged documents and bribery. He was then using this liquidity to purchase huge amounts of shares across industry verticals. The banking fraud was later estimated at just over a billion dollars.[4]

The stock markets, which had doubled in value in just the course of the last year, immediately crashed. Chairmen of several banks, which had found themselves to be short of hundreds of millions of dollars, had to resign. Rao ordered a special court to try those linked with the scandal. Harshad Mehta was put behind bars. He was eventually released on bail three months after being in custody. It was only in October 1997 that the special court would piece together criminal charges against Mehta and in September 1999 that the Bombay High Court would sentence him to five years' rigorous imprisonment.[5]

Dalal still laments that most politicians who had colluded with the scamsters remained unaffected by the scam, as did most bankers.[6] But the only positive outcome of the crisis was that it provided a trigger for an unprecedented pace of capital market reforms. The chairman of the Securities and Exchange Board (SEBI), the market regulator of the country, was G.V. Ramakrishna—a person Dalal described as its 'best chairman yet'.[7] He told the *New York Times* that 'Most players in the capital markets felt they were beyond regulation. We are now trying to bring about some sensible regulations of the market in line with other developing countries' capital markets.'

Soon, Ramakrishna enthusiastically introduced regulation into the sector bringing 'order to a rag-tag community of brokers, twenty stock exchanges and a variety of intermediaries,' in Dalal's words.[8] Brokers were now required to register themselves for a fee. A new stock exchange, the National Stock Exchange (NSE), was also instituted to keep the Bombay Stock Exchange (BSE) in check. He did so despite a serious threat to his life during this period.[9] The stock markets soon began to run professionally. It also needs to be highlighted that Ramakrishna was later transferred to the Planning Commission after he refused to water down a report against a company which involved the prime minister's son.[10]

Although Rao did not completely understand the stock markets, he understood the importance of reforms after the scam was exposed. In September 1992, foreign institutional investors (FIIs) were given entry into India. This was a massive step for a country that was absolutely sceptical of foreign capital. Some restrictions were imposed to prevent the money from flowing in and out of the country too quickly. But these precautions helped India emerge largely unaffected from the Asian financial crisis of the late 1990s. These FIIs went on to become major drivers of the Indian stock market and the economy itself, being pipped by domestic investment only recently.[11]

* * *

If 1991 had changed India forever, the year 1992 did the same in a very cruel manner by the time it ended. The Babri Masjid issue, which had led to the fall of the V.P. Singh government and had increased the parliamentary presence of the BJP in the 1991 elections, climaxed in December 1992. While the BJP was focusing more on being a political party with a broader focus on issues of economic and social interest, the temple-versus-mosque question did not subside. Hindu organizations like the Vishwa Hindu Parishad (VHP) and the Rashtriya Swayamsevak Sangh (RSS), the parent body of the BJP, kept the spotlight on Ayodhya.

The two bodies acquired the land around Babri Masjid in October 1991 and began levelling it to prepare for a temple construction. This was being done in clear violation of court orders, which demanded that the status quo be maintained. Moreover, the Uttar Pradesh government had an old RSS hand, Kalyan Singh, as its chief minister, who was turning a blind eye to all these activities.[12] It was only in July 1992, when the Supreme Court intervened, that the construction stopped.[13]

In anticipation of any escalation in tensions, the home ministry had already prepared a contingency plan for the imposition of President's Rule in the state. Such a step would have been necessary for the Central government to take control of the police in Uttar Pradesh as law and order was a state subject. But Rao wanted to try and resolve the dispute with talks.

Then, on 30 October, the VHP announced that it would perform a *kar seva*, or religious service, right next to the mosque, on 6 December. That day would also mark the beginning of the construction of the temple. They promised to leave the mosque untouched, but a melee of around 100,000 Hindu *kar sevak*s in close proximity of the disputed structure was a disaster waiting to happen.

By the middle of November, volunteers began streaming into Ayodhya. Kalyan Singh made arrangements to house and feed the volunteers coming from outside the state. Rao still dithered on imposing Central rule and taking control of the situation. Journalist Vinay Sitapati in his biography of Narasimha Rao has outlined in detail the series of actions taken by Rao in the days leading up to 6 December and why he never imposed the President's Rule.[14] Rao had witnessed the consequences of sending troops to resolve tensions in both the Golden Temple and Sri Lanka. So by all means, he wanted to avoid a violent confrontation. He held multiple meetings with his inner Cabinet to consider the possibility of resorting to President's Rule. But no one in the Cabinet suggested so because it could not be imposed in mere anticipation of trouble.

Eventually, he approached the Supreme Court to hand over control of the mosque to the Central government, but Kalyan Singh promised to protect the mosque during the proceedings and the court rejected Rao's request. Nevertheless, 20,000 troops were placed within an hour's march from the town of Ayodhya, ready to move in when required.

On the last day of November, L.K. Advani, who had led the procession of kar sevaks in 1990, announced that he would depart for Ayodhya as well. 'I cannot give any guarantee at the moment about what will happen on 6 December. All I know is that we are going to perform kar seva,' he said.[15]

The prayers were supposed to begin at 11.30 in the morning on the fateful day. The UP police were patrolling the boundary walls of the mosque. The Central forces had not been moved in. Around the time the prayers were supposed to begin, some kar sevaks began to make threatening moves towards the mosque. The police constables and RSS workers tried to stop them but to no avail. Soon, a teenaged kar sevak made his way to the top of one of the domes of the mosque. This signalled the others to join and, by noon, thousands began chipping away its domes. Within five hours, all three domes had been flattened. The President's Rule was eventually imposed at 9 p.m. that night.[16]

As the domes of Babri Masjid came crashing down, the idea of a secular India took a fatal blow as well. Deadly riots broke out all across India, sometimes initiated by triumphant Hindus, and at other times by defiant Muslims. More than 2,000 lives across India were lost in an orgy of violence. The VHP leader Ashok Singhal remarked in 1994 that the demolition of the Babri Masjid was 'a catalyst for the ideological polarization which was nearly complete'.[17]

The issue still awaits judgment in the Supreme Court and status quo has been maintained on the site. But the land dispute had further repercussions a decade later in 2002. The VHP continued to organize tours by kar sevaks from across the country to Ayodhya. One such tour held in February 2002 was attended by hundreds of kar sevaks from Gujarat. While returning home, they got into a dispute with some Muslim vendors at the Godhra railway station. The altercation got violent and the kar sevaks boarded the train to flee. But on the outskirts of the station, the train had to stop as one of its coaches caught fire for unknown reasons. Fifty-eight people died. As news reached Gujarat, a wave of retributory violence spread across the state. Muslim homes were selectively burned, and families killed. The police did little to stem the communal violence.[18]

The Babri issue, therefore, created permanent fissures between the Hindus and Muslims living in India. The secular fabric of the country, which Mahatma Gandhi had tried to secure until his final days and which Nehru had successfully carried forward, was permanently damaged on 6 December 1992. *Time* magazine went so far as to claim, 'Like the three domes that crowned the 464-year-old Babri mosque, the three pillars of the Indian state—democracy, secularism and the rule of law—are now at risk from the fury of religious nationalism.'[19] In hindsight, Indian democracy proved more resilient than commentators at the time imagined, but it is true that, since the issue of Babri began to pay electoral dividends, Hindu communalism became a prominent reality in the country's politics.

* * *

The demolition of the mosque is the biggest taint in Narasimha Rao's legacy in office. His inaction has been scrutinized time and again. But Rao emerged unscathed from the affair. The BJP passed a no-confidence motion against his government on 17 December but failed. On 24 October 1994, the Supreme Court passed a judgment on the Babri incident and absolved Rao of any guilt while pinning the entire blame on the Kalyan Singh government.

If it were any other politician, such an incident would have marked the end of the cycle of bold reforms that were being undertaken in the economy. Rajiv Gandhi, for instance, could not continue on his liberalization mission after Bofors. But Rao saw it as an opportunity to go the distance. The opposition parties were so alarmed by BJP's rise that all their attacks on economic reforms were now shifted to the growth of religious fundamentalism.

'The primacy of secular politics and the need to contain BJP's further expansion was one important reason why economic liberalization did not face significant hurdles, even though the Congress lacked a majority in Parliament,' writes Zoya Hasan, a political scientist.[20]

So, a month after the demolition of Babri Masjid, the government introduced a reform that would have infuriated the Opposition and even Congress in normal circumstances. The RBI, with the approval of the government, allowed private entry into India's banking system, two and a half decades after Indira Gandhi went on a nationalization drive. Ten new banks, including ICICI Bank, HDFC Bank, Axis Bank and IDBI Bank, were formed as a result.[21]

The reform in capital markets and the banking sector was huge steps forward to make foreign investors comfortable with India's business environment. But Rao was aware that mere tweaks in legislation would not suffice in building enough confidence to attract investment, especially into traditional sectors like consumer goods. That would require the Indian political class cajoling global companies and investors at summits around the world. Narasimha Rao took up the task in stride. He became the first Indian prime minister to visit Davos for the World Economic Forum in 1992, and went back again in 1994, carrying a message of reform and shaking the hands of CEOs. He similarly appealed to foreign industrialists on his visits abroad.

These efforts went a long way in altering India's global image of a closed economy with socialist leanings. Meanwhile, to alter the aversion to foreign investment at home, he stressed the domestic origins of some of these investors—a tactic that Deng had perfected in China. During the inauguration of a steel plant set up by Lakshmi Mittal, he questioned his audience, 'If our own people want to come back, if they want to set up some factories in India . . . should we put obstacles in their way as soon as they land here?'[22] Such arguments paid off. The opinion foreign investors held about India and that Indians held about them changed quite rapidly during Rao's tenure. By July 1993, around USD 3.2 billion had flown into India in the form of foreign equity investment.[23]

Sure enough, a consumer revolution swept India. Success in the liberalization of services was its biggest contributor. Banking was the first major services sector to be opened up. Others like television, airlines and telecommunications needed a little more handholding. It could be said that television was more a reform of omission and the other two were acts of commission.

In October 1992, Indian television viewers saw the launch of India's first privately owned channel, Zee TV. But more than a year ago, just a month before Rao became prime minister, an unknown foreign network called Satellite Television Asian Region, or STAR TV, began to broadcast all over Asia and made inroads into the Indian television market. Soon, a galaxy of cable operators put up satellites in their backyards and offered middle-class neighbourhoods the variety of channels that STAR offered. In the first six months of 1992, cable operators across India were connecting almost 4,500 homes per day, which shot up to 9,450 homes daily on an average in the second half of the year. A growing satellite and cable industry was, thus, born out of the available technology rather than any deliberate reforms.[24]

The growth of the television industry, however, was on dubious legal grounds. There was no regulation of what Indians were watching.

Anyone could fix a dish on their roof and see anything from around the world. But Rao was sceptical of banning satellite TV as it would send out the wrong image to the world about India, an image he was trying so hard to change.[25] So, he let the status quo prevail. This legal ambiguity lasted until 1995 when the Supreme Court passed a ruling that the airwaves belonged to the public and not the government. All satellite channels immediately became legal in India.[26]

Airlines and telecom were sectors where Rao played a more instrumental role in reform. It made sense to open up both of these sectors to better connect India to the world. Liberalization would have little meaning if India and its people were not linked to the global economy with an efficient means of transport and communication.

In airlines, state-owned carriers were the sole provider of air services since the Nehru government enacted the Air Corporations Act of India, 1953. But since the government had placed restrictions on their expansion, the airlines were highly limited in capacity. So the export promotion policies under Rajiv Gandhi were facing severe hurdles due to poor air services.[27] To overcome the challenge, the government adopted an 'open-sky policy' in April 1990 where air-taxi operators were allowed to operate flights from any airport in India and set their own schedules and fares. East-West Airlines became the first national private airline to operate flights in the country after a span of almost thirty-seven years.[28]

The Narasimha Rao government repealed the Nehru-era law and replaced it with the Air Corporations (Transfer of Undertaking and Repeal) Act, 1994, which formally enabled private players to operate scheduled services of flights. A number of private players made their foray into the market, including Jet Airways, Air Sahara and Modiluft. The aviation sector has grown exponentially since then and, currently, India is the third-largest and the fastest-growing domestic aviation market in the world.[29]

However, the liberalization of the airlines sector was marred with cases of political favouritism. When Ratan Tata was launching his Vistara airlines in 2015, he said that J.R.D. Tata was excited to begin airline operations when the Narasimha Rao government allowed private entry into the sector. 'That never happened . . . The same government that asked us to start an airline . . . made sure that this airline would never happen,' he claimed.[30]

While for satellite television, Rao chose to look the other way, and for aviation he mostly tried to get the government out of the way, for the telecom sector, he actively made an effort to push for reforms. India never had an efficient telephone network. Sam Pitroda had helped increase access to telephony with public call offices (PCOs), but it was a Herculean task to get a phone connection at home or in offices. In fact, by the late eighties, 700,000 people were on the waiting list to get a telephone connection.

When the mobile telephone came into India in the early 1990s, the most pertinent question was if private players should be allowed entry. Rao initially called for bids from private players to provide mobile phone services in four big cities—Bombay, Delhi, Calcutta and Madras. Two companies were licensed in each city and were asked to partner with a foreign firm with telecom experience. But the move got bogged down in legal quagmires created by unsuccessful applicants.[31]

Even while these issues were being ironed out in courts, the government issued a National Telecom Policy in May 1994, which allowed Indian businesses, in minority partnership with foreign firms, the right to bid to provide telecom services across twenty-one geographical circles. However, Rao made the mistake of taking up the suggestion of his telecom minister to impose onerous licensing rules on mobile operators.[32] It would require later governments to ease these norms and unleash the full potential of the sector.

As these major sectors were being liberalized, a similar reform went unnoticed by most of the software industry. But it would turn out to be a policy move that would be widely accepted as the 'poster boy' of the reforms. Until now, like any other part of the economy, the software industry was mired under the same web of bureaucracy that was stifling the rest of the economy.

The business of software exports required the existence of three crucial components: computers, telecommunication and a liberal foreign exchange regime for conducive trade. No aspect of the business came easy before 1991. In a sector as fast-paced as software, overcoming the bureaucratic challenges was excruciatingly frustrating.

Applications for import of machines would take at least nine months to process and, by that time, the manufacturer would have released a newer model. N.R. Narayana Murthy, the founder of Infosys, claims that in the eighteen months between 1981 and 1982, he undertook forty trips to Delhi for such approvals from the Department of Electronics. He also remembers how the shortage of telephones in the eighties left foreign clients dumbfounded at the prospect of doing business with a company without a number to call.[33]

These challenges were overcome by the concept of 'body-shopping', which simply meant sending Indian engineers abroad to work on-site. But even that was fraught with complications. All over the world, the fees for services are paid after the job is completed. But Indian norms required exporters to first bring in dollars and then be allowed to utilize only half of it. So a lot of time was exhausted in getting clearances from the RBI to send software engineers abroad. Moreover, company employees were expected to file travel reports detailing beforehand the places they would visit, and if any changes were made during the trip, the company risked losing clearances.

All of these impediments ceased to be a problem with the economic reforms package of 1991. The Indian software industry was ready to make its mark on the world markets. However, it needs to be highlighted that a series of preconditions had come together over time to contribute to the eventual rise of software firms in India. The story probably began with Nehru's foresight to establish high-quality engineering schools and assertiveness to retain English as the medium of higher education. The former gave India a healthy supply of skilled engineers, while the latter led to the creation of an English-speaking workforce, who could communicate with the rest of the world with ease, unlike their Chinese counterparts.

Also, the location of the country at GMT+5.5 hours provides the fortuitous advantage of 'same-day operations'. As America goes to sleep on the other side of the world, India gets up to work. So, by the time Americans wake up again, the job, which is outsourced to India, is completed. Thus, industries like data-processing and software development were already poised for takeoff and were only awaiting market reforms to free themselves from the shackles of controls that were holding them back.

* * *

Towards the fag end of Rao's term in office, most Indians had come to terms with the idea of liberalization. The critics had quietened down. Rao had survived through it all—politically explosive reforms, divisive countrywide riots, and even three no-confidence motions that were moved against him in Parliament by the Opposition. It was beyond doubt that he was well on his way to complete his full term in office, a first for any minority government in Indian political history. So, he decided to use his secure standing to navigate India into the very depths of the emerging global liberal order at the time.

Since 1948, most of the countries across the world, including India, had been a part of the General Agreement on Tariffs and Trade (GATT), a forum for discussion and negotiations on international trade issues. In the eighth round of negotiations held in Uruguay in 1986, it was decided to extend the trade rules into newer areas that had been previously too difficult to liberalize, like agriculture and textiles, or had been increasingly pertinent over time, like intellectual property rights.

These proved to be the most complex set of terms to negotiate for the world as every party was cautious about not being shortchanged in the deal. The two developed blocks—the United States and the European Union—were constantly fighting on agricultural reform. Meanwhile, India had reservations about including services and intellectual property rights, among other areas, in the negotiations.

Arthur Dunkel, the director general of GATT almost throughout the entire period of negotiations, made tireless efforts to break the deadlock between countries. Since India was still averse to the idea of liberalization, especially sectors like agriculture, he became the subject of a public hate campaign in India that often ended in burning of his effigies on countless occasions.[34] After many delays, the negotiations finally came to an end in December 1993. Five months later, on 15 April 1994, 124 governments signed the deal. Subsequently, as per the agreement, the World Trade Organization (WTO), a global body for resolution of trade disputes, came into existence on 1 January 1995. India was one of the signatories and, thus, became a member of the WTO.

The Opposition was furious. *India Today* noted that 'it would appear that New Delhi had bartered its economic sovereignty to a latter-day East India Company'.[35] But Rao, being more confident of his position than ever, stood his ground. Time would vindicate his stand. The services boom that followed in India owes in large part to the integration of the country into the new trading regime that was established in 1994.

* * *

All of Rao's efforts in his three years in office were beginning to pay off by 1994. Foreign exchange reserves that had touched USD 1 billion in 1991 had soared to USD 13 billion. With the opening up of capital markets, foreign inflows had also followed a similar trend. Between 1993 and 1994, they had exceeded USD 3 billion, which was higher than all the previous investments made since Independence. In the same period, exports also jumped by 20 per cent. Inflation, which had been another cause for concern during the 1991 crisis when it was around 17 per cent, halved to a manageable 8.5 per cent.[36]

The world was also taking note of India's changing economic policies. Coca-Cola, which had left India during the Janata rule, returned in 1994, now that it was not forced to partner with a local firm. Pepsi was already back. So were IBM, General Motors and

Kelloggs'.[37] When Narasimha Rao was about to make a visit to the United States in the summer of 1994, the *New York Times* commented that 'Mr Rao has become, in effect, the Deng Xiaoping of India—an ageing party leader who, in his sunset years, has abandoned many, if not all, of the economic precepts that had guided earlier governments, challenging not only the old orthodoxies but an entrenched network of vested interests that had built up under the old system'.[38]

Rao had decisively moved India far away from the old system. The socialist principles of the Nehruvian era had been finally jettisoned. Such an outcome was hard to imagine even a year before the reform process began. But, with the collapse of the Soviet Union, the last aspirations that were held for a socialist economy died with it. New Delhi was isolated. It became a lone bastion of socialism in a world that was fast moving towards open borders and free markets. It made little sense to be the contrarian.

Rao understood this and made sure India was not left behind from the day he joined office. By the time he signed the deal to make India a member of the WTO, the economy was growing at a comfortable 6.7 per cent. The reforms had begun to pay dividends. The economy would go on to record a growth rate of above 7 per cent for the rest of his term in office.

The reforms also did more than just revive the economy. A less-talked-about contribution of the reform process has been the improvement in government revenues, which left more to spend on welfare schemes. When Rao had joined office, the total receipts (or, income) with the Central government were merely 302 billion rupees (in real terms). These had escalated by 22 per cent by the time he left. This revenue has increased exponentially since then.[39] So, evidently more has been left for welfare schemes.

This was the biggest drawback with all the previous regimes. All the rhetoric of socialism could not match up to the resources that were available to the government. Indira Gandhi's grandiose plans of eradicating poverty were no more than just plans because an economy growing at an average of 3 per cent could not spare much for redistribution.

The most dramatic benefit of the increase in government revenue during Rao's tenure was to the field of education. Rao had previously held the education ministry in Rajiv Gandhi's Cabinet and was aware of its challenges. More importantly, he was conscious of the crucial role that health and education sectors play in a country's development. On a visit to South Korea, he was impressed by how the country's economic growth had occurred alongside an improvement in the well-being of the masses. He remarked to a diplomat accompanying him, 'This is what we have to do. We have to emphasize education and health at home. Look at the way young people are coming up.'[40] Sure enough, the Central government expenditure on education doubled during his term in office.[41]

Of course, Rao could not reform every aspect of the economy. The biggest missing link in the entire reform process was labour. The Indian economy has historically suffered the most because of its rigid labour laws. Manufacturers in India have always found it difficult to hire and fire people, which disincentivizes them from hiring at all. So, firms find it more lucrative to be capital-intensive (reliant on machines) than labour-intensive (reliant on humans).

The nature of the labour laws in India is the leading reason why the country has moved directly from being an agriculture-led economy to a services-led one, bypassing the manufacturing sector, against the typical trend for global economies. It also explains why India could not replicate China's success in becoming the manufacturing hub of the world. So, a lot was lost when Rao refrained from initiating labour reforms. But then again, he held a minority government, and labour laws are a politically sensitive topic for even the most stable governments. That is the only reason the subject has not been touched more than two and a half decades after the economic reforms were introduced.

Nevertheless, Narasimha Rao had played a stellar role in putting India on a new growth trajectory, one whose results became quite evident in the final years of his term in terms of higher growth rates. One would expect such a performance to be rewarded with electoral dividends. With elections a year away, Rao even became populist, from mid-1995, to appease his voters.[42] In his election campaign, he even gave reforms a populist face by linking its impact on the economy with employment.[43]

But the BJP was riding on the Hindu wave. No one had forgotten the Babri issue. When the election results were announced in May, Congress could only manage to scrape together 140 seats, down more than 100 seats from last time. It was the worst result for the party till date. The BJP emerged as the single-largest party with 161 seats. They were far short of a majority, but as per custom the president invited the leader of the BJP, Atal Bihari Vajpayee, to form a government. He was sworn in as the prime minister on 16 May 1996, and was given two weeks to prove his majority in Parliament.

Thus, followed a period of political turmoil and instability, which created an environment that was simply unfavourable for constructive economic policymaking. Vajpayee had to resign after thirteen days in office as he failed to garner the required support in Parliament. Congress, wanting to keep the BJP at bay at all costs, decided to support the thirteen-party United Front, and H.D. Deve Gowda was made the prime minister.

It was an unlikely alliance, with market-oriented centrists, communists and regionalists, all tied together in one shaky coalition. After ten months in power, Congress withdrew its support as Gowda refused to block the BJP from forming a coalition government in Uttar Pradesh.[44] The government was on the verge of falling when Congress agreed to support a new government under Inder Kumar Gujral.

However, the compromise lasted seven months. The Congress wanted Gujral to oust a coalition party that was linked with the assassination of Rajiv Gandhi as per a judicial report published in November 1997.[45] Gujral refused and submitted his resignation after three weeks of acrimonious protests in Parliament. The president accepted his resignation and called for fresh elections in February.

Ultimately, despite all attempts by Congress to keep the BJP out of power, the Atal Bihari Vajpayee–led faction managed to win 182 seats and, combined with its allies, secured a thin majority with 286 members out of 545. The political drama of the late-1990s did not end there. The Vajpayee government lost a no-confidence motion against them in 1999 by a single vote after one of their coalition partners withdrew support. General elections were held again that year after Congress led by Sonia Gandhi, who had taken over as the party president in 1998, failed to garner enough support to form a government. In the end, BJP won the 1999 elections with an equal number of seats as they had won a year ago, but this time, the party would go on to complete its five-year term in office.

In the 1999 elections, Congress were reduced to a historic low of 114 seats. Not even the 1977 elections after the Emergency had sunk the party to such depths. It was clear that the party was losing its hold across the country. The only thing that had initiated this change in the 1990s was the property dispute in the small north Indian town, which had come to dominate the political discourse of the country. It was evident that issues of religious identity had now come to supersede matters of economic development and social reform in Indian politics.

* * *

As India was preparing to step into the new millennium, it was clear that in the last two decades of the twentieth century, apart from Indian politics, the Indian economy would never be the same as well. Since Independence, India's growth had been derisively termed as the 'Hindu rate of growth'. The infamous licence raj, which had become a model of inefficiency and stagnation, was quite evidently beginning to hold it back.

The pro-business reforms of the 1980s sparked a promising uptick in growth rate. Then, the pro-market reforms of the 1990s augmented it further. To be precise, the annual per capita growth rate in income, which was around 1.2 per cent in the period 1972–82, increased to 3 per cent in 1982–92 and 3.9 per cent in 1992–2002.[46] The most significant contributor to this boost in economic growth was the services sector. Throughout the 1990s, the sector grew at an average of slightly over 8 per cent per annum.

The software industry proved to be a major driver of India's services boom. In a span of ten years between 1990 and 2000, it grew at astounding rates of over 50 per cent per annum, expanding from a mere USD 197 million industry to an USD 8,000 million one. By the turn of the century, India had over 340,000 software professionals and was employing 50,000 new recruits each year, on an average.[47]

The services sector was not the only noteworthy arena of reforms. A less remarkable effect was witnessed in the manufacturing sector. As foreign firms found entry into India, a lot of production of international brands was increasingly outsourced to the country. By the beginning of the twenty-first century, Indian garment exporters serviced over twenty top global brands like GAP, Polo and Tommy Hilfiger, earning over USD 3 billion in revenue. Similarly, exports of auto ancillary units to leading car manufacturers like Ford, Hyundai and Benz amounted to about USD 1.5 billion.[48] Such forays were made into other manufacturing sectors as well. This led to a productivity boost in Indian manufacturing and a lowering of commodity prices.

With the opening up of the economy, foreign firms also became more interested in investing in the Indian markets. Between 1992 and 1997, the approved foreign direct investment into the country rose over hundred times, from Rs 500 crore to about Rs 55,000 crore.[49] Some of the most popular investments came from various global consumer brands, ranging from cars manufactured by Ford and Honda, to televisions by Samsung, and mobile phones by Nokia to soft drinks by Pepsi and Coca-Cola. Other multinationals like General Electric and Microsoft even set up research centres in India to develop cutting-edge technology for the global economy.

It can be argued that these effects of reform were only catering to the whims and demands of the Indian middle class without creating any impact on the poorer sections of society that constitute the majority of the masses. But it is now widely accepted that the reform process has brought about an irrefutable decline in absolute and relative poverty. Jagdish Bhagwati and Arvind Panagariya in their seminal work *Why Growth Matters* show how poverty rates were stagnant till 1980, after which they begin to decline and accelerated further after the 1991 reforms. Even the fiercest critics of reforms agree with this assessment.

However, reforms were not an all-encompassing panacea that solved all the ills facing the Indian economy. Even though the reform process pulled the economy out of a rut and accelerated the growth process, its fruits largely failed to percolate down to the countryside. The growth of the agricultural sector was painfully slow in the 1990s and has remained so even after the turn of the century. This is not necessarily a problem of the reform process but, in fact, the utter lack of it within the sector.

This was the state of the economy five decades after Independence. India was well on its way to becoming the services hub of the world. Manufacturing activity across the country was picking up in the face of foreign investment and competition. And agriculture was in a typical status quo with the memories of the Green Revolution just an aberration of the past. India had also just emerged largely unscathed from the Asian financial crisis that had gripped most of East Asia at the time. In the politically tumultuous years between 1996 and 1998, the country had also become the fourth-largest economy in the world. The promise and hopes presented by a newly emerging Third World that was just coming to terms with capitalism were immense. But even the optimists could not have foreseen the growth spurt that was to come next.

CHAPTER 17

CLASH OF IDEOLOGIES

India's entry into the twenty-first century was marked by a rare sense of confidence and enthusiasm. But it was not only the country's improving economic performance that was fuelling this sense of optimism. A series of developments after Rao left office, which involved India becoming a nuclear state and then emerging victorious in a war with Pakistan, further reinforced these feelings.

India had first conducted nuclear tests in 1974 when Indira Gandhi was in power. But the government had gone to great lengths to argue that the tests were conducted for peaceful civilian energy purposes. This argument seemed plausible since India had no capabilities to deliver the unwieldy bomb to enemy targets using a missile or an aircraft. Adopting such a stance was necessary for India because any indications of hostile intent would have resulted in heavy global sanctions, which the economy could not have survived at the time.

But a team of scientists kept working on a discreet nuclear programme to build a smaller bomb that could be launched using a missile or a plane. After numerous delays due to political and economic instability, India was ready to undertake nuclear tests for such a bomb by December 1995. But since the CIA had suspicions about the plans, Rao had decided to postpone them until after the elections, which he eventually lost.[1] The tests again came close to fruition when the BJP formed a short-lived government for thirteen days. But when Vajpayee realized that the government would not survive long enough to deal with its aftermath, he called them off.

Two years later, in March 1998, when the BJP returned with a stronger mandate, Vajpayee wasted no time in initiating the test authorizations. In the early morning hours of 1 May 1998, four army trucks left the Bhabha Atomic Research Centre (BARC) complex in Mumbai with nuclear devices. They were flown to Jaisalmer airport at dawn where the explosive devices were again transferred to a convoy of four trucks and taken into the desert city of Pokhran, all in utmost secrecy.

To the world's surprise, India exploded five nuclear devices between 11 and 13 May. Vajpayee soon declared in an interview:

> India is now a nuclear weapons state. We have the capacity for a big bomb now, for which a necessary command-and-control system is also in place. Ours will never be weapons of aggression.[2]

The 'big bomb' that Vajpayee was referring to was a 'thermo-nuclear device' in technical terms, which had an explosive power that was many times that of the atomic bombs dropped on Japan in 1945. With the tests, India was now a part of the exclusive club of the five nuclear-powered states: United States, Russia, United Kingdom, France and China. The rest of the world was furious. The United States cut off all aid to India except for humanitarian assistance. Japan did the same.[3]

Not everyone in India was elated at India's nuclear weaponization as well. N. Ram, the formidable editor of the *Hindu*, argued that after the BJP government came into power they have managed to 'hijack India's independent and peace-oriented nuclear policy and twist it perilously out of shape' with no regard to 'both the consequences for the region and the basic interests of the Indian people'.[4]

The real threat from these tests, it was believed, was to the economy. As India suffered cutbacks in aid from other countries and multilateral institutions like the World Bank and the IMF, investor confidence took a major hit. The international credit ratings agency, Standard and Poor, downgraded its outlook on India in its first review after the Pokhran tests. Indian stock markets immediately dipped, and the rupee plummeted to historic lows.[5]

Since India was adopting a belligerent stance, international investors were finding it hard to see it as a promising destination any more. These fears were kindled even further when Pakistan successfully conducted its own nuclear tests in the same month as India. The Indian subcontinent was quickly turning into the most volatile region in the world, which was not promising for international capital that is fickle in the best of times. However, in hindsight, most of these fears came to naught in the long run, mostly because the interests of foreign businesses, especially American, were now too tied up with the well-being of Indian markets.

In a bid to return to geopolitical normality, Atal Bihari Vajpayee made an unexpected diplomatic gesture. On 20 February 1999, he took a delegation across the Pakistan border on a bus that was coming from Delhi and bound for Lahore. Pakistani Prime Minister Nawaz Sharif himself received his Indian counterpart on the other side of the border. Both shook hands and engaged in a warm embrace as crowds on both sides of the border cheered.

The deteriorating relationships between the two sides since the Pokhran tests were somewhat beginning to thaw. A Lahore Declaration was also signed that promised bilateral consultation between the two countries on nuclear issues. These were promising signs for the concerned global community, but it remained to be seen whether the bus diplomacy would merely be symbolic in nature or evolve into a stronger bond of friendship between the two nations.

The verdict was out in a few months. Soon after the Vajpayee government lost the no-confidence motion by a single vote in April 1999, reports of intrusion from Pakistan began emerging from the Kargil district of Jammu and Kashmir. An Indian Army patrol was sent to assess the situation, which ended in five soldiers being captured and tortured to death. After a few days, the infiltration began in other sectors of Kargil as well. The Indian side claimed that the infiltrators were Pakistani troops disguised as Kashmiri militants, while Pakistan insisted, despite widespread disbelief, that the men were Kashmiri freedom fighters who were not acting at their behest.[6]

By 10 May, the Indian Army had moved its troops from Kashmir to Kargil and, two weeks later, the Indian Air Force had also joined in to fight the infiltrators. Soon a full-scale war had broken out, as Pakistan stepped up its attack. At the height of the conflict, the Indian intelligence agencies intercepted and released a telephonic conversation between then Pakistan Army Chief General Pervez Musharraf and Chief of General Staff Lt Gen. Aziz Khan about how the former had kept the Pakistan Air Force and Navy chiefs in the dark about the attack. The tape vindicated India's claims about the involvement of the Pakistani establishment.[7]

As a concerned world tensely watched two nuclear powers engage in conflict, US President Bill Clinton called Nawaz Sharif to ask him to pull out his men from Kargil. However, by the end of June, the Indian counterattack itself began yielding successes and Pakistan had to withdraw its forces behind the Line of Control (LoC). The withdrawal was complete by 26 July 1999. Atal Bihari Vajpayee announced that the operation to clear the Kargil sector, codenamed Operation Vijay, was a success.

India had fought three larger battles with Pakistan before Kargil: in 1947, 1965 and 1971. But Kargil was the first televised war in Indian history and the entire nation was gripped by its live coverage. More than 1 in 3 Indians owned a television set during the Kargil war as compared to less than 1 in 200 in 1971. So, naturally the country, which was increasingly witnessing growing divisions along caste and religious lines, underwent a renewed sense of unity during the war. And when the dust settled in Kargil, there was an unmistakable sense of pride in India's advancing strengths.

So, as India entered the new millennium, it carried with itself the hopes of a growing economy, the confidence of a nuclear nation, and the pride of regional dominance. The country only needed someone to carry on what Rao had started, and preferably improve upon it, to put India on a higher growth trajectory. Vajpayee was an unlikely fit for the job. But to do the needful he had to first strike a fine balance between what his party wanted and what the economy needed. This struggle of ideologies defined Vajpayee's time in office right from his first short stint.

* * *

The organizational structure of the BJP is quite unlike other political parties in existence. Since the party had originated from a movement of Hindu revival propagated by the RSS since Independence and supported by its sister organizations, the VHP and the Bajrang Dal (together known as the Sangh Parivar), there is always an inherent conflict in setting a political agenda and appeasing its parent body. There is no other precedent in independent India, or in any other democracy for that matter, where a ruling party recognizes the ideological authority of a cultural organization that has no political accountability. Vajpayee faced the complex task of balancing the interests of the BJP and the RSS, while at the same time taking into account the demands of his coalition partners in the NDA government.

The economic situation that Vajpayee had inherited was not conducive to reforms. Since Rao had slowed down the process of reforms in his final years owing to electoral compulsions and as the Indian political scene had become extremely unstable after his loss, the economy had taken a hit. The economic growth had slowed down, the industrial sector was in crisis, the Asian financial crisis brewing mainly in the East was threatening the subcontinent, and a newly formed government that lacked in experience had complicated things by going through with a series of nuclear tests that had resulted in economic sanctions which it could ill afford.

During such challenging times, it seemed impossible for any government to have any more political appetite for reforms. And everyone generally expected the NDA government to be more protectionist in nature. Yet Vajpayee made clear at several instances during his tenure that he favoured reforms as the path to higher growth. For instance, during his visit to the United States in 2000, he acknowledged the crucial role played by foreign direct investment (FDI) in India's economic development since it opened up.[8] This often put him at odds with the RSS, which favoured the idea of private enterprises but was opposed to the prospect of globalization as it hurt domestic enterprises.

The RSS had vehemently criticized India's membership in the WTO when the Narasimha Rao government had initiated it, arguing that it would impose unmanageable competition on domestic firms and would go against the swadeshi principles of economic self-reliance. The concept of swadeshi was considered to be an integral part of the economic philosophy that the RSS propagated and an essential means to protect Indian culture from foreign influence. Globalization was, thus, perceived as just another foreign invasion of the country by multinationals.

So, the BJP election manifesto even in 1998 declared the adoption of a 'carefully calibrated approach' to globalization.[9] The phrase was an attempt to satisfy both the RSS, which was suspicious of party members being too influenced by ideas of liberalization, and foreign investors who were worried that the process of reforms would be reversed.

But the conflict of ideas became problematic when it came to actual implementation. Reality could not be enshrouded under a veil of phraseology. The first budget that the Vajpayee government introduced after coming into power in 1998 introduced import duties across the board to provide interim protection to domestic manufacturers from foreign competition. The NDA government also adopted a National Agenda for Governance, which promised to 'continue with the reform process [and] give it a strong swadeshi thrust to ensure that the national economy grows on the principle that "India shall be built by Indians"'.[10] This expectedly spooked foreign investors who felt that India was abandoning the government policies of the Narasimha Rao government.

When the budget received a negative reaction from the international business community, Vajpayee decided to take personal control over the government's economic policy. He set up two pro-reform advisory councils and took a number of steps to open up the economy. Even before the government collapsed in 1998, he had moved proposals to open up the insurance sector, which Rao had failed to do, and amend the Patent Act as per the agreements with the WTO. The RSS, realizing that the government had completely deviated from its swadeshi principles, bitterly opposed the moves and even observed a 'warning day' (*Chetavani Diwas*) on 18 January 1999.[11]

After the 1999 elections, the balancing act continued as FDI in the insurance sector was limited to 26 per cent and the changes in patent law postponed to 2005, which was the deadline agreed under the WTO agreement. Simultaneously, other sectors like banking, telecom, pharmaceuticals, civil aviation and real estate were opened up to foreign investors. Also, all quantitative restrictions on imports were eliminated by 2002. But these were replaced with a system of tariffs to provide protection to domestic industries and, more importantly, keep the RSS ideologues at ease.

Yashwant Sinha, the finance minister in the Vajpayee government, who introduced the first swadeshi budget, went on to be more liberal in his subsequent budgets and policies. Over the years, he initiated a litany of major reforms like the initiation of the value-added tax regime, dismantling of administered price structure for fertilizers and petroleum products, extension of capital market reforms that Rao had missed, reduction in government equity in public sector banks and reduction in the size of the bureaucracy. However, some of these ideas were too bold for their time and failed to take off. For instance, the change in pricing mechanism of petroleum products proved unsuccessful due to half-hearted implementation, and the move to reduce state control of public sector banks did not even pass through Parliament.[12]

An important step towards reducing state control that was successfully taken up by the Vajpayee government was to set up a separate ministry of disinvestment in 1999. The department soon announced a plan to reduce the government's stake to 26 per cent in 210 publicly owned enterprises and use the resources gained to reduce fiscal deficit and increase spending on infrastructure and social services.

The spate of privatizations that followed sparked intense controversies. Labour unions were particularly unimpressed. The RSS launched scathing attacks against the government. Its publications *Organiser* and *Panchjanya* carried a series of articles in a 2002 issue which particularly criticized the government's move to sell the assets of Videsh Sanchar Nigam Ltd (VSNL), the government's monopoly over international telephony, to the Tatas and the sale of Indian Petrochemicals Corporation Ltd (IPCL), a profit-making state-owned oil company, to Reliance. The lead article lamented that these sales have 'confirmed the worst fears of privatization'.[13]

By this time, Vajpayee did not have enough political capital to ignore such attacks. The support of the RSS was necessary for the grass-roots support that it could garner. The BJP also began to lose a series of state assembly elections. Beginning from 2000, it failed to put up a strong performance in large states like Orissa, Bihar, Haryana, Tamil Nadu and West Bengal. This was seen as a worrisome precedent for the party's aspirations at the national level.

The ultimate test, however, was based on the electoral outcome of the 2002 Uttar pradesh elections. Since Uttar Pradesh commands the largest chunk of parliamentary seats among all Indian states, elections are won and lost from the state. Moreover, since the Babri Masjid issue, BJP had gained considerable political dominance over the state. But, in 2002, the party declined to third place, losing to the emerging Samajwadi Party and Bahujan Samaj Party, which targeted lower and backward castes in the state. The defeat in the UP elections, coming on top of similar setbacks in other states, allowed those critical of Vajpayee's policies within the party to argue for higher consultation of the government with the BJP leadership and the RSS.

Even before the streak of electoral defeats, a couple of corruption scandals involving the prime minister's closest advisers damaged his credibility. In March 2001, the *Tehelka* website released a video of Bengaru Laxman, the BJP President at the time, along with George Fernandes, the defence minister, and other key members of the NDA accepting bribes from reporters who were posing as arms dealers of a fictitious company. Both Laxman and Fernandes immediately resigned.[14] In response, the RSS leadership pressed for more regular meetings with Vajpayee and Advani and appointment of more RSS workers as full-time party workers.[15]

In July 2002, Advani, who was closer to the RSS leadership, was elevated to the position of deputy prime minister. The finance minister, Yashwant Sinha, who was accused of implementing budgets that were 'anti-people', was also removed. Jaswant Singh was appointed in his place instead. Even N.K. Singh, the pro-reform secretary of the prime minister, was transferred to the Planning Commission. It was clear to Vajpayee that he could not afford to push the reform agenda strongly any longer.[16]

Also, there was little to support the reform process in economic terms. When Jaswant Singh took over the finance ministry, the economy was in a shambles. Since 1999, the country had averaged a growth rate of 5 per cent and the fiscal deficit had also worsened every year, reaching 5.9 per cent in 2002–03.[17] Meanwhile, an unstable geopolitical situation due to consistent confrontation with Pakistan made oil prices and exchange rates heavily volatile. International investors were also spooked by the Gujarat riots in 2002 that had swept across the state after the infamous Godhra incident. While economic sentiments were already low that year, the worst drought in fifteen years worsened growth prospects even more.

Surprisingly, Jaswant Singh turned out to be more reformist than the RSS would have wanted. In his first budget, he removed more industries off the list that were reserved for small industries, allowed foreigners to own majority stakes in banks and lowered government-set interest rates on 'small savings' deposits, which reduced the subsidy paid on them.

These were not big-bang reforms, but they maintained a spirit of continuity in India's reform process. He also did not do much to rein in India's escalating fiscal deficit but was instrumental in pushing through the Fiscal Responsibility and Budget Management Act, 2003, which Yashwant Sinha had been working on during his time in office. The Act was an effort to encourage Central and state governments to commit to predefined fiscal targets and institutionalize a system of fiscal discipline.

Luckily for Singh, 2003 was a year when monsoons were finally good and agricultural production shot up, which pushed the growth rate of the economy to almost 8 per cent. Global economic demand was also beginning to pick up around 2003. Inflation dropped to new lows and foreign exchange reserves rose. This was just the beginning of the fastest growth phase that India would enter in its history. But more on that later.

In all, the Vajpayee government never reversed the reform process that Rao began as many had feared they would when they first came into office. The process of reform, albeit incremental in some respects, was carried on despite vehement opposition from within the party organization. Also, unlike Rao, as Panagariya states, 'Vajpayee openly and forcefully advocated reforms. With the notable exceptions of higher education and labour, he made progress in virtually all policy areas during his six-year rule.'[18]

A more resounding legacy of the Vajpayee era came in the telecom sector. Even though the duo of Rajiv Gandhi and Sam Pitroda are credited with sparking the telecom revolution in India, their efforts did not materialize in the form of telecom penetration. In the decade since Rajiv Gandhi left office in 1989, teledensity across India marginally rose from 0.6 per cent to 2.8 per cent in 1999.[19]

As soon as Vajpayee joined office in 1998, he appointed the National Task Force on Information Technology and Software Development, which was headed by Jaswant Singh and included N.R. Narayana Murthy of Infosys and Azim Premji of Wipro. The task force called for a complete overhaul of India's telecom policy. It resulted in the New Telecom Policy (NTP) of 1999, which improved upon the telecom policy introduced by Narasimha Rao in 1994.

Most importantly, licensing norms were altered to make it more lucrative for private players to enter the market. In the same year, the government also made a separation between policy formulation and service provision, which led to the creation of Bharat Sanchar Nigam Limited (BSNL) in 2000. This move freed the telecom sector from political control. Later, the government also effected favourable fiscal changes like reducing import duties on mobile devices.

All of these reform initiatives in the telecom sector sparked the success story of the industry in the next decade. Against a target of teledensity of 15 per cent by 2010 in the NTP 1999, more than half the population of India was connected to a telecom device by the time.

Most recent estimates show a teledensity of almost 90 per cent.[20] The astounding growth of the Indian telecom industry, and especially mobile telephony, is a shining testament to how political clarity and focused reform can deliver favourable outcomes.

Vajpayee would also be popularly known for his large-scale infrastructure projects, something that Rao had overlooked. Two of his most memorable achievements on this front were the Golden Quadrilateral, a network of highways connecting four capital cities of India located in four different corners, and the Pradhanmantri Gramin Sadak Yojna, an initiative to build a network of all-weather roads for unconnected villages across the country.[21]

There were some noteworthy initiatives on the social front as well. Sarva Shiksha Abhiyan, a scheme to provide universal access to primary education for children aged 6–14, was introduced in 2001. Although the programme was a promising step to address the poor basic education levels across the country, it has failed to be truly universal up until now due to high dropout rates and poor resource management.

* * *

The Vajpayee government, much like the Rao government, also had a troubling legacy of communal rioting. As described earlier, kar sevaks returning to Gujarat from Ayodhya on 27 February 2002, got into an altercation with Muslim vendors at Godhra station, which ended in a train coach catching fire as soon as it left the station for reasons that are still debatable. As the news of the deaths of fifty-eight people on the train spread, a wave of retributory violence spread across Gujarat. Different estimates put the number of deaths arising from the bloody violence that followed anywhere between 1,000 to over 2,000.[22]

The role of the administration has often been questioned in quelling the violence that raged across the state unchecked and for quite a prolonged period. Just like in Uttar Pradesh in 1992, the BJP government was in power in Gujarat in 2002. Narendra Modi, the future prime minister of the country, had been appointed as the chief minister of Gujarat a few months ago. He attributed the time taken to curb the violence to the resource limitations and the outnumbered police force in the state.[23]

Nevertheless, calls for Modi's dismissal grew loud, but Vajpayee chose to ignore them. He also chose to visit Gujarat after a month and, later, when he spoke at the BJP National Executive Committee meeting in Goa in April, he pinned the blame for the riots on the Godhra incident. He rejected all accusations that India's secular fabric was under any threat. The nation was shocked at his stance. But it must be noted that by this time Vajpayee had lost all political appetite to go against the stance of the Sangh Parivar. With the 2004 general elections so close, he needed the support of the RSS to sustain in the government.[24]

But as the elections drew close, Vajpayee insisted that Godhra and the subsequent communal issues should not be used as election issues. Instead, the BJP should contest the elections on more pertinent issues of development and good governance.[25] This proved to be a successful approach in the 2003 state assembly elections of Rajasthan, Madhya Pradesh and Chhattisgarh, which had been under Congress rule until then.

The success of the BJP in state assembly polls in 2003 prompted the party to call for elections slightly early in April–May 2004. India was doing well economically, and it was widely believed that the voters held a favourable view of the Vajpayee government. Building on the development agenda, the BJP launched its 'India Shining' campaign, which symbolized the overall feeling of optimism across the country. Everyone expected a triumph of the NDA riding on the 'Atal wave'.[26]

The Congress campaign on its part was led by Sonia Gandhi, the widow of Rajiv Gandhi, who ferociously challenged the performance of the prime minister and the NDA government. She criticized the government for failing to provide jobs to the youth, neglecting the poor and creating a crisis in agriculture. She travelled across the country and tried connecting with the masses using the campaign slogan 'Congress *ka haath, aam aadmi ke saath*' (The hand of the

Congress is with the common man). This was a careful dig at the BJP's India Shining campaign that seemed to target only an affluent minority.

But no one expected what came next.

The upset of the election results stunned the country. The BJP managed to win only 138 seats, a significant drop from its 182-seat win in 1999. The setback to the NDA government as a whole was even more stunning. The coalition lost more than 100 seats, falling from 298 in the previous elections to a mere 186. The Congress, by contrast, emerged as the single-largest party with 145 seats. Combined with its pre-election allies, it accounted for a total of 216 seats. This was still far from the majority mark, but the left parties, which reached an all-time high of 60 seats, offered their support to form the Congress-led coalition, the United Progressive Alliance (UPA).

CHAPTER 18

TOO MUCH OF A GOOD THING

The UPA government inherited an economy that was in better shape than it had ever been since Independence. After more than a decade of reforms, the last year of the NDA rule had shown the first signs of an economic breakthrough with the GDP growth rate almost touching 8 per cent after a prolonged period of slowdown. Exports were growing at a robust 20 per cent; foreign exchange reserves were at a comfortable level north of a USD 100 billion; food stocks were bountiful; and a low-inflation, low-interest regime was prevalent. Portfolio investments were pouring into India. The country was beginning to make its mark on the global information technology markets. New lines of exports were also opening up in the automobile and pharmaceutical sectors. Confidence in the Indian economy had never been better.[1]

The new government's own Economic Survey reflected this sentiment. As the 2003–04 document stated, 'The economy appears to be in a resilient mode in terms of growth, inflation and balance of payments, a combination that offers large scope for consolidation of the growth momentum with continued macroeconomic stability.'[2] It can be safely said that no previous government had passed on an economy to a successor government in better circumstances. It is, therefore, curious as to why NDA lost the election in the first place.

There was also no disconnect between what the NDA had achieved during its term and what the voters perceived. Political scientist Yogendra Yadav wrote soon after the 2004 elections, based on recently surveyed data: 'If there was one thing that was not working against the ruling NDA, it was the popular perception of its governance and leadership . . . The level of satisfaction with the working of the NDA government at the Centre was easily one of the most positive assessments of any government at the end of its full term.'[3]

The inevitability of a win due to these factors might have led to a complacency in building strong coalition partners across states. But, since India is a particularly large heterogeneous country, the states have their individual social structure that often does not cross boundaries. As a result, most states have developed dominant regional parties over time that had greater appeal among the regional population. So, to perform well at a national level, it is necessary to form alliances with these dominant parties. In 2004, the Congress proved more adept at doing so than the BJP-led NDA. This became especially evident in the state of Tamil Nadu where the DMK, which had earlier been alienated by the BJP, went on to win all 39 seats of the state and joined the UPA.

The electoral dynamics played a decisive role in defining the subsequent path that the Congress-led UPA went on to follow in its entire term, which would last for a decade. In a historical perspective, adopting bold reforms had not yielded high electoral gains. Both Rao and Vajpayee had paid a heavy price for being reformist. So, between productive reform and a strategy of redistribution, Congress chose the latter and termed it 'economic reforms with a human face'.[4]

The Congress had adopted such a stance right from the election campaign where they had criticized Vajpayee's 'India Shining' slogan for being too disassociated from the masses. On the contrary, they claimed to stand for the masses. Moreover, electoral compulsions had also forced their hand to pump the brakes on the reform process. In a bid to get a majority in Parliament, the Congress had to enter into an alliance with the Left, which included the Communist Party of India (CPI) and the Communist Party of India (Marxist). The Left had been staunch critics of India's reforms since 1991. So, adopting a distributive strategy for government policy was the logical choice.

There was another reason for adopting a strategy that would appeal to the lower sections of the society. Since Congress was always an all-encompassing body, having grown out of the freedom struggle, it was finding it difficult to cope with recent political changes where emerging parties like the BJP had captured new social blocs. So, Congress opted to target the poor and marginal communities, including Dalits and Muslims, which formed a major part of the general population. Understandably, the party chose a strategy that favoured this section of society where economic and social programmes were especially designed around their needs and demands. This approach was not flawed in itself but it came at the cost of continued reforms. In fact, the reform process would come to a stand-still for the entire term of the UPA with damning outcomes in the long run.

* * *

In an ironic twist of fate, the party which had so forcefully introduced reforms in 1991 was now hesitant to carry them forward. The irony grew even stronger when the man called upon to lead the government was a man who had played an instrumental role as the finance minister under Narasimha Rao, Dr Manmohan Singh. The Congress President, Sonia Gandhi, who had led the party to victory, should have logically taken the role of prime minister. However, she chose to place Singh in the office instead, since her Italian origins had already created a lot of unnecessary clamour in the opposition camp during the election campaign.

Singh was a career economist. He did not have a political base of his own, nor had he ever won a legislative seat through direct elections. He had been elevated to the highest office in the country by sheer happenstance. But, the locus of power still lay with Sonia Gandhi. Singh's former media adviser, Sanjay Baru, brings out this queer arrangement in his remarkable account on the political relationship of the duo. While Singh held the formal authority, Gandhi commanded the effective power of the office without being politically accountable.[5]

Mrs Gandhi set up a National Advisory Council (NAC) to maintain her say in matters of public policy. The body was integrated into the government structure in the formulation of social and economic policy and, in some cases, even rivalled the functions of the Cabinet and the Planning Commission. It consisted of social activists and technocrats who advised in the development of entitlement programmes for the poorer sections of society. Above anything else, the body ensured that Sonia Gandhi reigned supreme in the decade-long UPA rule. She was the chairperson of the NAC in addition to being the chairperson of UPA and the president of the Congress party.

The NAC was responsible for drafting all the key legislations passed by both UPA governments. A commendable aspect of UPA's redistributive policies have been the rights-based approach that was adopted in implementing them. Most of the major developmental initiatives have been made legally binding as rights of the people, which has ensured their longevity beyond the UPA rule.

One of the first such rights-based policy is the National Rural Employment Guarantee Act (NREGA) of 2005, which was launched as early as February 2006. The idea was to provide an adult from every household a legal guarantee of at least 100 days of employment in a financial year to do unskilled manual work. This provides an individual not only the right to work on demand but also a right to a minimum wage, timely payment and workplace safety.

It was the largest public works programme in the world throughout the UPA rule, providing social security to almost 182 million people by 2014, about 15 per cent of the Indian population.[6] Several studies also point to the fact that rural wages and female workforce participation have unmistakably gone up after the implementation of the programme.[7]

But to the critics, the programme was too expensive and unproductive in nature, which only distorted labour markets by artificially raising the wages for labour and contributed to inflation in the economy. It was also accused of being ridden with corruption and leakages. Economists like Jagdish Bhagwati and Arvind Panagariya argue that the programme was a hallmark of inefficiency where five rupees needed to be spent to transfer one rupee to NREGA workers.[8]

The problem of leakage in government schemes was not something new. As a matter of fact, Rajiv Gandhi had famously stated, 'Out of Rs 100 crore allocated to an anti-poverty project, I know that only Rs 15 crore reaches the people. The remainder is gobbled up by middlemen, power brokers, contractors and the corrupt.'[9] But that is where the problem in the policy of 'reforms with a human face' lay. For the common man, the face of the government is the average official encountered in daily lives, whether it be the electricity linesman or the local banker. When no action was taken to make them more responsive than before, the distributive policies, even though well-intentioned, were bound to be less effective than their potential.

The other major rights-based economic policy initiatives pushed through by the NAC were the Right to Education (RTE) Act and the Right to Food Act. The RTE Act passed in 2009 made it the responsibility of the state to ensure that every child in the age group of 6 to 14 gets at least eight years of education. Again, this was a game-changer as it put the onus of providing education on the state, and primary education had long evaded the focus of public policy in India. But issues of implementation have consistently plagued the Act.

Even though universal enrolment has been achieved, high levels of school dropouts have been an unfortunate reality as critical requirements like adequate teachers and basic infrastructure are lacking. The Education Department data shows that even by 2015–16, around 33 per cent of schools around the country did not have adequate number of teachers.[10]

It also turns out that the students are mainly drawn by the allure of the mid-day meal schemes in schools, but there is very little learning. Each year the findings of the Annual Survey of Education Report (ASER) released by an NGO, Pratham, provide for immense shock value at the scale of learning in India. In 2015, five years after the beginning of the RTE programme, when the first cohort of children would have reached class V, it revealed that less than half of those children could read a class II text.[11]

While RTE makes education a basic right for Indian citizens, the Right to Food Act makes food security a legal entitlement as well. The flagship programme of the UPA government that was made into a law in 2013 aims to provide foodgrains to approximately two-thirds of the Indian population at a drastically subsidized rate. The criticism of the Act again lies in the financial burden that it imposed on the government. There have been various estimates of the government spending on the programme, all of which turn out to be higher than 1 per cent of India's GDP.[12] As the Act was pushed through towards the end of UPA's second term in office, when things were going rapidly downhill for them, it was also accused of being politically motivated to a large extent.

All of these programmes of the Congress were intended to advance the idea of 'inclusiveness' or 'inclusive growth', a term that had been popularly used as the maxim for the entirety of the UPA rule. The government was of the view that 'economic growth has failed to be sufficiently inclusive, particularly after the mid-1990s'. The aim was, therefore, to 'restructure policies to achieve a new vision based on faster, more broad-based inclusive growth'.[13]

India was hardly alone in striving towards inclusivity. Although different countries used different terms, like 'harmonious growth' in China and 'sufficiency philosophy' in Thailand, the reason for the approach was the same—high growth had not distributed the benefits of growth equitably and large parts of the population were poor and vulnerable.[14]

India's strategy for inclusive growth as per the Eleventh Five-Year Plan was one that 'aims at achieving a particular type of growth process which will meet the objectives of inclusiveness and sustainability' and 'not just a conventional strategy for growth to which some elements aimed at inclusion have been added'.[15] It is hard to argue that the UPA went on to adopt such an innovative strategy of inclusive growth.

Instead, all of the major initiatives introduced by the government during the period were attempts at short-term income redistribution that did little to make the intended beneficiaries more productive, which needs to be the aim of inclusive growth strategies. On the contrary, these schemes burdened the government on the fiscal front, which eventually contributed to high inflationary tendencies that brought more harm to the ones who were supposed to benefit from them.

* * *

The entry of the UPA government into office coincided with the period of fastest growth in Indian economic history. In the period between 2003-04, a year before UPA was voted into power, and 2007-08, the year of the worst global financial crisis after the Great Depression, India entered a dream run, growing at an average of 9 per cent annually—one of the highest in the world in the period, just behind China. Poverty rates were falling, and urbanization was accelerating. Briefly, it even seemed that India would surpass China's growth rate.

'It was a strange experience for us. Never since Independence did we have the problem of plenty,' Y.V. Reddy, the former Reserve Bank head commented. 'That is the time when my fellow economists began to mention double-digit growth. I used the word "over-heating".'[16] And the Indian economy was, in fact, over-heating. The high growth of the economy had little to do with the policies of UPA itself but was driven largely by a world economy on steroids in the years preceding the 2008 financial crisis.[17] The fortuitous turn of events, however, proved to be a blessing for the government as it could pursue its distributive strategy without restraint as public revenue soared due to the growth acceleration.

Unfortunately, there was a virtual absence of reforms during these years as the government fell into a sense of complacency as if the growth rate was a given. Eminent economist Shankar Acharya ominously commented in 2008, 'Not many reforms occurred in 2004–08, for which we will pay the price in future. Indeed, reform thrusts were rolled back in some areas, such as privatization, oil pricing, tax policy and interest rate controls.'[18]

The only promising effort on the part of the UPA government was probably in bringing down the fiscal deficit, which almost halved from 4.5 per cent of GDP in 2003-04 to just above 3 per cent in 2007-08. This helped fuel a savings and investment boom in the period. But, as the second term of UPA began, it became clear that even the narrowing of the fiscal deficit had less to do with the fiscal responsibility of the government than the unprecedented growth phase that the economy experienced, which allowed for higher public revenue. Columnist Harish Damodaran commented, 'The lowering of deficits . . . was simply a result of revenue buoyancy from growth, not rediscovery of the virtues of belt-tightening by a morally upright administration.'[19]

Contrary to belt-tightening, the government increased its expenditure well beyond its means throughout its tenure. Higher government expenditure is not necessarily a bad thing as long as it is devoted to productive activities. But in the UPA government, government subsidies for food, fertilizer and fuel saw a notable boost. These subsidies were also not entirely for the benefit of the poor. The benefits from fuel subsidies, for instance, mainly accrue to the middle class and the rich. In the election year of 2008-09 alone, India's subsidy bill ballooned by over 80 per cent from the previous year.[20]

As the global economy slowed after the 2008 crisis, the government managed to keep India's growth rate buoyant for two more years by expanding public expenditure. The FRBM (Fiscal Responsibility and Budget Management) limit of keeping the fiscal deficit below 3 per cent by 2008 was momentarily postponed. But the fiscal deficit soon began widening to unmanageable levels and the stimuli had to be tapered off by 2012. The growth rate soon faltered, which further worsened the fiscal situation.

Thus, the growth acceleration was financially enabling for the government, and it was the only factor preventing fiscal deterioration despite its costly policies of redistribution and inclusivity. As soon as the growth slowed, the mirage of fiscal consolidation ended. Due to high levels of public spending, the fiscal deficit never dipped below 3 per cent in both terms of the UPA.

While liquidity in the economy increased due to such high public expenditure financed by borrowings, inflation also rose to unprecedented double-digit levels. In fact, the second term of the UPA was the most prolonged inflationary episode since Independence.[21] During the bout of high inflation, food prices skyrocketed, which hurt the poor the most, the very segment of population that the UPA was aiming to uplift. Thus, the aim of social inclusion was thwarted at the altar of poor macroeconomic management.

Meanwhile, the slowdown in economic activity was being worsened by a numbing policy paralysis in the government. Issues of land acquisition and environmental clearances had stalled investment activity across the country. As the UPA entered the final years of its second term, the economic growth rate had sunk to below 5 per cent, its lowest in over a decade. The government estimated that in 2013 about 215 projects worth Rs 7 trillion awaited various clearances, while 127 new projects worth Rs 3.5 trillion were also in limbo.[22]

A part of the policy paralysis stemmed from an explosion in rent-seeking under the UPA government. The unusual arrangement between Sonia Gandhi and Manmohan Singh, where the locus of political power rested with the former while the latter only held the formal authority of the office, had far-reaching repercussions that affected the functioning of the government. Since almost all ministers owed their office to their loyalty to Sonia Gandhi rather than the prime minister, they hardly worked together as a team with him and, instead, ran their ministries as independent fiefdoms, at times even against his wishes.[23]

This arrangement allowed ministers in the UPA to indulge in rent-seeking on an unprecedented scale. Corruption and bribery were not new to India. They had been a part of Indian society in colonial times as well as during the socialist regime in the form of the 'licence and permit raj'. There was some relief from bribery after liberalization in areas like obtaining a telephone connection or making railway bookings. But the nature and scale of corruption has evolved substantially since then. Between the liberalization of 1991 and the time the UPA left office in 2014, the economy expanded from

USD 274 billion to over USD 2 trillion. Amidst such an explosion of economic growth, new avenues for corruption opened up and their sheer scale was simply astounding.

A few noteworthy cases of corruption, all of which came undone in the second term of the UPA, were the allocation of the 2G telecom spectrum, coal mines and the contracts for the 2010 Commonwealth Games. In the first case, the telecom minister, A. Raja, was accused of manipulating the decision-making process in the allocation of 2G spectrum to favour certain companies instead of using a transparent auction mechanism. According to the Comptroller and Auditor General (CAG) of India, this caused the Indian government a presumptive loss of somewhere between Rs 580 billion to Rs 1.76 trillion, while admitting that it was impossible to determine an exact loss to the exchequer.[24] However, a special court acquitted everyone accused in the scam in December 2017 due to the failure of the prosecution to prove the charges beyond reasonable doubt. As of 2018, the verdict stands challenged in the Delhi High Court.

In the coal mining scam, popularly known as 'Coalgate', a similar discretionary decision-making mechanism was used by the government to allocate coal mines to companies for a period of eight years instead of a transparent auction process. According to the CAG, the total losses to the government were approximately Rs 1.86 trillion based on the coal prices that existed in the year of allocation.[25] Similarly, when the 2010 Commonwealth Games took place in India, the government was accused of handing out bloated contracts to private companies for purchase of equipment for the event.

The incessant media coverage of the litany of scams that were uncovered throughout the second term of the UPA created a public furore against the establishment. The country witnessed mass displays of protests on the streets. Even though the prime minister's integrity was beyond reproach, his passivity in these matters generated general discontent with the government.

As cases of corruption piled up against the government, subsequent investigations often led to raids at the residences of officials who were suspected of being involved, which ended in their arrests at times. Such events made government officials reluctant to make any decisions, as it was safer not to take initiative than to do so and appear to be favouring private parties in return for bribes. This inertia of the bureaucracy added to the problem of policy paralysis in the government and the economy began grinding to a halt.

* * *

As growth slowed and fiscal deficit kept spiralling out of control, while inflation levels became unmanageable, the government tried to accumulate resources through questionable means. The most infamous instance is that of retroactive taxation in the case of Vodafone. The company had taken over operations of Hutchison Essar in 2007 and the two had sewn up a deal through their subsidiary in Cayman Islands beyond the jurisdiction of Indian tax authorities. The Indian IT department claimed over USD 2 billion in lost taxes, but, in 2012, the Supreme Court ruled in favour of Vodafone.

That year itself, the finance minister, Pranab Mukherjee, introduced a General Anti-Avoidance Rule (GAAR) in his budget speech, with an objective 'to counter aggressive tax avoidance schemes'. He announced that the rule would be effective retroactively, which implied that the Vodafone deal would fall under its purview. Investor sentiment, which was already low during the time, took an immediate hit. Although the government postponed the implementation of GAAR after immense criticism, such actions proved inimical to the economy and its growth.

Foreign investors grew sceptical of the Indian economy and withdrew money. As the rupee plummeted, India was infamously placed in the company of the 'Fragile Five' economies, which included Turkey, Brazil, South Africa and Indonesia apart from India. These five countries were described as 'economies that have become too dependent on skittish foreign investment to finance their growth ambitions'.[26]

As the 2014 general elections drew near, it was evident that the UPA was facing imminent defeat. Nothing was going right for them.

The economy was in tatters, their party was mired in corruption scandals, and they seemed to lack a leader to take on the Opposition that was led by the formidable chief minister of Gujarat, Narendra Modi.[27]

The results proved to be far worse than expected for Congress. The party was reduced to its worst performance in history, winning merely 44 seats, down 162 seats from the previous elections. The BJP, on the other hand, passed the majority mark on its own account with 282 seats, the first time for any party to do so since the 1984 elections, ending an era of coalition politics.

The Congress and the UPA had no one to blame but themselves. Since the very beginning, the priority to distributive measures with an utter disregard for fiscal prudence had made the domestic economy extremely vulnerable to external shocks. When the inevitable happened in 2008, the economy's financial vulnerabilities, which had been enshrouded in a cover of accelerated growth, stood exposed. The government managed to pull through the crisis using the same unsustainable means of heavy public spending, which eventually fell apart as well.

The phase of fast-paced growth in the first term was a time to push through bolder reforms and strengthen the country's macroeconomic fundamentals. But India chose the opposite path and had to pay a heavy price for it. If the UPA is guilty of any crime, it is this. The country's fastest growth phase in history was floundered in policies that helped no one, especially not the intended beneficiaries.

The distributive strategy did have substantial justification, given the state of poverty and abysmal social indicators. But the economic strategy used to implement these policies needed to be better aligned towards providing productive employment rather than pushing through with redistribution that only took the country off the path of fiscal consolidation. Nevertheless, the new prime minister had promised to put India back on the path of recovery and a lot of hopes were pinned on the performance of his government.

CHAPTER 19

GREAT EXPECTATIONS

Narendra Modi, the prime minister, was a product of the mass exasperation against the misdeeds of the previous government. The regular revelation of corruption scandals, the frustrating policy paralysis, the incessant price hikes and the widespread unemployment in a virtually stalled economy had made the average voter restless for change. So, when a figure emerged making expansive assurances to revive the moribund Indian economy by eliminating corruption, creating millions of jobs and extricating millions out of the depths of poverty, the choice was hardly a complex conundrum for the voters.

Modi also had the backing of his economic record as the chief minister of Gujarat for an unbroken stint of thirteen years since 2001. He had an integral role to play in developing a business-friendly image for his state. For a large part of his tenure, the state grew close to 10 per cent on an annual basis, making it one of the fastest-growing states in the country. Gujarat also boasted of a greater intensity of jobs and industry than the rest of the country.[1]

Even though the Gujarat model had its fair share of critics, Indians voted for him in large numbers in 2014 with the hope that he could replicate his achievements, in Gujarat, for the entire nation as well. India's dream run in the years preceding the 2008 economic crisis had given rise to hopes of the country becoming an economic superpower and there seemed simply no place for the inefficiencies that had become the unfortunate hallmark of the UPA rule. So, Modi, who campaigned on an appealing vision of economic growth, good governance and reforms, seemed like the inevitable choice.

The landslide victory for Modi was a reflection of how the burgeoning aspirations of Indians had made them more open to extending the baton of governance to those beyond the established elite. He was looked upon as a self-made politician from a humble background in a nation that was too accustomed to the prevalence of dynasty politics.

The BJP's thumping victory also marked a crucial change in India's political system that had grown noticeably weaker with time. Since the advent of regional parties, the authority of Congress and BJP had been undermined, resulting in shaky coalition governments in New Delhi. The decision-making process at the Centre had, thus, become linked to the varied, and often conflicting, interests of coalition partners. The scale of the electoral victory for BJP in 2014 restored the power centre back in the national capital. It gave the BJP government a mandate to follow through on its policies without restraint.

* * *

While in office, one of the first acts that Modi initiated was to dismantle the long-standing relic of economic planning, the Planning Commission, and also eliminate the distinction between planned and non-planned expenditure in the country's annual budgets. These changes signalled the completion of India's ideological shift in economic thinking, away from the state-led planning of the Nehruvian era towards a market-oriented approach of development.

A major drawback of the Planning Commission had been that it created rigid national schemes, which required states to implement them by setting aside a significant share of funds. This left the states grossly disempowered. With the dismantling of the institution, the states were now left with more discretion over how to use their funds. The government also accepted a proposal of the Finance Commission to give state governments 42 per cent of Central tax receipts, up from 32 per cent.

The devolution of powers to the states allows for more resources and authority to rest with entities that are better attuned to local challenges than the Central government. This was a necessary step in a large country like India where individual states are comparable in size to other countries around the world. As Modi once commented, '[A] one-size-fits-all approach does not work in India.'[2]

In a similar spirit of allowing market forces to define outcomes, the government also managed to deregulate diesel and petroleum prices, which formed a substantial part of the subsidy bill. As a result, India joined the club of select countries like USA and Australia where fuel prices are revised on a daily basis. Deregulation was also partially achieved in case of natural gas, but has yet to be taken up for fertilizer and kerosene. The use of the latter two commodities by people at the bottom of the pyramid makes it more difficult to tick them off the subsidy bill.

Advancing further on the reform process, the private sector was given further leeway in sectors where the state was proving incompetent. A cap on foreign investment in the defence sector was lifted from 26 per cent to 49 per cent. Similarly, furthering Vajpayee's initiative to allow private entry into the insurance sector, the cap for foreign investment in it was raised to 49 per cent as well. A similar push towards greater liberalization of India's FDI policy was made in crucial sectors like e-commerce and pharmaceuticals. As a result, a record average of USD 52 billion in annual FDI inflow has materialized till 2018.[3]

These moves were a concerted attempt to signal to the world that India was becoming more welcoming of private capital. But a more direct attempt at developing a business-friendly image on a global stage was in Modi's ambitious promise of advancing India to the 50th place on the World Bank's Ease of Doing Business rankings, by the end of his five-year term, from a lowly 142 when he joined office. To his credit, India has broken into the top 100 for the first time, owing to the government's consistent efforts at ushering in reforms in various aspects of business operations. The World Bank noted in its 2018 Doing Business report that India had adopted thirty-seven reforms since 2003 and nearly half of them had been introduced in the last four years.[4] Even though the Doing Business rankings might not be the sole determinant for attracting investment, it will reinforce global investor confidence in India as it reflects the government's commitment to undertaking reforms.

A few of the key reforms that the World Bank alludes to have been game-changing in their expected long-term impact on the economy. The first arose from a strenuous legacy of rising non-performing assets (NPA) with public sector banks that the BJP government had inherited. During India's high growth phase before the crisis, and for a brief period following it when the government was pumping in money to stimulate the economy, investor sentiments were high. So, a flurry of investments were undertaken based on some over-optimistic assumptions, with banks failing to carry out appropriate checks on the creditworthiness of its borrowers.

Vijay Mallya was created in this era of imprudent lending. During the boom years, Indian banks recklessly lent out exorbitant sums of money to his now-grounded Kingfisher Airlines. There have also been allegations of some political involvement at the time to allow his airline to stay afloat.[5] But when the growth phase abruptly came to an end, the corporates found it increasingly difficult to pay back these sums of money. As a result, balance sheets of both banks and corporates plummeted in quality, resulting in the so-called 'twin balance-sheet' problem. Mallya, for instance, still owes about Rs 90 billion to more than a dozen Indian bankers for his airlines.[6]

When the UPA left office, the share of bad loans with banks stood at 4.11 per cent. But since the RBI tightened NPA regulations under the then governor, Raghuram Rajan, in 2015, the share of declared NPAs by banks escalated quickly and eventually went past 10 per cent by the end of 2017. As over 70 per cent of these NPAs have arisen out of loans extended to the corporate sector, the credit growth to industries had virtually come to a standstill since the problem was highlighted by the RBI.[7]

A long-term solution was needed to fix the problem of bad loans inherent in India's state-run banks. It is often suggested to adopt the path of higher privatization of banks to infuse efficiency and eliminate political interference. But global markets show that privatization of banks is not always the optimal choice. The economic crisis of 2008, which was triggered by the economic mismanagement of private banks in America, is a case in point.

Instead, a better remedy for the Indian case was found in directly targeting the problem of growing number of insolvent companies and individuals in the country. According to World Bank statistics, it takes an average of 4.3 years in India to resolve insolvency, and lenders eventually recovered just over 26 cents to the dollar. These numbers were among the poorest in emerging economies.

The Insolvency and Bankruptcy Code, 2016, was passed in Parliament to address the issue. The Code allows either the creditor or the borrower to approach the National Company Law Tribunal (NCLT) to initiate insolvency proceedings. It further lays down provisions for debt resolution within a span of 3–5 months. The success of the move will depend on how well the NCLT is able to manage the wave of cases filed with it. By the end of 2017, over 4,300 petitions had been filed within eighteen months of operation.

The second major reform by the BJP government on the economic front came in the form of the biggest tax reform in Indian history with the implementation of the goods and services tax (GST), after well over a decade in the making. The tax, which aims at simplifying the tax structure of the country by replacing the erstwhile multi-layered complicated tax system, was introduced in 2017. It brings a multitude of taxes and levies under one uniform tax system. Soon after the bill relating to the tax was cleared by the Parliament in 2016, the *Economist* wrote, 'The government of Narendra Modi, never averse to over-hyping what turn out to be modest policy tweaks, has enacted its most important reform to date.'[8]

Apart from easing the taxation framework of the country, the move truly integrated India into a single market, allowing for easy movement of goods across state borders. The new tax system eliminated the maze of check posts at state borders, where lorries transporting goods typically used to languish for hours. It is expected to transform into higher ease of doing business in the economy and translate into facilitation of a high-growth trajectory.

The tax, however, has not been free of criticism. First, the tax was introduced with five tax slabs to have the minimum effect on the price of the goods compared to the previous tax regime. But this was said to defeat the very purpose of simplification of taxes. Over time, the government seems to be addressing this issue by shifting most of the goods to lower-rate brackets, which might eventually result in the reduction of the number of tax slabs.[9]

Second, the tax was expected to have deleterious effects on the unorganized sector, which does not pay taxes by definition. Considering it employed over 90 per cent of the Indian workforce at the time of the implementation of the GST, there were expected concerns on its impact on small informal businesses and on the overall economy itself. Too little time has passed since the implementation of the GST, in 2017, to pass a definite verdict on this front.

Finally, the haste in which the tax was implemented without ironing out the complexities has often been criticized as well. Nevertheless, even though the challenges facing the GST system can prove to be daunting, the long-term benefits of the reform are many as tax evasion will become difficult due to its inbuilt self-regulatory mechanism, and the cost of doing business will fall across the country owing to fewer tax complications.

Therefore, the BJP government has been proactive in kickstarting India's stalled reform process in sharp contrast to the previous one. There are at least three other cases where this is true for the economy as well. One has been its take on fiscal deficit. After a profligate regime of the UPA government, a sense of fiscal responsibility was imperative, and, as luck would have it, global crude oil prices began to fall since 2014. This allowed the government to collect higher excise taxes on petroleum products. The increase in tax revenue and a focus on achieving predefined fiscal targets allowed the deficit to narrow down to 3.5 per cent of GDP in 2018 from 4.5 per cent when the UPA left office. Notably, the FRBM Act target of a fiscal deficit of 3 per cent, which was to be achieved by 2008, has not been met since the Act was implemented.[10]

The other varied approach from the UPA government came in tackling the problem of inflation, which had been sharply impacting the purchasing power of consumers. Again, the falling crude oil prices played a significant impact in bringing down inflation across Indian markets. But an institutional change was brought about when the RBI began the process of inflation-targeting, through which it aimed at keeping inflation levels for the economy within a predefined band. An independent Monetary Policy Committee (MPC) was also set up to adjust interest rates based on inflation levels. Such a mechanism was aimed at maintaining public confidence in a low-inflation regime.

The third major contrast in the BJP government to the previous one has been in its approach towards combating corruption. While the second term of the UPA had been mired in corruption scandals right at the top, the complete absence of any such cases since then has been refreshing. The government has also been focused on addressing the problem of black money in the economy. A successful effort has been made in managing to end the data secrecy of money stashed in Swiss banks, which has long been perceived as a haven for illicit wealth.[11]

A more controversial step by the government against black money has been the move to demonetize 86 per cent of India's currency overnight, with the expectation that the illicit part of it will not be returned to banks for fear of being penalized. As it turned out, almost all of the demonetized currency returned to the central bank. The other motive of the move to shift the economy towards a less cash-based society also come to naught as people began to prefer cash as their primary currency soon after the circulation was normalized. The New York Times penned a scathing editorial against the move, calling it 'atrociously planned and executed'.[12] The only long-term impact it had was to create a cash crunch in the economy which slowed down India's growth to its lowest level since the BJP came into power and set the economy back by at least a few months.[13]

Despite such setbacks, the economic record of the BJP government has been fairly satisfactory. Beginning from a point where the economy was in unenviable company of the 'Fragile Five', it has been an impressive feat to achieve the 'fastest-growing major economy' tag. More importantly, this growth has not come at the cost of high fiscal deficits or inflation levels. In fact, the finances of the state were brought under control with considerable restraint and cutting back on a few costly subsidy programmes. At the same time, a spate of reforms was also pushed through, which are expected to yield economic dividends in the long run. The confidence in the Indian economy has been renewed due to these efforts, which is evident from the record foreign investments that have been pouring in from large multinationals, including Alibaba, Amazon, Apple, Uber, Walmart and Vodafone.

The prime minister has also been particularly indefatigable in initiating a series of initiatives: Swachh Bharat, to encourage cleanliness and construction of indoor toilets; Digital India, to make the country digitally empowered; and Jan Dhan Yojana, to ensure financial inclusion of citizens. A flagship initiative of the government is the Make in India programme, which aims at courting multinationals and addressing the impediments to their entry into India. The extent of success of these initiatives has been a matter of constant debate as the ground impact of these schemes has been mixed at best.

The Swachh Bharat Mission has managed to build over 80 million toilets for households across the country in the four years since the programme was launched, covering about 90 per cent of the country. The number of open defecation free (ODF) villages has also gone up from 47,000 to over 420,000 in the same period—about 70 per cent of the country's villages.[14] These are impressive statistics, but actual usage of these toilets is still debatable as open defecation has always been a behavioural issue. So, the true success of the programme can only be determined over time.

Similarly, the success of Digital India, which aims at broader digital inclusion of the masses to access new services, markets and information, will depend on the growth in digital literacy of the population. In a country as large as India, generating a wider acceptability of digital services will take dogged efforts. So, it might be too early to reflect on the performance of the initiative.

On the other hand, Jan Dhan Yojana has achieved some successes since its inception in 2014. The World Bank estimates that by March 2018, the scheme had added 310 million Indians into the formal banking system. The share of adults having an account in India has more than doubled since 2011 and the government policy has played a significant role in the process. A positive outcome of India's financial inclusion process has been that account ownership has increased faster among women and the poorest (40 per cent) than among men and the wealthiest (60 per cent).[15] Thus, the gender and wealth gap have been narrowing in India in this aspect.

But the report also highlights that 190 million adults in India are still without a bank account. So there remains a long way ahead before universal financial inclusion is achieved. Besides, almost half of the accounts in India are inactive, which is the highest in the world and twice as high as the developing country average of 25 per cent.[16] A litany of other challenges, including infrastructural ones like a shortage of bank branches and ATMs, also remain to be addressed.

Lastly, the Make in India programme was launched in 2014 with an aim to make India the manufacturing hub of the world, a centre for research and innovation, and an integral part of the global supply chain. The programme was initiated at an opportune time when China's growth was slowing down and a lot of global firms were pulling out of the country due to increasing labour costs. Even though numerous multinationals have shown an inclination towards setting up production plants in India since then, the programme has been unable to live up to its potential. The share of manufacturing in India's GDP has remained stagnant at 15 per cent since 2014. Notably, the Make in India programme had targeted increasing the share to a healthy 25 per cent, which seems unachievable now.[17]

Although the intent behind the programme is commendable, India's historical lacklustre performance in the manufacturing sector has not been a problem for attracting foreign investment. The country's rigid labour laws since Independence have been extremely inimical to the sector's development. The most onerous of such regulations includes a requirement for a firm that employs more than 100 workers to seek government approval before firing a worker. The prevalence of such complex stipulations incentivizes firms to stay small. Expectedly, small-sized firms employ 84 per cent of the workers in India. By contrast, China employs over 75 per cent of its workforce in medium- and large-scale firms.

A major outcome of firms remaining small is that despite being a labour-abundant economy, India has failed to 'have a comparative advantage in large-scale, labour-intensive manufacturing'.[18] On the contrary, successful sectors in India have been highly capital- or skilled labour–intensive. So, a push towards labour reforms is absolutely imperative for the Indian economy. Incidentally, even the BJP election manifesto had outlined the need to 'review our labour laws which are outdated, complicated and even contradictory'.[19]

The government did begin its term with some enthusiastic progress on labour reforms, but it has slowed down with time. Initially, plans were afoot to consolidate 44 labour laws into four codes. But that has been put on the backburner for now. Moreover, even the consolidation plan fails to repeal rules that make companies reluctant to expand.

These restrictive labour laws have also spawned one of the biggest challenges for the Indian economy—job creation. India has had a unique growth trajectory of developing a strong service sector before its manufacturing could account for a significant proportion of the economy. As manufacturing is usually labour-intensive, developing economies manage to provide employment to its expanding population within the sector. However, since India missed its industrial boom phase, jobless growth has been an uncomfortable reality for the country's masses. The situation has worsened of late. According to a recent study, latest Labour Bureau estimates show that there was an absolute decline in employment between 2013–14 and 2015–16, probably for the first time since Independence.[20]

Even though claims of job growth are always contestable in India, since most of its workforce is employed in the informal sector where employment becomes difficult to track, for a country in which 10 million people are expected to join the workforce annually for the near future, dismal job prospects could prove disastrous. Tackling this problem has always been a challenge for the economy, and reforming labour laws to kickstart manufacturing in India can partly address the problem. As firms are allowed to grow, economies of scale will kick in and create widespread employment opportunities.

Apart from ensuring labour market flexibility, land reforms are another aspect that have been left unaddressed by the BJP government. Historically, India's notoriously complex land acquisition laws have been a barrier to investment and development. The UPA government had introduced the Land Acquisition Act in 2013, but its framework involved a time frame for execution that made the entire process of acquiring land unviable. The Economic Survey of 2015 noted that land acquisition was the primary cause in the delay of 161 government projects. Economist Arvind Panagariya remarked, 'The Land Act, 2013 is an onerous Act under which by all calculations it will take up to five years for acquiring land, assuming that all steps progress smoothly.'[21] However, no progress on land reforms has been made as well in the four years that BJP has been in power.

Both land and labour reforms have been pushed down to the states for now. If India aims to achieve an export boom akin to what East Asia achieved towards the end of the previous century, these reforms need to be pushed through with urgency. The politically sensitive nature of these policies has made it difficult for any government to take them up. But more than half of India's population is below twenty-five years of age and as they begin to join the labour market each year, sufficient employment opportunities will be difficult to create.[22]

It bodes upon future governments to complete the job that has been left unfinished in India's reforms process. India has an unusual history of adopting major reforms only when a crisis ensues, from the Green Revolution to the economic reforms of 1991. Prime Minister Manmohan Singh had admitted quite candidly that the 1991 crisis was 'a blessing in disguise' as it helped introduce changes that would have been impossible without it.[23] Hopefully, the next phase of reforms for land and labour will not require the shadow of a crisis and instead prevent one.

CONCLUSION

Over seven decades have passed since Nehru had famously redeemed the pledge for India to make her 'tryst with destiny', which it had made 'long years ago'. He was referring to the glory days of the bygone years when the amorphous nation of India was a notable economy on the world stage before the British intervened, a time that many countrymen still love to reminisce about.

As India enters its eighth decade of freedom, it is all set to overtake its erstwhile colonizer and become the fifth-largest economy in the world. If nothing goes awry, it is expected that by the centenary of Indian independence, the power balance that existed for most of the past 2,000 years will be restored, where China and India would be much larger economies than Europe or America. The Asian economies will have compensated for the gains of the Industrial Revolution that the West had made.[1]

But the question still remains whether India is on its way to make her tryst with destiny. It is undeniable that India has come a long way since Independence. The average Indian is today seven times richer than what he was at the time of Independence. Education and health standards, despite being severely wanting, have witnessed significant gains as well. While only 18 per cent of the population was literate in 1951, the figure has now risen to account for approximately three-fourths of the country.

The gross enrolment in elementary education is also reaching near-universal levels, although a lot of challenges still remain to be addressed in the actual learning imparted to students. On the health front, Indians who used to survive up to an average age of thirty-two at the time of Independence, now live up to sixty-eight years of age. Infant mortality rate has declined from 146 in 1951 to less than thirty-four as of today.

But all of this seems less of an achievement when seen in relative terms. If the Human Development Index (HDI) is taken as an approximation of social indicators, India still ranks 131 out of 188 countries in the world. Meanwhile, on the economic front, an average Indian has an annual income of USD 1,940, which puts India firmly in the category of 'lower-middle income' economies by the World Bank.[2]

By comparison, China, which was at the same level of per capita income as India from Independence till 1980, has achieved 'middle income' country status with a per capita income of USD 8,827. At best, India could be where China is today in the next decade or so. And only if it continues growing at that pace can India become larger than Europe and America by the middle of the century.

Inarguably, the developmental path that India adopted since Independence has had outcomes that are not absolutely satisfactory. In particular, the adoption of the idea of a planned economy by Nehru and the subsequent controls imposed upon the economy are often blamed for the present scenario. The assertion is not completely out of place. The four-decade-long flirtation with planning did impose restrictions on the economy that were hardly conducive to growth and development. But the benefit of hindsight can often lead to erroneous conclusions.

The Nehruvian approach was by no means unique at the time. The idea that the state could plan to meet each and every demand and need of its citizens had quite a few takers in the post-War era, even if it might seem absurd today. In fact, Nehru had invited the best and brightest economists of the time to India for insights on the viability of a planned economy. I.G. Patel recalls in his memoir how a number of economists—Gunnar Myrdal, Ragnar Frisch, Jan Tinbergen, Oskar Lange and Richard Goodwin—came to India with a definite view that development could be plotted and planned till the last mile.[3] Even the business community in India favoured the idea of planning, at least in the first decade following Independence.

Added to the mix was the recent experience of colonialism, which made the appeal of self-reliance quite alluring. During the British rule, Indian economists led by Dadabhai Naoroji popularized the idea that the leading cause of poverty in India was the senseless drain of wealth from the country in favour of their colonizers. So there existed an understandable scepticism about the virtues of an open economy. It seemed imperative to plug the drain of wealth at the time by closing India's borders for trade. Thus, the choices made in selecting the path of economic development by a newly independent India cannot be faulted outright.

However, the mistake lay in persisting with the model even after its failures and inefficiencies became apparent. By the mid-1960s, the criticisms of planned development were hard to miss. The Swedish economist Gunnar Myrdal penned a telling account of the failures of development, *Asian Drama*, in which he remarked that 'India's promised social and economic revolution failed to materialize.'[4] Interestingly, Mahalanobis, the leading figure behind Indian planning, concurred with the assessment.[5]

The arguments of free marketeers led by Milton Friedman were also becoming dominant in the field of economics at the time. A few East Asian economies—mainly South Korea, Taiwan, Hong Kong and Singapore—began opening up their economies after becoming disillusioned with the central planning model. They adopted a unique approach of state-led capitalism with a substantial export-oriented focus. Over the next few decades, these economies entered a phase of sustained high growth that popularly came to be known as 'the East Asian miracle'. Therefore, India's continued fascination with the status quo becomes hard to defend after Nehru's death. Instead of evolving with the times, India became even more closed and state-controlled under Indira Gandhi.

India hardly made any policy shifts even when China began opening up its markets under Deng Xiaoping in the latter half of the 1970s. The inaction persisted despite the fact that between 1960 and 1990, at least a dozen committees were set up to examine almost every aspect of the control economy, each of which unfailingly came to the conclusion that the system of licensing was at fault.[6]

Only incremental changes were made through the eighties when Indira Gandhi returned for her final stint in office, with Rajiv Gandhi following along similar lines. Eventually, it was a disastrous crisis that allowed the Indian economy to shed the complex webs of licensing and controls that had been impeding its growth. The travails of central planning were finally put to rest.

The delicensing of industrial activity, slashing import tariffs and opening up different parts of the economy to the private sector ushered in a new era of economic growth. In sector after sector that was opened up to the private sector, government-owned companies were quickly outperformed. This was evident in sectors like telecom, aviation and banking where new entrants from the private sector became market leaders.

The story of the Indian economy since Independence is, in fact, accurately captured in the contribution of the private sector. Back in 1950–51, private corporate savings (or, profits) were less than 1 per cent of the GDP, while public sector savings stood at 2.1 per cent. The strength of the public sector in the economy accentuated under Nehru and further under Indira Gandhi's statist push. So, by 1976-77, private corporate savings were almost stagnant at 1.3 per cent while public sector savings had expanded to 5.6 per cent. However, a decade and half after liberalization, the tables had turned, and the private sector savings stood at 6.5 per cent of the GDP while public sector savings had deteriorated at 2.4 per cent.

The process of liberalization, however, has been challenging in itself. The growth of the economy has undoubtedly picked up since it has been opened up and, as a result, India has managed to halve the share of population living in poverty in the two decades following reforms.[7] But, as the country accumulates more wealth, the pattern of its distribution is raising quite a few eyebrows.

The growth of the Indian economy in the post-liberalization era has given rise to three distinct forms of capitalism: state capitalism, crony capitalism and entrepreneurial capitalism. The first two trends are a matter of the most concern for the development of the economy. Yet again, the problem lies in too much government control.

The public sector enterprises in India command significant or even complete control in a variety of crucial sectors. Such companies are notoriously operated as extensions of the state and carry a familiar hallmark of inefficiency and apathy. Political needs play a decisive role in their operations. The power sector is a typical case in point which is a commercially unviable business in India, as huge power subsidies have to be shelled out to appease the vast rural electorate.

An even more pernicious aspect of Indian capitalism has been the unfortunate prevalence of crony capitalism, where businesses have thrived due to an unhealthy nexus with the political class instead of entrepreneurship and risk. The phenomenon has taken two distinct forms within the economy. In sectors like airline and telecommunications, the practice of cronyism has taken place simultaneously with entrepreneurship. There have been definite instances where licences in these sectors have been handed out in an unfair manner, but the competition among firms has ensured immense benefits to the masses. In other sectors like mining and real estate, businesses have operated simply as crony capitalists, where vast fortunes have been amassed by a select few in conjunction with the state through highly extractive mechanisms.

The final flavour of capitalism is the highlight of the country's liberalization process. Over the last few decades, entrepreneurial efforts have been adequately rewarded in sectors that have been disassociated from governmental intervention. These mainly include knowledge-intensive industries, capital markets and consumer goods. The success of information technology in India has been a child of such entrepreneurial capitalism. These outcomes are the ones that need to be enthusiastically encouraged throughout the economy.

On the other hand, the prevalence of former streams of capitalism has led to undesirable consequences. Corruption has been an obvious byproduct. Even though India has been ridden with shades of corruption long before Independence, liberalization has created newer and grander avenues of graft for the unscrupulous. The litany of scams that was uncovered in the second term of the UPA stands testimony to the extent of corruption that pervades the economy, especially as a result of crony capitalism. The market reforms themselves cannot be blamed for the outcome. Countries such as Poland have managed to implement reforms without succumbing to a wave of cronyism.

A more unsettling outcome of the liberalization process is the highly unequal distribution of wealth. In the early 1990s, there was no Indian on the annual billionaire ranking released by *Forbes*. Soon, a constellation of Indian names began appearing on the list. Two and a half decades later, more than a hundred billionaires emblazoned the global rankings. This seems like a favourable outcome in the sense that the economy clearly created avenues for prosperity following the market reforms of 1991. But the facade of opulence falls flat when considered in relative terms.

In 2008, Jayant Sinha, a Harvard Business School graduate and the son of Yashwant Sinha, the finance minister under Atal Bihari Vajpayee, attempted to determine how India's richest compared to other countries. The results were astounding. When the proportion of wealth held by the billionaires on the *Forbes* rankings was measured relative to the country's gross domestic product, India ranked second only to Russia, a country infamous for its exploitative oligarchy. 'We had been running a socialist economy for so long. And in only fifteen or sixteen years we had created this incredible wealth concentration, perhaps more quickly than any country in history,' he commented.[8]

To be clear, it is healthy for an economy to produce wealth. But the problem only surfaces when the wealth arises more out of political connections than the emergence of innovative and productive industries. The former is increasingly becoming the case in India. Using Sinha's data, Raghuram Rajan, the celebrated former central banker for India, asked a sinister question to the audience at the Bombay Chamber of Commerce in 2008: 'Is there a threat of oligarchy in India?'[9] Much before the series of scams came to light, he pointed out in his speech that scarce public resources were being handed out to favoured industrialists who are raking in excessive, undeserved profits. Simply put, '[T]oo many people have gotten too rich based on their proximity to the government.'[10]

The skewness in India's growth pattern gave rise to one of the most phenomenal academic debates in the country's history between two giants in the field of economics, Amartya Sen and Jagdish Bhagwati. The debate revolved around the appropriate governance priority for India to pursue. Sen put forward the argument that Indian policymakers should invest more in social infrastructure, which would improve the productivity of its people and thereby drive growth. On the other hand, Bhagwati opines that a policy focus on growth can yield the adequate resources for the government to invest in social sector schemes.

To be clear, Sen also argues that growth is essential to economic development, but it needs to be combined with commensurate investments in improving the health and education levels of a society. Not doing so would only widen inequality and impede the growth process itself. Bhagwati, on his part, acknowledges that economic growth may initially raise inequality but believes that maintaining growth over a sustained period will allow the state to raise enough resources to undertake redistribution and negate the effects of the initial rise in inequality.

The growth-versus-redistribution debate is only one of the multitude of conundrums facing the Indian economy today. But, despite all of its challenges, the only thread holding the country together has been the institution of democracy. The founders of independent India chose to adopt the path of democracy at a time when large swathes of the population were largely unaware of the concept itself. As Sunil Khilnani wrote in *Idea of India*, 'India became a democracy without really knowing how, why or what it meant to be one.'[11] In fact, Indian leaders chose the path of universal adult franchise at a time when quite a few advanced Western powers had not taken it up and at a scale that nobody in history had ever attempted before. Yet, the democratic spirit allowed the survival and progress of the country when almost everyone expected it to fall apart at some point due to its diverse mix of people, interests and ideas.

The only question that needs to be asked today after more than seven decades of independence is a question that was put forward by B.R. Ambedkar in 1949 during the closing debates of the Constituent Assembly, which had been set up to produce India's Constitution. He had pointedly asked:

> On the 26th of January 1950, we are going to enter a life of contradictions. In politics, we will have equality and in social and economic life, we will have inequality. In politics, we will be recognizing the principle of one man, one vote and one vote, one value. In our social and economic life, we shall, by reason of our social and economic structure, continue to deny the principle of one man, one value. How long shall we continue to live this life of contradictions? How long shall we continue to deny equality in our social and economic life? If we continue to deny it for long, we do so only by putting our political democracy in peril.[12]

These questions remain pertinent even today. The principle of one man, one value is still largely elusive in the social and economic life of Indian citizens. But it is probably the equitable access to political rights itself that has compensated for it and ensured the resilience of the India experiment. Nevertheless, long after the British have departed, India remains a work in progress.

EPILOGUE

If one insight has to be drawn from the daunting breadth of the Indian economic history, it is that the country needs to evolve with the times to stay abreast of the ever-changing dynamics of the world economy. Time has shown this can be a complex task. Most evidently, the persistence with the socialist model despite developing evidence of its flaws (both within India and outside it) is a case in point. India's current economic situation would have been substantially different had it moved towards more freer markets around the time the East Asian economies were beginning to find merits in such an approach. But the country failed to keep up with the times until crisis struck.

With this historical background, Indian policymakers need to be extremely wary of any emerging threats to the economy. In recent times, the most pertinent concern for the world economy lies in the repercussions of the exponential spurt in technological breakthroughs where modern computers are increasingly encroaching into domains that were previously considered exclusive to humans. In 2015, a Google computer beat the world's finest player of the ancient Chinese game Go, which is highly intuitive and has exceptionally high number of possible moves. These developments have been nothing short of a revolution. Machine-learning has breached the bastion of strategic thought.

Such astonishing advances in the fields of automation, robotics, Internet of Things (IoT), artificial intelligence (AI) and other similar technological innovations are expected to change the nature of jobs in developed and developing countries alike. India particularly stands to lose out if it does not manage to keep pace with these changes as its economy is significantly capital-intensive, that is Indian manufacturers prefer processes that are more dependent on capital than labour. So, any shift towards higher technological dependence on the shop floor will appeal to the industrial class, leaving the workforce on the shorter end of the stick.

If the threat to employment due to technological advancement is not adequately addressed in time, it can have disastrous repercussions on the country's future generations. This has a lot to do with India's nascent demography. More than half the Indian population lies below twenty-five years of age. So, each year an increasing proportion of young adults will be added to the workforce. By estimates of the labour ministry, this would amount to an increment of over 10 million people each year. As per the UN data on world population, the working age population—that is, those between the ages of fifteen and sixty-four—will continue to expand until 2050. In case this burgeoning section of the population is not provided with adequate employment opportunities, India would fail to cash in on a rare opportunity of a demographic dividend.

The conjunction of the prospect of loss in employment due to automation and a young demography looking for jobs might be the biggest challenge that India faces today. A recent UN report claimed that if industrial robots increasingly undertake manufacturing, developing countries could lose about two-thirds of all jobs. It is imperative that the country makes a break from the past and address the issue before it festers into a crisis of unimaginable proportions. What can India do to embrace technology, create job opportunities and meet the requirements that the situation demands?

Previously, India has always lived through industrial revolutions on the sidelines. During the first industrial revolution that was triggered with the invention of the steam engine, and the second one, which was brought about by the invention of electricity and the assembly line, India found itself on the receiving end of colonial history. Only in the third industrial revolution, which began after the 1960s, driven by computers, digital technology and the internet, did India manage to make some economic gains for itself. But even those came much later in the day after adoption of these technologies became easier post liberalization. In the latest industrial revolution, however, India has a chance to be at the centre of it and not merely cope with its effects.

But, for this possibility to materialize, a series of structural policy responses are required to be implemented. The first line of action should be realigning the education system to emphasize more on accumulation of skills than degrees. The latter is an unfortunate legacy of the Anglo-Saxon system of education. A shift away from it towards a more hands-on learning in practical subjects is needed.

Secondly, the Indian workforce needs a major upgradation of skills. Added to a severe shortage of skilled manpower, there is a need to implement massive upgradation programmes in the new technologies that have been at the heart of the latest industrial revolution. The current institutes of higher education must reinvent themselves to cater to the issue of re-skilling.

Third, for India to completely bring itself at the centre of the revolution, India must fully embrace the new era of emerging technologies. The focus should be on percolating the benefits from these technologies at every level of society. In particular, the social sector, including education, health and nutrition, is where these new technologies can be used to improve the quality of life. These are also the segments of the economy where maximum jobs will be created. Countries around the world are still navigating through the nascent stages of this new industrial revolution. Can India jumpstart this transformation?

Amitabh Kant

APPENDIX

1.1. Letters between Mahatma Gandhi and Jawaharlal Nehru on the economic path India should adopt

Gandhi's letter to Nehru:

October 5, 1945

MY DEAR JAWAHARLAL,

I have been desirous of writing to you for many days but have not been able to do so before today. The question of whether I should write in English or Hindustani also entered my mind. I have at length preferred to write in Hindustani.

The first thing I want to write about is the difference in outlook between us. If the difference is fundamental, then I feel the public should also be made aware of it. It would be detrimental to our work for Swaraj to keep them in the dark. I have said that I still stand by the system of Government envisaged in Hind Swaraj. These are not mere words. All the experience gained by me since 1908 when I wrote the booklet has confirmed truth of my belief. Therefore, if I am left alone in it, I shall not mind, for I can only bear witness to the truth as I see it. I have not Hind Swaraj before me as I write. It is really better for me to dream the picture anew in my own words. And whether it's the same as I drew in Hind Swaraj or not is immaterial for both you and me. It is not necessary to prove rightness of what I said then, it is essential only to know what I feel today. I am convinced that if India is to attain true freedom and through India the world also, then sooner or later the fact must be recognized that people will have to live in villages, not in towns, in huts, not in palaces. Crore of people will never be able to live at peace with one another in towns and palaces. They will then have no recourse but to resort to both violence and untruth. I hold that without truth and non-violence there can be nothing but destruction for humanity. We can realize truth and non-violence only in the simplicity of village life and this simplicity can best be found in the Charkha and all that the Charkha connotes. I must not fear if the world today is going the wrong way. It may be that India too will go that way and like the proverbial moth, burn itself eventually in the flame round which it dances more and more furiously. But it is my burden to protect India and, through India, the entire world from such a doom. The essence of what I have said is that man should rest content with what are his real needs and become self-sufficient. If he does not have this control, he cannot save himself. After all the world is made up of individuals just as it is the drops that constitute the ocean. I have said nothing new. This is a well-known truth.

But I do not think I have stated this in Hind Swaraj. While I admire modern science, I find that it is the old looked at in the true light of modern science which should be reclothed and refashioned aright. You must not imagine that I am envisaging our village life as it is today. The village of my dreams is still in my mind. After all, every man lives in the world of his dreams. My ideal village will contain intelligent human beings. They will not live in dirt and darkness as animals. Men and women will be free and able to hold their own against anyone in the world. There will be neither plague nor cholera nor smallpox; no one will be idle, no one will wallow in luxury. Everyone will have to contribute his quota of manual labour. I do not want to draw a large-scale picture in detail. It is possible to envisage railways, post and telegraph offices, etc. For, me it is material to obtain the real article and the rest will fit into the picture afterwards. If I let go the real thing, all else goes.

On the last day of the working committee, it was decided that this matter should be fully discussed, and the position clarified after a two or three days' session. I should like this. But whether the working committee sits or not, I want our position vis-à-vis each other to be clearly understood by us for two reasons. Firstly, the bond that unites us is not only political work. It is immeasurably deeper and quite unbreakable. Therefore, it is that I earnestly desire that in the political field also should we understand each other clearly. Secondly, neither of us thinks himself useless. We both live for the cause of India's freedom and we would both gladly die for it. We are not in need of the world's praise. Whether we get praise or blame is immaterial to us. There is no room for praise in this service. I want to live to 125 for the service of India but I must admit that I am now an old man. You are much younger in comparison and I have therefore named you as my heir. I must, however, understand my heir and my heir should understand me. Then alone shall I be content.

One other thing. I asked you about joining the Kasturba Trust and the Hindustani Prachar Sabha. You said you would think over the matter and let me know. I find your name in the Hindustani Prachar Sabha. Nanavati reminded me that he had been to [see] both you and Maulana Sahib in regard to this matter and obtained your signature in 1942. That, however, is past history. You know the present position of Hindustani. If you are still true to your signature, I want to take work from you in this Sabha. There won't be much work and you will not have to travel for it.

The Kasturba Fund work is another matter. If what I have written above does not and will not go down with you, I fear you will not be happy in the Trust and I shall understand.

The last thing I want to say to you is in regard to the controversy that has flared between you and Sarat Babu. It has pained me. I have really not grasped it. Is there anything more behind what you have said? If so, you must tell me.

If you feel you should meet me to talk over what I have written, we must arrange a meeting.

You are working hard. I hope you are well. I trust Indu too is fit.

Blessings from
BAPU

Nehru's response to Gandhi:

October 9, 1945

MY DEAR BAPU,

I have received today, on return from Lucknow, your letter of 5th October. I am glad you have written to me fully and I shall try to reply at some length, but I hope you will forgive me if there is some delay in this, as I am at present tied up with close-fitting engagements. I am only here now for a day and a half. It is really better to have informal talks but just at present I do not know when to fit this in. I shall try.

Briefly put, my view is that the question before us is not one of truth versus untruth or non-violence versus violence. One assumes as one must that true co-operation and peaceful methods must be aimed at and a society which encourages these must be our objective. The whole question is how to achieve this society and what its content should be. I do not understand why a village should necessarily embody truth and non-violence. A village, normally speaking, is backward intellectually and culturally and no progress can be made from a backward environment. Narrow-minded people are much more likely to be untruthful and violent.

Then again, we have to put down certain objectives like a sufficiency of food, clothing, housing, education, sanitation, etc., which should be the minimum requirements for the country and for everyone. It is with these objectives in view that we must find out specifically how to attain them speedily. Again, it seems to me inevitable that modern means of transport as well as many other modern developments must continue and be developed. There is no way out of it except to have them. If that is so, inevitably a measure of heavy industry exists. How far that will fit in with a purely village society? Personally, I hope that heavy or light industries should all be decentralized as far as possible and this is feasible now because of the development of electric power. If two types of economy exist in the country, there should be either conflict between the two or one will overwhelm the other.

The question of independence and protection from foreign aggression, both political and economic, has also to be considered in this context. I do not think it is possible for India to be really independent unless she is a technically advanced country. I am not thinking for the moment in terms of just armies, but rather of scientific growth. In the present context of the world, we cannot even advance culturally without a strong- background of scientific research in every department. There is today in the world a tremendous acquisitive tendency both in individuals and groups and nations, which leads to conflicts and wars. Our entire society is based on this more or less. That basis must go and be transformed into one of co-operation, not of isolation which is impossible. If this is admitted and is found feasible, then attempts should be made to realize it not in terms of an economy which is cut off from the rest of the world, but rather one which co-operates. From the economic or political point of view, an isolated India may well be a kind of vacuum which increases the acquisitive tendencies of others and thus creates conflicts.

There is no question of palaces for millions of people. But there seems to be no reason why millions should not have comfortable up-to-date homes where they can lead a cultured existence. Many of the present overgrown cities have developed evils which are deplorable. Probably, we have to discourage this overgrowth and at the same time encourage the village to approximate more to the culture of the town.

It is many years ago since I read Hind Swaraj and I have only a vague picture in my mind. But even when I read it 20 or more years ago, it seemed to me completely unreal. In your writings and speeches since then I have found much that seemed to me an advance on that old position and an appreciation of modern trends. I was therefore surprised when you told us that the old picture still remains intact in your mind. As you know, the Congress has never considered that picture, much less adopted it. You yourself have never asked it to adopt it except for certain relatively minor aspects of it. How far it is desirable for the Congress to consider these fundamental questions, involving varying philosophies of life, it is for you to judge. I should imagine that a body like the Congress should not lose itself in arguments over such matters which can only produce great confusion in people's minds, resulting in inability to act in the present. This may also result in creating barriers between the Congress and others in the country. Ultimately of course, this and other questions will have to be decided by representatives of free India. I have a feeling that most of these questions are thought of and discussed in terms of long ago, ignoring the vast changes that have taken place all over the world during the last generation or more. It is 38 years since Hind Swaraj was written. The world has completely changed since then, possibly in a wrong direction. In any event any consideration of these questions must keep present facts, forces and the human material we have today in view[;] otherwise it will be divorced from reality. You are right in saying that the world, or a large part of it, appears to be bent on committing suicide. That may be an inevitable development of an evil seed in civilization that has grown. I think it is so. How to get rid of this evil, and yet how to keep the good in the present as in the past is our problem. Obviously, there is good too in the present.

These are some random thoughts hurriedly written down and I fear they do injustice to the grave import of the questions raised. You will forgive me, I hope, for this jumbled presentation. Later, I shall try to write more clearly on the subject.

About Hindustani Prachar Sabha and about Kasturba Fund, it is obvious that both of them have my sympathy and I think they are doing good work. But I am not quite sure about the manner of their working and I have a feeling that this is not always to my liking. I really do not know enough about them to be definite. But at present I have developed distaste for adding to my burden of responsibilities when I feel that I cannot probably undertake them for lack of time. These next few months and more are likely to be fevered ones for me and others. It seems hardly desirable to me, therefore, to join any responsible committee for form's sake only.

About Sarat Bose, I am completely in the dark; as to why he should grow so angry with me, unless it is some past grievance about my general attitude in regard to foreign relations. Whether I was right or wrong, it does seem to me that Sarat has acted in a childish and irresponsible manner. You will remember perhaps that Subhash did not favour in the old days the Congress attitude towards Spain, Czechoslovakia, Munich and China. Perhaps this is a reflection of that old divergence of views. I know of nothing else that has happened.

I see that you are going to Bengal early in November. Perhaps I may visit Calcutta for three or four days just then. If so, I hope to meet you.

You may have seen in the papers an invitation by the President of the newly formed Indonesian Republic to me and some others to visit Java. In view of the special circumstances of the case, I decided immediately to accept this invitation subject of course to my getting the necessary facilities for going there. It is extremely doubtful if I shall get the facilities, and so probably I shall not go. Java is just two days by air from India, or even one day from Calcutta. The Vice-President of this Indonesian Republic, Mohammad Hatta, is a very old friend of mine. I suppose you know that the Javanese population is almost entirely Muslim.

I hope you are keeping well and have completely recovered from the attack of influenza.

Yours affectionately,
JAWAHARLAL

MAHATMA GANDHI,
NATURE CURE CLINIC,
6, TODIWALA ROAD, POONA

NOTES

Introduction

1. Interview in the *Adelaide Advertiser*, November 1981, quoted in *The Times Literary Supplement*, 9 March 2001.
2. Strachey, J. *India*. London: Kegan, Paul, Trench and Co., 1888, p. 2.
3. Tharoor, S. *India: From Midnight to the Millennium and Beyond*. New Delhi: Penguin, 1997, p. 7.
4. Khilnani, S. *The Idea of India*. New Delhi: Penguin, 1999, p. 16.

Part 1: The Nehru Years

Chapter 1: Radcliffe and His Line

1. Maddison, A. *The World Economy*, OECD Publishing, 2006, Vol. 1–2, p. 638.
2. Kotkin, S. *Magnetic Mountain: Stalinism as a Civilization*. University of California Press, 1997.

    Kotkin reports an interesting account of how during the Great Depression, the Soviet Union was bringing in large number of Americans to employ in its factories and farms. Unemployment in the Western world allowed the Soviet Union to benefit from the surplus labour as it began implementing its five-year plans in the 1930s. However, the Union was having economic problems of its own making during the decade, which were unrelated to the effects of the Great Depression. The forced collectivization of agriculture had resulted in the Soviet famine of 1932-33. But, since these instances of failure were hardly reported accurately to the outside world, socialism was perceived as a possible alternative to the crumbling capitalist system.

3. Beckett, F. *Clem Attlee: Labour's Great Reformer*. Hans Publishing, 2015.
4. Lapierre, Dominque, and Larry Collins. *Mountbatten and the Partition of India*. Delhi: Vikas Publishing House, 2015, p. 18.

5. It is clear from historical records that neither Gandhi nor Nehru ever accepted the idea of Partition. On 3 June, when Nehru announced the acceptance of Partition by Congress, he stated in his broadcast that: 'It is with no joy in my heart that I commend these proposals to you, though I have no doubt in my mind that this is the right course. For generations we have dreamt and struggled for a free and independent united India. The proposals to allow certain parts to secede, if they so will, are painful for any of us to contemplate. Nevertheless, I am convinced that our present decision is the right one even from the larger viewpoint.'

    Meanwhile on 5 July, a day after the Indian Independence Bill was introduced in the British Parliament, Gandhi told his prayer meeting that the bill contained poison. 'The British carried on their rule in India for 150 years and the British government accepted the fact that politically India was one nation . . . Having unified the country, it is not a very becoming thing for them to divide it. It is true that both the Congress and Muslim League gave their assent to the Bill. But accepting a bad thing does not make it good.' He ominously predicted that this would only result in war.

6. A colloquial Indian term for 'hack' that has come to be associated with frugal innovation.

7. Sir Cyril Radcliffe to Mark Tennant, 13 August 1947. Cited in Heward, E. *The Great and the Good: A Life of Lord Radcliffe*. Barry Rose Law Publishers, 1994, p. 42.

8. Keay, J. *India: A History*. Harper Press, 2000.

9. Collins, Larry, and Lapierre, Dominique. *Freedom at Midnight*. Delhi: Vikas Publishing, 1975, p. 263.

10. Wilcox, W. 'The Economic Consequences of Partition: India and Pakistan'. *Journal of International Affairs*, 1964, Vol. 18, No. 2, pp. 188–97.

11. Collins, Larry, and Lapierre, Dominique. *Freedom at Midnight*. Delhi: Vikas Publishing, 1975, p. 265.

12. Tunzelmann, A.V. *Indian Summer: The Secret History of the End of an Empire*. Simon & Schuster, 2007, p. 287.

13. Sir Laurence Grafftey-Smith to Philip Noel-Baker, 27 October 1947. 'TNA: DO 133/6'.

14. Tunzelmann, A.V. *Indian Summer: The Secret History of the End of an Empire*. Simon & Schuster, 2007, p. 267.

15. A detailed description of the Delhi riots can be found in Tunzelmann, A.V. *Indian Summer: The Secret History of the End of an Empire*. Simon & Schuster, 2007, pp. 269–72.

16. The *Times of India*, 10 September 1947, p. 1.

17. Tendulkar, D.G. *Mahatma, Vol. 8*. Ministry of Information and Broadcasting, 1951.

18. Gopal, S. *Jawaharlal Nehru: A Biography*. Oxford University Press, 2003.

19. Tunzelmann, A.V. *Indian Summer: The Secret History of the End of an Empire*. Simon & Schuster, 2007, p. 308.

20. UK High Commissioner (India) to Commonwealth Relations Office, 13 January 1948. 'TNA: DO 35/3162'.

21. National Archives of India, Mahatma Gandhi Murder Trial Papers, Statement of Accused in Original.

22. Tunzelmann, A.V. *Indian Summer: The Secret History of the End of an Empire*. Simon & Schuster, 2007, p. 313.

23. Ghoshi, A., 'We Missed Mahatma Gandhi'. The *Times of India*, 17 October 2006.

Chapter 2: A Middle Ground

1. Tomlinson, B. *The Economy of Modern India: From 1860 to the Twenty-First Century*. Cambridge University Press, 2013.

2. Galbraith, John Kenneth. 'Rival Economic Theories in India'. *Foreign Affairs*, 1958, Vol. 36, No.4, p. 591.

3. Nehru, J. *The Discovery of India*. New Delhi: The Signet Press, 1946.

4. Akbar, M. *Nehru: The Making of India*. Lotus, 2004.

5. Gopal, S. *Jawaharlal Nehru: A Biography*. Oxford University Press, 2003.

6. Nehru, J. *The Discovery of India*. New Delhi: The Signet Press, 1946.

7. Gandhi, M. *The Voice of Truth*. Ahmedabad: Navajivan Publishing House, 1968.

8. Gandhi, M. *Selected Works of Mahatma Gandhi: Vol. IV*. Ahmedabad: Navajivan Mudranalaya, 1968.

9. Nehru, J. *A Bunch of Old Letters*. Asia Publishing House, 1958, pp. 507–11.

10. Tendulkar, D. *Mahatma: Life of Mohandas Karamchand Gandhi*. New Delhi: Ministry of Information and Broadcasting, Government of India, 1953.

11. FICCI. Statement issued by FICCI to the press on 25 December 1942: 'India's vital interests in the economic, financial an[d] fiscal spheres have hitherto been subordinated to those of Britain and whenever they have been in conflict . . . Indian interests have in the past been sacrificed or relegated to a second place.' *Correspondence and Relevant Documents Relating to Important Questions Dealt with by the Federation during the Year 1942–43*.

12. Tata, J.R.D., and G.D. Birla. *A Brief Memorandum Outlining a Plan of Economic Development for India, Part 1*. Ed. Purushottamdas Thakurdas, Penguin Books, 1944.

13. Due to this appointment, Sir Dalal was the signatory of only Part 1 of the Bombay Plan and not Part 2, which was published in December 1944.

14. Hanson, A. *The Process of Planning: A Study of India's Five Year Plans 1950–1964*. Oxford, 1966.

15. Cited in NP (2018), p. 38.

16. Reprinted by Government of India. *Government of India Resolution on Industrial Policy 6th April 1948*, in *Report of the Indian Fiscal Commission 1949–50, Vol. 1*.

17. Address at the annual meeting of the Indian Chemical Manufacturers' Association, New Delhi, 26 December 1950.

18. Broadcast speech from New Delhi, September 1946, printed in Appadorai, A. *Select Documents on India's Foreign Policy and Relations, 1947–1972*. Delhi: Oxford University Press, 1982.

19. An insightful read on the complications in the Indo-US relations during the Nehru era can be found in Dennis Merrill's *Bread and the Ballot*.

20. Merrill, Dennis. *Bread and the Ballot*. The University of North Carolina Press, 1990.

21. Kaul, T. *Diplomacy in Peace and War: Recollections and Reflections*. Delhi: Vikas Publishing House, 1979.

Chapter 3: Planning Ahead

1. Granville, A. *The Indian Constitution: Cornerstone of a Nation*. Oxford, 1999.

2. Editorial of *The Economic Weekly* (Now *Economic and Political Weekly*). See Chaudhuri, S. 'The Sardar Departs'. *Economic and Political Weekly*, 1950, Vol. 2, No. 485.

3. Gandhi, R. *Patel: A Life*. Navajivan Publishing House, 1991.

4. Speech in the House of the People, New Delhi, 15 December 1952.

5. According to estimates by Sivasubramonian, S. *National Income of India in the Twentieth Century*. Oxford University Press, 2001, India's per capita national income grew at 0.1 per cent between 1900 and 1947.

6. Planning Commission. First Five-Year Plan, A Draft Outline.

7. Guha, R. *India after Gandhi: The History of the World's Largest Democracy*. Macmillan, 2007.

8. C. Rajagopalachari, the last Governor General of India, replaced Patel as the Minister of Home Affairs after his death. Differences between Nehru and him started coming to the fore by the end of 1951 on a range of issues. He ultimately parted ways with Congress just before the 1957 elections, along with a group of dissidents, and formed the Congress Reform Committee that eventually evolved into the Swatantra Party.

9. The First Amendment of the Indian Constitution was passed to insert two new Articles that broadly stated that no state law, which deals with land acquisition for the state, shall be deemed void on the ground that it is in

conflict with the Fundamental Rights provided. The Fourth Amendment was later introduced to bring more clarity as to the interpretation of these two Articles.

10. Speech delivered by Jawaharlal Nehru to the National Development Council on 9 November 1954.

11. Akbar, M. *Nehru: The Making of India*. Lotus, 2004.

12. Mahalanobis, P. 'The Approach of Operational Research to Planning in India'. *Sankhya, The Indian Journal of Statistics*, 1955.

13. Outlay, here, implies the total amount of funds of the Plan allocated towards something.

14. Planning Commission. Second Five-Year Plan, Ch. 3.

15. Heavy goods are described as 'machine-building complexes with a large capacity for the manufacture of machinery to produce steel, chemicals, fertilizers, electricity, transport equipment, etc. Cited from Joshi, P. 'Dimensions of Agricultural Planning: Reflections on the Mahalanobis Approach'. *Man and Development*, 1979, pp. 9–31.

16. Mahalanobis, P. *Talks on Planning*. Calcutta: Indian Statistical Institute, 1960. Cited in Balakrishnan, P. 'The Recovery of India: Economic Growth in Nehru Era'. In Kapila, Uma, *Indian Economy since Independence*, Academic Foundation, 2017, p. 258.

17. FICCI argued that 'the proper spheres of activities for the public sector in the future are the formation and maintenance of social capital. In an underdeveloped country like India, the task of providing the basic requirements, such as power or, from a long-term point of view, education, health, etc., and also the institutional framework within which private enterprise is to work, is in itself sufficient for any government administration to be fully occupied with.

'A revision in the official approach on the subject is urgently called for'.

18. Shenoy was a student of the renowned libertarian economist Friedrich Hayek. He became the first Indian economist to be published in an international journal. He critiqued Nehruvian economics all his life and proved to be quite accurate with his policy recommendations. Most of the policy changes in India since 1991 were on the lines of Shenoy's recommendations.

19. These include arms and ammunition; atomic energy; iron and steel; heavy castings and forgings of iron and steel; heavy plant and machinery required for iron and steel production; mining and machine tool manufacture; heavy electric plants; coal and lignite; mineral oils; mining and processing of specified ores, metals and minerals; aircraft; air and railway transport; shipbuilding; electricity; and public communications.

20. These include non-ferrous metals, machine tools, ferro-alloys and tool steels; and basic and intermediate products required by chemical industries

for making essential drugs, fertilizers and synthetic rubber, carbonizing coal—and for processing chemical pulp, road transport and sea transport.

21. Griffin, Keith. 'Alternate Strategies for Economic Development: A Report to the OECD Development Centre'. Basingstoke: Macmillan in association with the Organisation for Economic Co-operation and Development, 1989, p. 118.

22. Saha, M. *My Experiences in Soviet Russia*. Calcutta: The Bookman, 1945, gives an interesting account of the dams in Russia and how Indian river systems have higher untapped potential to generate hydroelectricity.

23. Hart, H.C. *New India's Rivers*. Bombay: Orient Longman, 1954.

24. Magnitogorsk was one of the largest steel companies in Soviet Russia at the time.

Chapter 4: First Signs of Crisis

1. Outlay for agriculture rose from Rs 234 crore to Rs 294 crore while it fell from Rs 384 crore to Rs 381 crore for irrigation facilities (Second Five-Year Plan, Ch. 3).

2. Public Law (P.L.) 480 was a bill passed by President Eisenhower on 10 July 1954 to allow food-deficient countries to pay in their own currencies and, simultaneously, create a foreign market for American agriculture. The agreement would go on to be a cause of national humiliation during the drought years of mid-1960s when India would be forced to live 'ship to mouth'.

3. Government of India. Lok Sabha Debates, Second Series, XIV, 1958.

4. This was the view held by the Foodgrains Enquiry Committee that was reluctantly appointed by A.P. Jain in May 1957 due to severe criticism in Lok Sabha of the ministry's handling of the food crisis.

5. Frankel, F. *India's Political Economy, 1947–2004*. New Delhi: Oxford University Press, 2005.

6. Industry and mining received an additional Rs 190 crore while allocations to social services, irrigation and power, and transport fell.

7. Quoted in *Keep the Flame Alive: A Thesis by a Group of Congress Workers*, New Delhi, 1 December 1957.

8. Ali, S. The General Election 1957: A Survey. New Delhi, 1959.

9. Samanth Subramanian, 'Long View: India's Very First Corruption Scandal', The *New York Times*, 9 May 2012.

10. Ibid.

11. Frankel, F. *India's Political Economy, 1947–2004*. New Delhi: Oxford University Press, 2005.

12. N.G. Ranga quit the Congress to form the Swatantra Party with C. Rajagopalachari on 4 June 1959. Ranga became the founder-president of the party.

13. Government of India. Lok Sabha Debates, Second Series, 25, 19 February 1959.

14. Tomlinson, B. *The Economy of Modern India: From 1860 to the Twenty-First Century*. Cambridge University Press, 2013.

15. Following the recommendation of the N.R. Sarkar Committee Report (1946), the first IIT at Kharagpur was established in May 1950. As the planned economy demanded a technically capable workforce, four more IITs, in Bombay, Madras, Kanpur and Delhi, were established during the decade to address the need.

16. These figures were quoted by Nehru in Lok Sabha while discussing the Third Five-Year Plan on 21 August 1961.

Chapter 5: War and Dissent

1. Planning Commission, *Summary Records*, Twelfth Meeting of the National Development Council, New Delhi, 1959.

2. At the end of the Second Plan, close to 9 million people were unemployed, with 6.5 million outside agriculture.

3. Figures from the Third Five-Year Plan, p. 58.

4. Indian Institute of Public Opinion. *An Analysis of Indian Political Behaviour*, Vol. 12, No. 7, 8, 9, 1967.

5. Malviya, H.D. *The Danger of Right Reaction*. Socialist Congressman, 1965.

6. The ridge was a point of conflict as per the McMahon Line. India claimed the ridge fell south of the Line while China argued otherwise.

7. The *New York Times* reports from 21–24 October 1962.

8. External Publicity Division, Ministry of External Affairs, 1962.

9. Menon helped Allen Lane establish Penguin Books back in 1935 and later had a falling out, leading to his ejection from the company in December 1938.

10. The rise in production was at 6.5 per cent in 1961–62 and 8 per cent in 1962–63.

11. Super Profits Tax Bill, 1963, and Compulsory Deposit Scheme Bill, 1963.

12. Ruthnaswamy, M. 'The Swatantra Idea of Planning'. *Swarajya*, 1963, p. 11.

13. Cited in the *Times of India*, 21 June 1963; and Frankel, F. *India's Political Economy, 1947–2004*. New Delhi: Oxford University Press, 2005, p. 227.

14. Frankel, F. *India's Political Economy, 1947–2004*. New Delhi: Oxford University Press, 2005, p. 229.

15. Nayar, K. *India after Nehru*. Delhi: Vikas Publishing House, 1975.

16. 'Resolution on Democracy and Socialism'. Reprinted in the *Times of India*, 1 January 1964.

17. Nehru's reservation with Morarji is described in Nayar, K. *India after Nehru*. Delhi: Vikas Publishing House, p. 6.

18. Malhotra, Inder. *Indira Gandhi: A Personal and Political Biography*. Hodder & Stoughton, 1989.

19. Television interview screened in New York on 18 May 1964. Quoted in Nayar, K. *India after Nehru*. Delhi: Vikas Publishing House, 1975.

20. Ghose, S. *Jawaharlal Nehru: A Biography*. Allied Publishers, 1993.

21. Nayar, K. *India after Nehru*. Delhi: Vikas Publishing House, 1975.

22. Balakrishnan, P. 'The Recovery of India: Economic Growth in Nehru Era'. In Kapila, Uma. *Indian Economy since Independence*. Academic Foundation, p. 258.

23. Guha, R. 'Verdicts on Nehru: The Rise and Fall of a Reputation'. *Economic and Political Weekly*, 2005, Vol. 40, No. 19, pp. 1958–62

Part 2: The Indira Years

Chapter 6: A Small Interlude

1. Guha, R. *India after Gandhi: The History of the World's Largest Democracy*. Macmillan, 2008, pp. 354–56.

2. Ibid., p. 399.

3. Wolpert, S.A. *India*. University of California Press, 1999, p. 227.

4. Ibid., p. 209.

5. Statement in Parliament on 19 September 1964. Quoted in Nayar, K. *India after Nehru*. Delhi: Vikas Publishing House, 1975, p. 19.

6. Letter to the Chief Minister dated 3 March 1953. Cited in Khosla, M. *Letters for a Nation: From Jawaharlal Nehru to His Chief Ministers 1947–1963*. Allen Lane, 2014.

7. Planning Commission. *Twenty-first Meeting of the National Development Council, Summary Record*. New Delhi, 27 and 28 October 1964, p.1.

8. Ibid., p.2.

9. The *Times of India*, 11 January 1965.

10. The *Times of India*, 10 January 1965.

11. The world at the time followed a fixed exchange rate system. The value of one rupee was fixed at one dollar at the time of Independence and it had remained so since. However, when the balance of payments situation for a country becomes precarious, it is advisable to go for devaluation—that is to reduce its value so that exports become cheaper and imports costlier.

12. The *Times of India*, 18 July 1965.

13. Frankel, F. *India's Political Economy, 1947–2004*. New Delhi: Oxford University Press, 2005, p. 275

14. Srinath Raghavan, 'The War We Forgot', *Outlook*, 25 May 2015.

15. Government of India, *Economic Survey, 1966–67*. Delhi: Ministry of Finance, Appendix, Statistical Table 5.1.

16. Kudaisya, M.M. *The Life and Times of G.D. Birla*. Oxford University Press, 2006.
17. Mishra, D.P. *The Post-Nehru Era: Political Memoirs*. Har Anand Publications, 1993, p. 36.
18. The *Times of India*, 4 January 1966.
19. The *New York Times*, 11 January 1966.

Chapter 7: The Dumb Doll

1. The socialist Ram Manohar Lohia had infamously called Indira Gandhi '*goongi gudiya*' (the dumb doll) on account of her lacklustre public-speaking skills. The label even stuck with her long after she began to find her voice. Cited in Frank, K. *Indira: The Life of Indira Nehru Gandhi*. HarperCollins, 2001, p. 296.
2. Frank, K. *Indira: The Life of Indira Nehru Gandhi*. HarperCollins, 2001, pp. 284–85.
3. Gopal, S. *Radhakrishnan*. Oxford University Press, 1989, pp. 344–46.
4. Gandhi, I. *My Truth*. Delhi: Vision Books, 1981, p. 115.
5. Interview by Inder Malhotra, Morarji Desai, New Delhi, 30 August 1973.
6. Both Indira and Desai had abstained from voting.
7. By 1966, the world had five nuclear powers: US, Soviet Union, UK, France and China, with the latter being the latest entrant in 1964. India would eventually go on to conduct its first nuclear test in 1974.
8. Dhar, P. *Indira Gandhi, the 'Emergency' and Indian Democracy*. New Delhi: Oxford University Press, 2000, p. 134. The 'Kitchen Cabinet' consisted of her closest advisers—Dinesh Singh; Inder Gujral; Nandini Satpathy, a young MP from Orissa; Umar Shankar Dikshit; D.P. Mishra, the chief minister of Madhya Pradesh; C. Subramaniam; Asoka Mehta and Fakhruddin Ali Ahmed.
9. Frank, K. *Indira: The Life of Indira Nehru Gandhi*. HarperCollins, 2001 p. 296.
10. Nayar, K. *India: The Critical Years*. Delhi: Vikas Publications, 1971, p. 92. Based on Bhattacharya's promise the World Bank released a loan of Rs 150 crore from a total package of Rs 675 crore.
11. Malhotra, I. *Indira Gandhi: A Personal and Political Biography*. Hodder & Stoughton, 1989, p. 95.
12. Frank, K. *Indira: The Life of Indira Nehru Gandhi*. HarperCollins, 2001, p. 297.
13. Gupte, P. *Mother India: A Political Biography of Indira Gandhi*. Charles Scribner's Sons, 1992, p. 290.
14. Jayakar, P. *Indira Gandhi: A Biography*. Penguin Books, 1992, p. 196.
15. Ibid., p. 197.
16. Jayakar, P. *Indira Gandhi: A Biography*. Penguin Books, 1992, p. 196.
17. Malhotra, I. *Indira Gandhi: A Personal and Political Biography*. Hodder & Stoughton, 1989, p. 101.

18. Interview published in the *Times of India*, 26 December 1966.

19. Malhotra, I. *Indira Gandhi: A Personal and Political Biography*. Hodder & Stoughton, 1989, p. 105.

20. Brecher, M. 'Succession in India'. *Asian Survey*, 1967, Volume XVII, No. 7, p. 434.

Chapter 8: Sharp Left Ahead

1. It was called the Prime Minister's Secretariat then and was renamed as the Prime Minister's Office in 1977 by Morarji Desai.

2. Malhotra, I. *Indira Gandhi: A Personal and Political Biography*. Hodder & Stoughton, 1989, p. 107.

3. Frankel, F. *India's Political Economy, 1947–2004*. New Delhi: Oxford University Press, 2005, p. 400; and Malhotra, I. *Indira Gandhi: A Personal and Political Biography*. Hodder & Stoughton, 1989, p. 112.

4. Gupte, P. *Mother India: A Political Biography of Indira Gandhi*. Charles Scribner's Sons, 1992, p. 351.

5. Tomlinson, B. *The Economy of Modern India: From 1860 to the Twenty-First Century*. Cambridge University Press, 2013, p. 171.

6. Aiyar, S. *Accidental India: A History of the Nation's Passage through Crisis and Change*. Aleph Book Company, 2012, p. 114.

7. Warrier, S. 'Our farmers are second to none'. Rediff News, 6 October 2009.

8. Paul R. Ehrlich, a professor of biology at the Stanford University and author of *The Population Bomb*, had painted a depressing picture of the state of the world. He stated that the ever-expanding population of countries like India would soon be impossible to feed and hundreds of millions will die of starvation within a decade. Ehrlich was not alone.

    There were others like William and Paul Paddock who predicted a widespread famine that will grip the world by 1975. In response to the Green Revolution, Ehrlich merely commented that the world had postponed the inevitable.

9. Nobel Presentation Speech by Aase Lionaes, Chairman of the Nobel Committee, 1970.

10. Malhotra, I. *Indira Gandhi: A Personal and Political Biography*. Hodder & Stoughton, 1989, p. 114.

11. Contents of the Nijalingappa diaries were disclosed by the veteran Indian journalist Kuldip Nayar. Cited in Gupte, P. *Mother India: A Political Biography of Indira Gandhi*. Charles Scribner's Sons, 1992, p. 352.

12. Nayar, K. *India: The Critical Years*. Delhi: Vikas Publications, 1971, pp. 67–68.

13. Gupte, P. *Mother India: A Political Biography of Indira Gandhi*. Charles Scribner's Sons, 1992, p. 368.

14. Ibid., p. 369.
15. Masani, Z. *Indira Gandhi: A Biography*. Hamish Hamilton Ltd, 1975, p. 211.

Chapter 9: That Woman

1. Aiyar, S. *Accidental India: A History of the Nation's Passage through Crisis and Change*. Aleph Book Company, 2012, p. 39.
2. Mehta, V. *The Sanjay Story*. Bombay: Jaico Publishing Company, 1978, p. 56.
3. Quoted in Merchant, Minhaz. *Rajiv Gandhi: The End of a Dream*, Viking, 1991, p. 46.
4. Malhotra, I. *Indira Gandhi: A Personal and Political Biography*. Hodder & Stoughton, 1989, p. 124.
5. Sahgal, N. *Indira Gandhi: Her Road to Power*. New York: Frederick Ungar, 1981, p. 66.
6. Nayar, K. *India: The Critical Years*. Delhi: Vikas Publications, 1971, p. 69.
7. Frank, K. *Indira: The Life of Indira Nehru Gandhi*. HarperCollins, 2001, p. 326.
8. Masani, Z. *Indira Gandhi: A Biography*. Hamish Hamilton Ltd, 1975, p. 230.
9. Planning Commission. *Towards Self-Reliance, Approach to the Fifth Five Year Plan*, p. 4.
10. Bhutto, B. *Daughter of the East*. London: Hamish Hamilton, 1988, p. 53.
11. Ibid.
12. Dhar, P. *Indira Gandhi, the 'Emergency' and Indian Democracy*. New Delhi: Oxford University Press, 2000, p. 156.
13. Kissinger, H. *White House Years*. London: Weidenfeld & Nicolson, 1979, pp. 880–81.
14. Malhotra, I. *Indira Gandhi: A Personal and Political Biography*. Hodder & Stoughton, 1989, p. 137.
15. Dhar, P. *Indira Gandhi, the 'Emergency' and Indian Democracy*. New Delhi: Oxford University Press, 2000, p. 176.
16. The *Hindustan Times*, 12 November 1986.
17. Malhotra, I. *Indira Gandhi: A Personal and Political Biography*. Hodder & Stoughton, 1989, p. 139.
18. Gandhi, I. *Speeches in Parliament*. New Delhi: Jainco Art India, 1996, pp. 808–09.

Chapter 10: Power Pangs

1. Frank, K. *Indira: The Life of Indira Nehru Gandhi*. HarperCollins, 2001, p. 346.
2. Lamb, A. *Kashmir: A Disputed Legacy, 1846–1990*. Roxford Books, 1991, p. 211.

3.   Dhar, P. *Indira Gandhi, the 'Emergency' and Indian Democracy*. New Delhi: Oxford University Press, 2000, p. 210.
4.   Gupte, P. *Mother India: A Political Biography of Indira Gandhi*. Charles Scribner's Sons, 1992, p. 347.
5.   Government of India. *Economic Survey, 1975–76*. New Delhi: Ministry of Finance, p. 92.
6.   Minhas, B. 'Mass poverty and strategy of rural development in India'. Economic Development Institute, International Bank for Reconstruction and Development, p. 3.
7.   Planning Commission. The Fourth Mid-Term Appraisal, p. 50.
8.   Planning Commission. Fourth Five-Year Plan, a Draft Outline, pp. 106–08.
9.   Government of India. *Economic Survey, 1975–76*. New Delhi: Ministry of Finance, p.59.
10.   Planning Commission. The Fourth Plan Mid-Term Appraisal, p. 43.
11.   Malhotra, I. *Indira Gandhi: A Personal and Political Biography*. Hodder & Stoughton, 1989, p. 144.
12.   Ibid., p. 145.
13.   Ibid., p. 145.
14.   Frank, K. *Indira: The Life of Indira Nehru Gandhi*. HarperCollins, 2001, p. 350.
15.   Ibid., p. 352.
16.   Joshi, V., and I. Little. *India: Macroeconomics and Political Economy*. Delhi: Oxford University Press, 1994, p. 105.
17.   Malhotra, I. *Indira Gandhi: A Personal and Political Biography*. Hodder & Stoughton, 1989, p. 154.
18.   Gujral, M. *Economic Failures of Nehru and Indira Gandhi: A Study of Three Decades of Deprivation and Disillusionment*. Delhi: Vikas Publishing House, 1979, p. 156.
19.   Frank, K. *Indira: The Life of Indira Nehru Gandhi*. HarperCollins, 2001, p. 360.
20.   Gandhi, I. *Speeches in Parliament*. New Delhi: Jainco Art India, 1996, p. 511.
21.   Frank, K. *Indira: The Life of Indira Nehru Gandhi*. HarperCollins, 2001, p. 367.

Chapter 11: Democracy Interrupted

1.   Gupte, P. *Mother India: A Political Biography of Indira Gandhi*. Charles Scribner's Sons, 1992, p. 426.
2.   Nayar, K. *India after Nehru*. Delhi: Vikas Publishing House, 1975, p. 3–4.
3.   Frank, K. *Indira: The Life of Indira Nehru Gandhi*. HarperCollins, 2001, p. 373–74.
4.   Ibid., p. 375.

5. Gandhi, I. *Selected Speeches and Writings of Indira Gandhi, Volumes I–V*. New Delhi: Publications Division, Ministry of Information and Broadcasting, 1971–86, Vol III, pp. 177–79.

6. Borders, William. 'Authoritarian Rule Gains Wide Acceptance in India'. The *New York Times*, 8 September 1975.

7. Government of India. *Economic Survey, 1976–77*. New Delhi: Ministry of Finance, p. 4.

8. Toye, J. 'Economic Trends and Policies in India during the Emergency'. *World Development*, 1977, Vol. 5, No. 4, 303–31, p. 304.

9. Government of India. *Economic Survey, 1976–77*. New Delhi: Ministry of Finance, pp. 79–80.

10. The *New York Times*, 3 July 1975.

11. Frankel, F. *India's Political Economy, 1947–2004*. New Delhi: Oxford University Press, 2005, pp. 550–56.

12. Planning Commission. Third Five-Year Plan. Ch. 2.

13. A detailed commentary on the excesses of Sanjay Gandhi during the Emergency can be found in Frank, K. *Indira: The Life of Indira Nehru Gandhi*. HarperCollins, 2001, pp. 400–47.

14. Jayakar, P. *Indira Gandhi: A Biography*. Penguin Books, 1992, p. 306.

15. Frank, K. *Indira: The Life of Indira Nehru Gandhi*. HarperCollins, 2001, pp. 396–67.

16. Bhutto, Benazir. *Daughter of the East*. London: Hamish Hamilton, 1988, p. 305.

17. Gandhi, I. *My Truth*. Delhi: Vision Books, 1981, p.166.

Chapter 12: United We Fall

1. Schwarz, Walter. 'Two-Party Democracy Faces a Test Run'. *Guardian*, 14 May 1977.

2. *New York Times Magazine*, 27 March 1977, p. 88.

3. Bhutto, Benazir. *Daughter of the East*. London: Hamish Hamilton, 1988, pp. 372–73.

4. *Statement on Economic Policy*, adopted by the Janata Party on 14 December 1977, p. 1.

5. Ibid., p. 2.

6. Ibid., p. 4.

7. Tharoor, S. *India: From Midnight to the Millennium and Beyond*. Penguin Books, 1997, p. 165.

8. Eventually, the multinational Hindustan Lever would take over Modern Food Industries in 2000.

9. Frank, K. *Indira: The Life of Indira Nehru Gandhi*. HarperCollins, 2001, p. 417.

10. Ibid., pp. 400, 418.
11. Shah Commission Report, I, p. 1.
12. Moraes, D. *Mrs Gandhi*. London: Jonathan Cape, 1980, p. 277.
13. Shah Commission Report, III, p. 234.
14. The *Times of India*, 6 June 1978.
15. Kidwai, A. *Indira Gandhi: Charisma and Crisis*. New Delhi: Siddi Books, 1996, p. 33.
16. Bobb, Dilip, and Arul Louis. 'Indian Airlines Boeing 737 Hijacking: A black political comedy'. *India Today*, 9 December 2014.
17. Joshi, V., and I. Little. *India: Macroeconomics and Political Economy*. Delhi: Oxford University Press, 1994, p. 148.
18. Ibid., p. 143.

Chapter 13: Crash and Burn

1. Frank, K. *Indira: The Life of Indira Nehru Gandhi*. HarperCollins, 2001, p. 440.
2. Ibid., p. 348. Indira had displayed tendencies towards centralization even before she became the prime minister. In 1959, when she was the Congress President, she practically forced her father to dismiss the communist Kerala ministry of E.M.S. Namboodiripad as the government began making changes that were not appreciated in New Delhi, like schools replacing portraits of Gandhi with those of Lenin and Marx. Nehru did not object as the government had been democratically elected. This was the first instance of Indira's aversion to pluralism in politics. Cited from Malhotra, Inder. 'India's trial run in Kerala'. The *Indian Express*, 3 February 2014.
3. Frank, K. *Indira: The Life of Indira Nehru Gandhi*. HarperCollins, 2001, p. 445.
4. Jayakar, P. *Indira Gandhi: A Biography*. Penguin Books, 1992.
5. Frank, K. *Indira: The Life of Indira Nehru Gandhi*. HarperCollins, 2001, p. 449.
6. Manor, J. 'Parties and the Party System'. In Kohli, A., *India's Democracy: An Analysis of Changing State-Society Relations*. Princeton University Press, 1988.
7. Joshi, V., and Little, I. *India: Macroeconomics and Political Economy*. Delhi: Oxford University Press, 1994, pp. 148–49.
8. *India Today*. 'IMF Loan: Leash or Lease'. 15 December 1981.
9. The *Times of India*. 22 February 1981.
10. Kohli, A. 'Politics of economic liberalization in India'. *World Development*, 1989, Vol. 17, No.3, pp. 305–28.
11. Ibid., pp. 308–39.

12. Cited in Kohli, A. 'Politics of Economic Growth in India, 1980-2005, Part 1'. *Economic and Political Weekly*, Vol. 41, No. 14, pp. 1251–59.

13. The *Times of India*, 10 July 1980.

14. Frank, K. *Indira: The Life of Indira Nehru Gandhi*. HarperCollins, 2001, p. 456.

15. Ibid.

16. Ibid., p. 462.

17. Nehru, B.K. *Nice Guys Finish Second*. Delhi: Viking Penguin, 1997, p. 611.

18. Frank, K. *Indira: The Life of Indira Nehru Gandhi*. HarperCollins, 2001, p. 472.

19. Rajiv Gandhi owned the first Toshiba laptop computer in India.

20. Frank, K. *Indira: The Life of Indira Nehru Gandhi*. HarperCollins, 2001, pp. 482–83.

21. Nehru, B.K. *Nice Guys Finish Second*. Delhi: Viking Penguin, 1997, p. 627.

22. Smith, William E. 'Indira Gandhi: Death in the Garden', *Time*, 12 November 1984.

23. Malhotra, I. *Indira Gandhi: A Personal and Political Biography*. Hodder & Stoughton, 1989, p. 309.

Part 3: The Reform Years

Chapter 14: Pangs of Change

1. Bedi, Rahul. 'Indira Gandhi's death remembered'. BBC, 1 November 2009.

2. Editorial. 'Bhopal's deadly legacy'. The *New York Times*, 4 December 2014.

3. *Business India*, 31 December 1984 –13 January 1985.

4. Tokas, J. *Rajiv Gandhi: Future of India*. New Delhi: Pustkayan, 1987, p. 43.

5. Quoted in The *Times of India*, 6 January 1986.

6. Ghoshal, Sumantra. *World Class in India: A Casebook of Companies in Transformation*. New Delhi: Penguin Books, 2001, p. 167.

7. Ponkshe, S. *Rajiv Gandhi: The Pragmatic Prime Minister of India*. Pune: Bhate & Ponkshe Publications, 1986, p. 272.

8. Kohli, A. 'Politics of economic liberalization in India'. *World Development*, 1989, Vol. 17, No. 3, pp. 305–28.

9. Ninan, T.N., 'Rise of the Middle Class'. *India Today*, 31 December 1985.

10. Kohli, A. 'Politics of economic liberalization in India'. *World Development*, 1989, Vol. 17, No. 3, p. 313.

11. See *Hindustan Times*, 6 December 1985.

12. Midha, Tania. 'Finance Minister V.P. Singh fails to stay in line with his own long-term policy'. *India Today*, 31 December 1986.

13. Ninan, T.N., 'Rise of the Middle Class'. *India Today*, 31 December 1985.

14. The *Statesman*, 19 December 1985.

15. Srinivasan, Kannan. 'The ASI Report'. The *Hindu*, 14 October 2003.

16. Veer, P.V. 'God Must be Liberated'. *Modern Asian Studies*, 1987, Vol. 21, No. 2, pp. 283–301.

17. Guha, R. *Verdicts on Nehru: The Rise and Fall of a Reputation*. *Economic and Political Weekly*, 2005, 1958–62, p. 583.

18. Rushdie, Salman. 'India Bans a Book for Its Own Good'. The *New York Times*, 19 October 1988. Rushdie accused Rajiv Gandhi of banning his book for the 'Muslim vote' in an open letter to him. Rushdie would, however, call his reaction 'arrogant' in a later book.

19. Guha, R. *India after Gandhi: The History of the World's Largest Democracy*. Macmillan, 2007, p. 594.

20. Frankel, Francine. *India's Political Economy, 1947–2004*. New Delhi: Oxford University Press, 2005, pp. 587–88.

21. Polgreen, Lydia. 'Right-to-Know Law Gives India's Poor a Lever'. The *New York Times*, 28 June 2010. Rajiv Gandhi made the assertion during a visit in 1985 to the drought-affected Kalahandi district of Orissa.

22. Guha, R. *India after Gandhi: The History of the World's Largest Democracy*. Macmillan, 2007, p. 598.

23. Ninan, T.N., and Jagannath Dubashi. 'Dhirubhai Ambani: The Super Tycoon'. *India Today*, 30 June 1985.

24. Giridharadas, Anand. 'Indian to the Core, and an Oligarch'. The *New York Times*, 15 June 2008.

25. Dehejia, Vivek. 'Is India's Rising Billionaire Wealth Bad for the Country'. The *New York Times*, 30 October 2012. The threat of oligarchy in India has also been famously highlighted by Raghuram Rajan in a speech to the Bombay Chamber of Commerce, 10 September 2008.

26. Rajan, Raghuram. 'Is There a Threat of Oligarchy in India'. Speech to the Bombay Chamber of Commerce, 10 September 2008.

27. Banerjie, Indranil. 'The New Maharajahs'. *Sunday*, 17–23 April 1988.

28. Thakurta, Paranjoy Guha. 'Foreign Investments: V.P. Singh government's economic policies cause concern'. *India Today*, 15 February 1990.

29. Interview with Anil Padmanabhan. Livemint, 5 February 2016.

30. Jaffrelot, C. 'Communal Riots in Gujarat: The State at Risk?'. Heidelberg Papers in South Asian and Comparative Politics, 2003, pp. 345–47.

31. Guha, R. *India after Gandhi: The History of the World's Largest Democracy*. Macmillan, 2007, p. 609.

32. Hazarika, Sanjay. 'India's Prime Minister Loses His Parliamentary Majority in Temple Dispute'. The *New York Times*, 24 October 1990.

33. Ibid.

34. The foreign exchange reserves had been at Rs 5,277 crore on 31 December 1989. They fell to Rs 2,152 crore by December 1990. Meanwhile, the

current account deficit increased from Rs 11,350 crore in 1989-90 to Rs 17,350 crore in 1990-91.

35. Singh, D. *Strictly Personal: Manmohan & Gursharan.* New Delhi: HarperCollins, 2014, p. 373.
36. Sinha, Y. *Confessions of a Swadeshi Reformer.* New Delhi: Penguin, 2007, pp. 7-8.
37. Sinha, Y., and V. K. Srivastava. *The Future of Indian Economy: Past Reforms and Challenges Ahead.* New Delhi: Rupa Publications, 2017.

Chapter 15: The Perfect Crisis

1. Natwar Singh K. 'How PV became PM'. The *Hindu,* 6 July 2012.
2. Sitapati, V. *Half Lion: How P.V. Narasimha Rao Transformed India.* Gurgaon: Penguin Random House India, 2016, p. 67.
3. Ibid., p. 79.
4. Ramesh, J. *To the Brink and Back: India's 1991 Story.* New Delhi: Rupa Publications, 2015, pp. 5, 8.
5. Ibid., p. 11.
6. Rao, P.N. *P.V. Narasimha Rao, Selected Speeches: 1991-1992.* New Delhi: Publications Division, Ministry of Information and Broadcasting, 1993, p. 106.
7. The *Times of India.* 'Economy must be put back on the rails'. 20 June 1991.
8. Rao, P.N. *P.V. Narasimha Rao, Selected Speeches: 1991-1992.* New Delhi: Publications Division, Ministry of Information and Broadcasting, 1993, pp. 3-4.
9. Sitapati, V. *Half Lion: How P.V. Narasimha Rao Transformed India.* Gurgaon: Penguin Random House India, 2016, p. 106.
10. Ramesh, J. *To the Brink and Back: India's 1991 Story.* New Delhi: Rupa Publications, 2015, p. 18.
11. Ibid., p. 42.
12. Rao, P.N. *P.V. Narasimha Rao, Selected Speeches: 1991-1992.* New Delhi: Publications Division, Ministry of Information and Broadcasting, 1993, p. 155.
13. Hazari, Rabindra Kishen. *Industrial Planning and Licensing Policy: Interim Report to Planning Commission.* New Delhi: Manager of Publications, 1967.
14. Friedman, Milton. 'Indian Economic Planning'. May 1963, as quoted by Shah, Parth J. 'Friedman on India'. New Delhi: The Centre for Civil Society, 2000.
15. Shankar, Kalyani. 'Industrial Licensing to Go'. *Hindustan Times,* 11 July 1991.
16. Ramesh, J. 'To the Brink and Back: India's 1991 Story'. New Delhi: Rupa Publications, 2015, p.87.
17. Ibid., p.95.

18. Ibid., p. 98.
19. Panagariya, A. 'India in the 1980s and 1990s: A Triumph of Reforms'. In W. Tseng. *India's and China's Recent Experience with Reform and Growth.* London: Palgrave Macmillan, 2005, p. 191.
20. Budget 1991-92. Speech of Manmohan Singh, 24 July 1991. Available at https://www.indiabudget.gov.in/bspeech/bs199192.pdf.
21. Sitapati, V. *Half Lion: How P.V. Narasimha Rao Transformed India.* Gurgaon: Penguin Random House India, 2016, p. 72.
22. Rao, P.N. *P.V. Narasimha Rao, Selected Speeches: 1991-1992.* New Delhi: Publications Division, Ministry of Information and Broadcasting, 1993, p. 161.

Chapter 16: Going the Distance

1. Hasan, Z. *Congress after Indira: Policy, Power, Political Change (1984-2009).* Oxford University Press, 2012, p. 50.
2. Baru, Sanjay. 'Remembering Narasimha Rao'. *Business Standard,* 20 January 2013.
3. Devarajan, A. 'Tirupati Plenary – down the memory lane'. The *Hindu,* 21 January, 2006.
4. Gargan, Edward A. 'Huge Financial Scandal Shakes Indian Politics'. The *New York Times,* 9 June 1992.
5. Reuters. 'Indian Broker Sentenced'. The *New York Times,* 29 September, 1999.
6. Dalal, Sucheta. 'Harshad Mehta scam broke 20 years ago. What has changed?'. *Moneylife,* 3 May 2012.
7. Ibid.
8. Ibid.
9. Sitapati, V. *Half Lion: How P.V. Narasimha Rao Transformed India.* Gurgaon: Penguin Random House India, 2016, p. 145.
10. Sucheta Dalal, 'Harshad Mehta scam broke 20 years ago. What has changed?'. *Moneylife,* 3 May 2012.
11. Modak, Samie, and Hamsini Karthik. 'Mutual funds pip FIIs in net investments'. *Business Standard,* 8 August 2017.
12. Guha, R. *India after Gandhi: The History of the World's Largest Democracy.* Macmillan, 2007, p. 638.
13. Rao, P.N. *P.V. Narasimha Rao: Selected Speeches: 1992-1993.* New Delhi: Publications Division, Ministry of Information and Broadcasting, 1994, pp. 8–10.
14. Sitapati, V. *Half Lion: How P.V. Narasimha Rao Transformed India.* Gurgaon: Penguin Random House India, 2016, pp. 225–56.
15. Quoted in *Sunday,* 6–12 December 1992.

16. The sequence of events is detailed in the Report of the Liberhan Ayodhya Commission of Inquiry, 2009, pp. 119–258.

17. McKean, L. *Divine Enterprise: Gurus and the Hindu Nationalist Movement.* Chicago: University of Chicago Press, 1996, p. 315.

18. Dugger, Celia W. 'More than 200 die in 3 days of riots in western India'. The *New York Times*, 2 March 2002.

19. Serril, Michael S. 'India: The Holy War'. *Time*, 21 December 1992.

20. Hasan, Z. *Congress after Indira: Policy, Power, Political Change (1984-2009).* Oxford University Press, 2012, p. 58.

21. 'IDFC and Bandhan make the cut for banking licences'. *Business Standard*, 3 April 2014.

22. Rao, P.N. *P.V. Narasimha Rao, Selected Speeches: 1991-1992.* New Delhi: Publications Division, Ministry of Information and Broadcasting, 1993, p. 185.

23. ———. *P.V. Narasimha Rao: Selected Speeches: 1993-1994.* New Delhi: Publications Division, Ministry of Information and Broadcasting, 1995, p. 24.

24. Kumar, S. *Gandhi Meets Primetime: Globalization and Nationalism in Indian Television.* Champaign: University of Illinois Press, 2005, p. 4.

25. Sitapati, V. *Half Lion: How P.V. Narasimha Rao Transformed India.* Gurgaon: Penguin Random House India, 2016, p. 159.

26. The Secretary. *Ministry of Information and Broadcasting vs Cricket Association of Bengal,* 1995, *SCC*, No. 2, p. 161.

27. Mazumdar, A. 'Deregulation of the Airline Industry in India: Issues, Causes and Rationale'. *The Indian Journal of Political Science*, Vol. 70, No. 2, p. 460.

28. Chronology of Events of Indian Civil Aviation Sector, *Association of Private Airport Operators.*

29. Government of India. *Economic Survey 2017-18, Volume II.* Ministry of Finance, p. 139.

30. Times News Network. 'Narasimha Rao govt asked Tata to start airline, then backed out'. The *Times of India*, 31 January 2015.

31. Jeffery, Robin, and Assa Doron. *Cell Phone Nation: How Mobile Phones Have Revolutionized Business, Politics and Ordinary Life in India.* Hachette India, 2013, p. 46.

32. Sinha, Y. *Confessions of a Swadeshi Reformer: My Years as Finance Minister.* New Delhi: Penguin, 2007, p. 161.

33. Aiyar, S. *Accidental India: A History of the Nation's Passage through Crisis and Change.* Aleph Book Company, 2012, pp. 234–35.

34. Obituary of Arthur Dunkel in the *Guardian*, 16 June 2005.

35. 'Defend GATT Aggressively', *India Today*, 15 May 1994.

36. Burns, John F. 'Unlikely Reformer Coaxes India toward a Market Economy'. The *New York Times*, 8 May 1994.

37. Gargan, Edward A. 'A Revolution Transforms India: Socialism's Out, Free
     Market In'. The *New York Times*, 29 March 1992.

38. Burns, John F. 'Unlikely Reformer Coaxes India toward a Market Economy'.
     The *New York Times*, 8 May 1994.

39. Sitapati, V. *Half Lion: How P.V. Narasimha Rao Transformed India*. Gurgaon:
     Penguin Random House India, 2016, p. 172.

40. Ibid., p. 173.

41. Estimates from the budget documents during Rao's tenure.

42. Agha, Zafar. 'Fighting for Survival'. *India Today*, 15 June 1995.

43. 'Reforms Mainstay of Congress Manifesto'. The *Economic Times*, 25 March
     1996.

44. Cooper, Kenneth J. 'India's Government Collapses after 10 Months'. The
     Washington Post, 12 April 1997.

45. Burns, John F. 'Premier of India Quits, Deepening Political Bedlam'. The
     New York Times, 29 November 1997.

46. CSO data, author estimates.

47. Guha, R. *India after Gandhi: The History of the World's Largest Democracy*.
     Macmillan, 2007, p. 696.

48. Shankkar Aiyar. 'Propelled by reforms, Indian manufacturers arrive as big
     players in global supermarket'. *India Today*, 1 December 2003.

49. Nagaraj, R. 'Foreign Direct Investment in India in the 1990s: Trends and
     Issues'. *Economic and Political Weekly*, p. 1703.

Part 4: The New Millennium

Chapter 17: Clash of Ideologies

1.   The sequence of events is discussed in detail in Sitapati, V. *Half Lion:
     How P.V. Narasimha Rao Transformed India*. Gurgaon: Penguin Random
     House India, 2016, pp. 279–95.

2.   Burns, John F. 'New Delhi Premier Indicates Resolve to Produce Nuclear
     Weapons'. The *New York Times*, 16 May 1996.

3.   BBC America. 'US imposes sanctions on India'. BBC Press Release, 13 May
     1998.

4.   Ram, N. 'What wrong did this man do?'. *Frontline*, 8–21 May 1999, Vol. 16,
     No. 10.

5.   Ghosh, Jayati. 'On sanctions and being sanctimonious'. *Frontline*, Vol. 15,
     No. 12, 6–19 June 1998.

6.   Duggar, Celia W. 'Kashmir War, Shown on TV, Rallies India's Unity'. The
     New York Times, 18 July 1999.

7.   Raman, B. 'Release of Kargil Tape: Masterpiece or blunder?'. *Rediff News*,
     27 June 2007.

8. Speech by US Ambassador to India Robert D. Blackwill, American Chamber of Commerce in India/Indo-American Chamber of Commerce lunch, New Delhi, 28 January 2002.

9. Frankel, Francine. *India's Political Economy, 1947–2004.* New Delhi: Oxford University Press, 2005, p. 731.

10. Rediff Press Release. 'National Agenda for Governance'. *Rediff News*, 29 March 1998.

11. The 'warning day' was especially observed against the new patent law by RSS and the BJP student wing, ABVP.

12. Bhattacharya, A.K. 'What about the deficit Mr. Sinha?'. *Rediff.com*, 21 June 2007.

13. Gupta, Smita. 'RSS organs snap at government for IPCL disinvestment'. The *Times of India*, 15 June 2002.

14. Luce, Edward. 'The man who wouldn't go away'. *Financial Times*, 15 August 2003.

15. Gupta, Smita. 'BJP turns to RSS in search for lost ideology'. The *Times of India*, 16 May 2001.

16. Frankel, F. *India's Political Economy, 1947-2004.* New Delhi: Oxford University Press, 2005, pp. 736, 758.

17. Bhattacharya, A.K. 'What about the deficit Mr. Sinha?', *Rediff.com*, 21 June 2007.

18. Panagariya, Arvind. 'Indian Economy: Retrospect and Prospect', Richard Snape Lecture, Melbourne, 6 November 2013.

19. Mantri, Rajeev, and Harsh Gupta, 'The story of India's telecom revolution'. Livemint, 8 January 2013.

20. Estimates from TRAI Press Releases.

21. Chawla, Prabhu. 'The Vajpayee Years'. *India Today*, 10 December 2015.

22. Jaffrelot, C. 'Communal Riots in Gujarat: The State at Risk?' Heidelberg Papers in South Asian and Comparative Politics, 2003, p. 16.

23. Interview of Narendra Modi by BBC reporter, Rajyasri Rao, 30 December 2002.

24. Sahey, Tara Shankar. 'RSS forces Vajpayee to change tack on Modi issue'. *Rediff.com*, 13 April 2002.

25. Frankel, F. *India's Political Economy, 1947-2004.* New Delhi: Oxford University Press, 2005, p. 762.

26. Ibid., p. 771.

Chapter 18: Too Much of a Good Thing

1. Nayar, B.R. 'India in 2004: Regime Change in a Divided Democracy'. *Asian Survey*, 2005, Vol. 45, No. 1, p. 73.

2. Government of India. *Economic Survey, 2003-04*. New Delhi: Ministry of Finance, 2004, p. 1.

3. Yadav, Y. 'The Elusive Mandate of 2004'. *Economic and Political Weekly*, Vol. 39, No. 51, p. 5393.

4. Ramgopal, Ram. 'Singh: Reforms with "human face"'. CNN, 20 May 2004.

5. Baru, S. *The Accidental Prime Minister: The Making and Unmaking of Manmohan Singh*. Gurgaon: Penguin, 2014, p. 91.

6. Honorati, M., U. Gentilini and R. Yemtsov. *The State of Social Safety Nets 2015*. Washington, D.C.: World Bank Group, 2015, p. 13; and media reports of the study.

7. Azam, M. 'The Impact of Indian Job Guarantee Scheme on Labor Market Outcomes: Evidence from a Natural Experiment'. *Forschungsinstitut zur Zukunft der Arbeit*, Institute for the Study of Labor (IZA), No. 6548, p. 20.

8. Bhagwati, Jagdish, and Arvind Panagariya. 'Rural inefficiency act: Despite protests about diluting NREGA, the PM is right to confine it to 200 poorest districts'. The *Times of India*, 23 October 2014.

9. Jalan, B. *India's Politics: A View from the Backbench*. New Delhi: Penguin, 2007, p. 169.

10. Dwivedi, Maninder Kaur. 'The ABC of RTE'. The *Hindu*, 12 January 2018.

11. Nanda, Prashant K. 'India disappoints in educational outcome test'. Livemint, 14 January 2015.

12. Kaul, Vivek. 'Food security is the biggest mistake India might have made till date'. Firstpost, 20 December 2014.

13. Government of India. *Towards Faster and More Inclusive Growth: An Approach to the 11th Five Year Plan (2007-2012)*. New Delhi: Planning Commission, 2006, p. 89.

14. Nayar, B.R. 'The Political Economy of Reforms under the UPA, 2004-2014'. *India Review*, 2015, Vol. 14, No. 2, p. 185.

15. Government of India. *Eleventh Five Year Plan 2007-12: Volume I: Inclusive Growth*. New Delhi: Oxford University Press, 2008, p. 5.

16. Crabtree, J. *The Billionaire Raj*. Noida: HarperCollins, 2018, p. 47.

17. Indrawati, Sri Mulyani. 'The global economy off steroids', *World Economic Forum*, 6 February 2014.

18. Acharya, Shankar. 'The Halcyon Years, 2003-8'. *Business Standard*, 9 October 2008.

19. Damodaran, Harish. 'Shed the Deficit Obsession'. *Hindu Business Line*, 8 June 2014.

20. Government of India Planning Commission data tables.

21. Rajadhyaksha, Niranjan. 'Inflation: The War is Still On'. Livemint, 22 July 2014.

22. Bandyopadhyay, Tamal. 'Three Challenges before the New Finance Minister'. Livemint, 25 May 2014.

23. Nayar, B.R. 'The Political Economy of Reforms Under the UPA, 2004-2014'. *India Review*, 2015, Vol. 14, No. 2, p. 193.

24. Government of India. *Performance Audit of Issue of Licences and Allocation of 2G Spectrum of Union Government, Ministry of Communications and Information Technology.* New Delhi: Comptroller and Auditor General of India, 2010, p. 56.

25. Government of India. *Performance Audit of Allocation of Coal Blocks and Augmentation of Coal Production, Ministry of Coal 2012.* New Delhi: Comptroller and Auditor General of India, 2012, p. 30.

26. Thomas Jr., Landon. '"Fragile Five" Is the Latest Club of Emerging Nations in Turmoil'. The *New York Times*, 28 January 2014.

27. The *Economist*. 'Watery sunrise'. The *Economist*, 18 January 2014.

Chapter 19: Great Expectations

1. The *Economist*. 'The Gujarat Model'. The *Economist*, 8 January 2015.

2. ———. 'How to run a continent'. The *Economist*, 23 May 2015.

3. Thakker, Aman. '4 Years of the Modi Government: Taking Stock of Economic Performance'. The *Diplomat*, 29 May 2018.

4. World Bank Press Release. 'India Jumps Doing Business Rankings with Sustained Reform Focus'. *World Bank*, 31 October 2017.

5. Crabtree, J. *The Billionaire Raj.* Noida: HarperCollins, 2018, p. 47.

6. Tripathy, Devidutta. 'Vijay Mallya seeks to sell $2 billion in assets to settle bank dues'. Livemint, 26 June 2018.

7. RBI data.

8. The *Economist*. 'One nation, one tax'. The *Economist*, 6 August 2016.

9. Sapra, Bipin. 'GST tax structure should move towards lower tax brackets'. Livemint, 31 July 2018.

10. Government of India. 'Table 1'. Planning Commission, Data Tables. The closest India has come to achieving the fiscal deficit target had been just before the 2008 crisis when the central fiscal deficit reached a low of 3.11 per cent of the GDP.

11. ET bureau. 'Narendra Modi government finally manages to break the Swiss bank black money vault'. The *Economic Times*, 18 June 2017.

12. The Editorial Board, 'The Cost of India's Man-Made Crisis'. The *New York Times*, 9 January 2017.

13. Safi, Michael. 'India's slowing growth blamed on "big mistake" of demonetisation'. The *Guardian*, 1 June 2017.

14. Swachh Bharat Mission Database, Ministry of Drinking Water and Sanitation.

15. Demirgüç-Kunt, A., L. Klapper, D. Singer, S. Ansar and J. Hess. 'The Global Findex Database 2017: Measuring Financial Inclusion and the Fintech Revolution'. Washington DC: The World Bank, 2018, p. 65.

16. Ibid.

17. Dubey, Jyotindra. 'Share of manufacturing in India's GDP falling despite "Make in India"'. CNBCTV18, 24 July 2018.

18. NITI Aayog and IDFC Institute. *Ease of Doing Business: An Enterprise Survey of Indian States*. New Delhi: NITI Aayog, 2017, p. 10.

19. BJP Election Manifesto 2014, p. 31.

20. Abraham, V. 'Stagnant Employment Growth'. *Economic and Political Weekly*, 2017, Vol. 63, Issue No. 38, pp. 13–17.

21. Sharma, Yogima Seth. 'Land acquisition a difficult task in India: Arvind Panagariya'. The *Economic Times*, 1 August 2015.

22. Jack, Ian. 'India has 600 million young people – and they're set to change our world'. The *Guardian*, 13 January 2018.

23. Aiyar, S. *Accidental India: A History of the Nation's Passage through Crisis and Change*. Aleph Book Company, 2012, p. 15.

Conclusion

1. McRae, Hamish . 'This year, India will surpass the UK to be the fifth largest economy – but we shouldn't worry much'. *Independent*, 10 March 2018.

2. The statistics have been obtained mainly from the World Bank database.

3. Patel, I. *Glimpses of Indian Economy: An Insider's View*. New Delhi: Oxford University Press, 2002.

4. Myrdal, Gunnar. *Asian Drama – An Inquiry into the Poverty of Nations*. Harmondsworth: Penguin, 1968.

5. Khilnani, S. *The Idea of India*. New Delhi: Penguin, 1999, p. 86.

6. Aiyar, S. *Accidental India: A History of the Nation's Passage through Crisis and Change*. Aleph Book Company, 2012, p. 45.

7. Narayan, Ambar. 'India lifted 133 million people out of poverty between 1994 and 2012'. World Bank, 13 July 2016.

8. Crabtree, J. *The Billionaire Raj*. Noida: HarperCollins, 2018, pp. 60–61.

9. Rajan, Raghuram. 'Is there a threat of oligarchy in India?'. *Bombay Chamber of Commerce*, 10 September 2008.

10. Ibid.

11. Khilnani, S. *The Idea of India*. New Delhi: Penguin, 1999, p. 17.

12. Ambedkar, B. *Dr. Babasaheb Ambedkar: Writings and Speeches, Vol. 13*. New Delhi: Ministry of Social Justice and Empowerment, 1994, Government of India, p. 1216.

BIBLIOGRAPHY

Aiyar, Shankkar. *Accidental India: A History of the Nation's Passage through Crisis and Change*, Aleph Book Company, 2012.

Akbar, M.J. *Nehru: The Making of India*. Lotus, 2004.

Ali, Sadiq. 'The General Election 1957: A Survey'. New Delhi.

Appadorai, A. *Select Documents on India's Foreign Policy and Relations,1947–1972*. Delhi: Oxford University Press, 1982.

Azam, Mehtabul. 'The Impact of Indian Job Guarantee Scheme on Labor Market Outcomes: Evidence from a Natural Experiment'. *Forschungsinstitut zur Zukunft der Arbeit*, No. 6548, Institute for the Study of Labor (IZA), 2012.

Balakrishnan, P. 'The Recovery of India: Economic Growth in Nehru Era'. In Uma Kapila, *Indian Economy since Independence*, Academic Foundation, 1988, p. 258.

Baru, Sanjaya. *The Accidental Prime Minister: The Making and Unmaking of Manmohan Singh*. New Delhi: Penguin, 2014.

Beckett, Francis. *Clem Attlee: Labour's Great Reformer*. Hans Publishing, 2015.

Bhutto, Benazir. *Daughter of the East*. London: Hamish Hamilton, 1988.

Brecher, Michael. 'Succession in India'. *Asian Survey*, 1967, Volume XVII, No. 7, 967.

Burns, W. *Sons of the Soil: Studies of the Indian Cultivator, 2nd Edition*. Delhi: Manager of Publications, 1944.

Chaudhuri, Sachin. 'The Sardar Departs'. *Economic and Political Weekly*, Vol. 2, No. 48, 1950.

Collins, Larry, and Dominique Lapierre. *Freedom at Midnight*. Delhi: Vikas Publishing House, 1975.

Demirgüç-Kunt, Asli, Leora Klapper, Dorothe Singer, Saniya Ansar and Jake Hess. *The Global Findex Database 2017: Measuring Financial Inclusion and the Fintech Revolution*. Washington DC: The World Bank, 2018.

Dhar, P.N. *Indira Gandhi, the 'Emergency' and Indian Democracy*. New Delhi: Oxford University Press, 2000.

Frank, Katherine. *Indira: The Life of Indira Nehru Gandhi*. HarperCollins, 2001.

Frankel, Francine. *India's Political Economy, 1947–2004*. New Delhi: Oxford University Press, 2005.

Galbraith, J.K. 'Rival Economic Theories in India'. Vol. 36, No. 4591, *Foreign Affairs*, 1958.

Gandhi, Indira. *My Truth*. Delhi: Vision Books, 1981.

———. *Selected Speeches and Writings of Indira Gandhi, Volumes I–V*. New Delhi: Publications Division, Ministry of Information and Broadcasting, 1971–86.

———. *Speeches in Parliament*. New Delhi: Jainco Art India.

Gandhi, M.K. *Selected Works of Mahatma Gandhi: Vol. IV*. Ahmedabad: Navajivan Mudranalaya, 1968.

———. *The Voice of Truth*. Ahmedabad: Navajivan Publishing House, 1968.

Gandhi, Rajmohan. *Patel: A Life*. Navajivan Publishing House, 1991.

Ghose, Sankar. *Jawaharlal Nehru: A Biography*. Allied Publishers, 1993.

Ghoshal, Sumantra. *World Class in India: A Casebook of Companies in Transformation*. New Delhi: Penguin Books, 2001.

Ghosh, Avijit. 'We Missed Mahatma Gandhi'. The *Times of India*, 17 October 2006.

Government of India. *Economic Survey, 2003–04*. New Delhi: Ministry of Finance, 2004.

———. *Eleventh Five Year Plan 2007–12: Volume I: Inclusive Growth*. New Delhi: Oxford University Press, 2008.

———. *Performance Audit of Allocation of Coal Blocks and Augmentation of Coal Production, Ministry of Coal*. New Delhi: Comptroller and Auditor General of India, 2012.

———. *Performance Audit of Issue of Licences and Allocation of 2G Spectrum of Union Government, Ministry of Communications and Information Technology*. New Delhi: Comptroller and Auditor General of India, 2010.

———. *Towards Faster and More Inclusive Growth: An Approach to the 11th Five Year Plan (2007–2012)*. New Delhi: Planning Commission, 2006.

Gopal, Sarvepalli. *Jawaharlal Nehru: A Biography*. Oxford University Press, 2003.

———. *Radhakrishnan*. Oxford University Press, 1989.

Granville, Austin. *The Indian Constitution: Cornerstone of a Nation*. Oxford, 1999.

Griffin, Keith. 'Alternate Strategies for Economic Development: A Report to the OECD Development Centre'. Basingstoke: Macmillan in association with the Organisation for Economic Co-operation and Development, 1989, p. 118.

Guha, Ramachandra. *India after Gandhi: The History of the World's Largest Democracy*. Macmillan, 2007.

Guha, Ramachandra. 'Verdicts on Nehru: The Rise and Fall of a Reputation'. *Economic and Political Weekly*, 2005, pp. 1958–62.

Gujral, M.L. *Economic Failures of Nehru and Indira Gandhi: A Study of Three Decades of Deprivation and Disillusionment.* Delhi: Vikas Publishing House, 1979.

Gupte, Pranay. *Mother India: A Political Biography of Indira Gandhi.* Charles Scribner's Sons, 1992.

Hanson, A.H. *The Process of Planning: A Study of India's Five Year Plans 1950–1964.* Oxford, 1966.

Hart, Henry C. *New India's Rivers.* Bombay: Orient Longman, 1954.

Hasan, Zoya. *Congress after Indira: Policy, Power, Political Change (1984–2009).* Oxford University Press, 2012.

Hazari, Rabindra Kishen. *Industrial Planning and Licensing Policy: Interim Report to Planning Commission.* New Delhi: Manager of Publications, 1967.

Heward, Edmund. *The Great and the Good: A Life of Lord Radcliffe.* Barry Rose Law Publishers, 1994.

Honorati, Maddalena, Ugo Gentilini and Ruslan G. Yemtsov. *The State of Social Safety Nets 2015.* Washington, D.C.: World Bank Group, 2015.

Jaffrelot, Christophe. *India's Silent Revolution: The Rise of the Lower Castes in North India.* Columbia University Press, 2003.

———. 'Communal Riots in Gujarat: The State at Risk?' Heidelberg Papers in South Asian and Comparative Politics, 2003.

Jalan, Bimal. *India's Politics: A View from the Backbench.* New Delhi: Penguin, 2007.

Jayakar, Pupul. *Indira Gandhi: A Biography.* Penguin Books, 1992.

Jeffery, Robin, and Assa Doron. *Cell Phone Nation: How Mobile Phones Have Revolutionized Business, Politics and Ordinary Life in India.* Hachette India, 2013.

Joshi, P.C. 'Dimensions of Agricultural Planning: Reflections on the Mahalanobis Approach'. *Man and Development,* 1979, pp. 9–31.

Joshi, Vijay, and I.M.D. Little. *India: Macroeconomics and Political Economy.* Delhi: Oxford University Press, 1994.

Kaul, T.N. *Diplomacy in Peace and War: Recollections and Reflections.* Delhi: Vikas Publishing House, 1979.

Keay, John. *India: A History.* Harper Press, 2000.

Khosla, Madhav. *Letters for a Nation: From Jawaharlal Nehru to His Chief Ministers 1947–1963.* Allen Lane, 2014.

Kidwai, Ansar. *Indira Gandhi: Charisma and Crisis.* New Delhi: Siddi Books, 1996.

Kissinger, Henry. *White House Years.* London: Weidenfeld & Nicolson, 1979.

Kohli, Atul. 'Politics of Economic Growth in India, 1980–2005, Part 1'. *Economic and Political Weekly,* 2006, Vol. 17, No. 3, pp. 1251–59.

———.'Politics of economic liberalization in India'. *World Development,* 1989, Vol. 17, No. 3, pp. 305–28.

Kotkin, Stephen. *Magnetic Mountain: Stalinism as a Civilization.* University of California Press, 1997.

Kudaisya, Medha M. *The Life and Times of G.D. Birla.* Oxford University Press, 2006.

Kumar, Shanti. *Gandhi Meets Primetime: Globalization and Nationalism in Indian Television.* Champaign: University of Illinois Press, 2005.

Lamb, Alastair. *Kashmir: A Disputed Legacy, 1846–1990.* Roxford Books, 1991.

Lapierre, Dominique, and Larry Collins. *Mountbatten and the Partition of India.* Delhi: Vikas Publishing House, 2015.

Maddison, Angus. *The World Economy,* OECD Publishing, 2006, Volume 1–2, p. 638.

Mahalanobis, P.C. *Talks on Planning.* Calcutta: Indian Statistical Institute, 1960.

———. 'The Approach of Operational Research to Planning in India'. *Sankhya: The Indian Journal of Statistics,* Vol. 16, No. 1/2, 1955.

Malhotra, Inder. *Indira Gandhi: A Personal and Political Biography.* Hodder & Stoughton, 1989.

———. *Indira Gandhi: A Personal and Political Biography.* Hodder & Stoughton, 1989.

Malviya, Harsh Dev. *The Danger of Right Reaction.* Socialist Congressman, 1965.

Manor, James. 'Parties and the Party System'. In Kohli, Atul. *India's Democracy: An Analysis of Changing State-Society Relations.* Princeton University Press, 1988.

Masani, Zareer. *Indira Gandhi: A Biography.* Hamish Hamilton Ltd, 1975.

Mazumdar, Arijit. 'Deregulation of the Airline Industry in India: Issues, Causes and Rationale'. *The Indian Journal of Political Science,* 2009, Vol. 70, No. 2, 451–69.

Mehta, Vinod. *The Sanjay Story.* Bombay: Jaico Publishing Company, 1978.

Merrill, Dennis. *Bread and the Ballot.* The University of North Carolina Press, 1990.

Minhas, B.S. 'Mass poverty and strategy of rural development in India'. *Economic Development Institute, International Bank for Reconstruction and Development,* 1971.

Mishra, Dwarka Prasad. *The Post-Nehru Era: Political Memoirs.* Har Anand Publications, 1993.

Moraes, Dom. *Mrs Gandhi.* London: Jonathan Cape, 1980.

Nagaraj, R. 'Foreign Direct Investment in India in the 1990s: Trends and Issues'. *Economic and Political Weekly,* 2003, Vol. 38, No. 17, pp. 1701–12.

Nayar, Baldev Raj. 'India in 2004: Regime Change in a Divided Democracy'. *Asian Survey,* 2005, Vol. 45, No. 1, pp. 71–82.